THE AFRICAN ORIGIN
OF CIVILIZATION

Myth or Reality

1. The Sphinx, as the first French scientific mission found it in the nineteenth century. This profile is neither Greek nor Semitic: it is Bantu. Its model is said to have been Pharaoh Chephren (circa 2600 B.C., Fourth Dynasty), who built the second Giza pyramid.

Cheikh Anta Diop

THE
AFRICAN
ORIGIN
OF
CIVILIZATION

Myth or Reality

Translated from the French by
MERCER COOK

LAWRENCE HILL & COMPANY

Westport

This book consists of selections from
NATIONS NÈGRES ET CULTURE, first published by
Présence Africaine, Paris, 1955.
ANTÉRIORITÉ DES CIVILISATIONS NÈGRES:
Mythe ou Vérité Historique?,
first published by Présence Africaine, Paris, 1967
Copyright © Présence Africaine, 1955 and 1967.

This translation and edited condensation
copyright © Lawrence Hill & Co., 1974

ISBN clothbound edition: 0-88208-021-0
ISBN paperback edition: 0-88208-022-9
Library of Congress Catalogue card number: 73-81746

First edition February, 1974
Lawrence Hill & Co., Publishers, Inc.
Manufactured in the United States of America
4 5 6 7 8 9 10

**Library of Congress
Cataloging in Publication Data**
Diop, Cheikh Anta.
The African origin of civilization.
Translation of sections of Antériorité des civilisations nègres
and Nations nègres et culture.
Includes bibliographical references.
1. Negroes in Egypt. 2. Egypt—Civilization—
To 332 B.C. 3. Negro race—History. I. Title.
DT61.D5613   913.32′06′96   73-81746
ISBN 0-88208-021-0   ISBN 0-88208-022-9 (pbk.)

Table of Contents

v

vi

List of Illustrations

Translator's Preface

To introduce Cheikh Anta Diop to English-speaking readers, we present, with the author's consent, ten chapters from his first published volume: *Nations nègres et culture* (1954), and three from his latest work: *Antériorité des civilisations nègres: mythe ou vérité historique?* (1967). For purposes of continuity and accessibility, this selection excludes most of the more technical discussions, especially the linguistic and grammatical passages, but nonetheless should give the reader a general idea of what Congolese author Théophile Obenga calls the "Historical Method and Conception of Cheikh Anta Diop."[1]

Dr. Diop's method is multi-faceted and reflects his varied background as "historian, physicist, and philosopher." Obenga singles him out as "the only Black African of his generation to have received training as an Egyptologist." As a Senegalese, he has had direct contact with the oral traditions and social structure of West Africa. From André Aymard, Professor of History and later Dean of the Faculty of Letters at the University of Paris, he has gained an understanding of the Greco-Latin world. As a student of Gaston Bachelard, Frédéric Joliot-Curie, André Leroi-Gourhan, and others, he has acquired proficiency in such diverse disciplines as rationalism, dialectics, modern scientific techniques, prehistoric archeology, and so on. More importantly, he has applied this encyclopedic knowledge to his researches on African history.

"While pursuing this research," he told the First International Congress of Black Writers and Artists in September 1956, "we have come to discover that the ancient Pharaonic Egyptian civilization was undoubtedly a Negro civilization. To defend this thesis, anthropological, ethnological, linguistic, historical, and cultural arguments have been provided. To judge their validity, it suffices to refer to *Nations nègres et culture* . . ."[2]

Thus he proceeded in *Nations nègres et culture* and subsequent volumes to document conclusions that form a coherent theory, controversial because it refutes many ideas previously presented by Egyptologists, anthropologists, archeologists, linguists, and historians.

---

1. Théophile Obenga, "Méthode et conception historiques de Cheikh Anta Diop." *Présence Africaine,* number 74, 2nd quarter, 1970, pp. 3–28.
2. *Présence Africaine,* numbers 8–10, June November, 1956, p. 339.

A good example of this is Chapter XII of the present volume in which he replies to a critical review of *Nations nègres*.

More than a decade ago Immanuel Wallerstein summarized Dr. Diop's contribution as follows:

Perhaps the most ambitious attempt to reconstruct African history has been the numerous writings of Cheikh Anta Diop. Diop has a theory that there is a basic global division of peoples into two kinds: the Southerners (or Negro-Africans), and the Aryans (a category covering all Caucasians, including Semites, Mongoloids, and American Indians). Each grouping has a cultural outlook based on response to climate, the difference between them being that the Aryans have had a harsher climate.

The Aryans have developed patriarchal systems characterized by the suppression of women and a propensity for war. Also associated with such societies are materialist religion, sin and guilt, xenophobia, the tragic drama, the city-state, individualism, and pessimism. Southerners, on the other hand, are matriarchal. The women are free and the people peaceful; there is a Dionysian approach to life, religious idealism, and no concept of sin. With a matriarchal society come xenophilia, the tale as a literary form, the territorial state, social collectivism, and optimism.

According to Diop's theory, the ancient Egyptians, who were Negroes, are the ancestors of the Southerners. This bold hypothesis, which is not presented without supporting data, has the interesting effect of inverting Western cultural assumptions. For, Diop argues, if the ancient Egyptians were Negroes, then European civilization is but a derivation of African achievement. . . .[3]

Born on December 29, 1923, at Diourbel, Senegal, Cheikh Anta Diop received his master of arts degree and his doctorate from the University of Paris. Since 1961 he has been on the staff of IFAN (Institut Fondamental de l'Afrique Noire)[4] in Dakar, where he directs the radiocarbon laboratory which he founded. In 1966, at the First

---

3. Immanuel Wallerstein, *Africa: The Politics of Independence.* New York: Vintage Books, 1961, pp. 129–130. A footnote on p. 130 reads: "The hypothesis is not original with Diop. Other scholars, such as W. E. B. DuBois, had earlier presented the argument that the ancient Egyptians were Negroes."
4. Fundamental Institute of Black Africa. Cf. Cheikh Anta Diop, *Le Laboratoire de radiocarbone de l'IFAN* (Dakar: IFAN, 1968). Diop dedicated this 110-page book "to the memory of my former professor Frédéric Joliot who welcomed me into his laboratory at the Collège de France."

World Festival of Negro Arts, he shared a special award with the late W. E. B. DuBois, as the writer who had exerted the greatest influence on Negro thought in the twentieth century.

All numbered footnotes in the present volume (except for inserted material included between square brackets and so indicated) are the author's and are placed at the end of the book. All asterisked footnotes within the text are the editor-translator's. For the reader's convenience, a list of Brief Biographical Notes on authors and authorities mentioned within the book but not identified exhaustively is given as an appendix. Most archeological terms used in the book are also listed and defined in an appendix.

M.C.

The Meaning of Our Work

I began my research in September 1946; because of our colonial situation at that time, the political problem dominated all others. In 1949 the RDA* was undergoing a crisis. I felt that Africa should mobilize all its energy to help the movement turn the tide of repression: thus I was elected Secretary General of the RDA students in Paris and served from 1950 to 1953. On July 4–8, 1951 we held in Paris the first postwar Pan African political congress of students, with the West African Student Union (from London) well represented by more than 30 delegates, including the daughter of the Oni of Ife, the late Miss Aderemi Tedju. In February 1953 the first issue of the *Voie de l'Afrique Noire* appeared; this was the organ of the RDA students. In it I published an article entitled "Toward a Political Ideology in Black Africa."

That article contained a résumé of *Nations nègres,* the manuscript of which was already completed. All our ideas on African history, the past and future of our languages, their utilization in the most advanced scientific fields as in education generally, our concepts on the creation of a future federal state, continental or subcontinental, our thoughts on African social structures, on strategy and tactics in the struggle for national independence, and so forth, all those ideas were clearly expressed in that article. As would subsequently be seen, with respect to the problem of the continent's political independence, the French-speaking African politicians took their own good time before admitting that this was the right political road to follow. Nevertheless, the RDA students organized themselves into a federation within France and politicized African student circles by popularizing the slogan of national independence for Africa from the Sahara to the Cape

---

*Rassemblement Démocratique Africain (Democratic African Rally), the RDA, founded in 1946, "was the first interterritorial movement in French West Africa, created before parties in territories other than Senegal or Ivory Coast had taken root." Ruth S. Morgenthau, *Political Parties in French-speaking West Africa.* Oxford: Clarendon Press, 1964, p. 302.

and from the Indian Ocean to the Atlantic, as our periodical attests. The archives of the FEANF (Federation of African Students in France) indicate that it did not begin to adopt anticolonialist positions until it was directed by RDA students.* We stressed the cultural and political content that we included in the concept of independence in order to get the latter adopted in French-speaking Africa: already forgotten is the bitter struggle that had to be waged to impose it on student circles in Paris, throughout France, and even within the ranks of RDA students.

The cultural concept especially will claim our attention here; the problem was posed in terms of restoring the collective national African personality. It was particularly necessary to avoid the pitfall of facility. It could seem too tempting to delude the masses engaged in a struggle for national independence by taking liberties with scientific truth, by unveiling a mythical, embellished past. Those who have followed us in our efforts for more than 20 years know now that this was not the case and that this fear remained groundless.

Admittedly three factors compete to form the collective personality of a people: a psychic factor, susceptible of a literary approach; this is the factor that would elsewhere be called national temperament, and that the Negritude poets have overstressed. In addition, there are the historical factor and the linguistic factor, both susceptible of being approached scientifically. These last two factors have been the subject of our studies; we have endeavored to remain strictly on scientific grounds. Have foreign intellectuals, who challenge our intentions and accuse us of all kinds of hidden motives or ridiculous ideas, proceeded any differently? When they explain their own historical past or study their languages, that seems normal. Yet, when an African does likewise to help reconstruct the national personality of his people, distorted by colonialism, that is considered backward or alarming. We contend that such a study is the point of departure for the

---

*Starting especially with the administration of Franklin, secretary general of the RDA students at Montpellier. Cf. the article by Penda Marcelle Ouegnin: "Un compte-rendu du Congrès de la FEANF organisé par les ERDA aux Sociétés savantes le 8 avril 1953," in the same bulletin cited above, May–June 1953.

Similarly, with a few exceptions, the PAI (African Independence Party) was organized by former RDA students who had returned to Africa. Various branches in France rallied to the new party which thus carried forward the RDA line and popularized the slogan of national independence that we had launched.

cultural revolution properly understood. All the headlong flights of certain infantile leftists who try to bypass this effort can be explained by intellectual inertia, inhibition, or incompetence. The most brilliant pseudo-revolutionary eloquence ignores that need which must be met if our peoples are to be reborn culturally and politically. In truth, many Africans find this vision too beautiful to be true; not so long ago some of them could not break with the idea that Blacks are non-existent culturally and historically. It was necessary to put up with the cliché that Africans had no history and try to start from there to build something modestly!

Our investigations have convinced us that the West has not been calm enough and objective enough to teach us our history correctly, without crude falsifications. Today, what interests me most is to see the formation of teams, not of passive readers, but of honest, bold research workers, allergic to complacency and busy substantiating and exploring ideas expressed in our work, such as:

1. Ancient Egypt was a Negro civilization. The history of Black Africa will remain suspended in air and cannot be written correctly until African historians dare to connect it with the history of Egypt. In particular, the study of languages, institutions, and so forth, cannot be treated properly; in a word, it will be impossible to build African humanities, a body of African human sciences, so long as that relationship does not appear legitimate. The African historian who evades the problem of Egypt is neither modest nor objective, nor unruffled; he is ignorant, cowardly, and neurotic. Imagine, if you can, the uncomfortable position of a western historian who was to write the history of Europe without referring to Greco-Latin Antiquity and try to pass that off as a scientific approach.

The ancient Egyptians were Negroes. The moral fruit of their civilization is to be counted among the assets of the Black world. Instead of presenting itself to history as an insolvent debtor, that Black world is the very initiator of the "western" civilization flaunted before our eyes today. Pythagorean mathematics, the theory of the four elements of Thales of Miletus, Epicurean materialism, Platonic idealism, Judaism, Islam, and modern science are rooted in Egyptian cosmogony and science. One needs only to meditate on Osiris, the redeemer-god, who sacrifices himself, dies, and is resurrected to save mankind, a figure essentially identifiable with Christ.

A visitor to Thebes in the Valley of the Kings can view the Moslem inferno in detail (in the tomb of Seti I, of the Nineteenth Dynasty), 1700 years before the Koran. Osiris at the tribunal of the dead is indeed the "lord" of revealed religions, sitting enthroned on Judgment Day, and we know that certain Biblical passages are practically copies of Egyptian moral texts. Far be it from me to confuse this brief reminder with a demonstration. It is simply a matter of providing a few landmarks to persuade the incredulous Black African reader to bring himself to verify this. To his great surprise and satisfaction, he will discover that most of the ideas used today to domesticate, atrophy, dissolve, or steal his "soul," were conceived by his own ancestors. To become conscious of that fact is perhaps the first step toward a genuine retrieval of himself; without it, intellectual sterility is the general rule, or else the creations bear I know not what imprint of the subhuman.

In a word, we must restore the historical consciousness of the African peoples and reconquer a Promethean consciousness.

2. Anthropologically and culturally speaking, the Semitic world was born during protohistoric times from the mixture of white-skinned and black-skinned people in western Asia. This is why an understanding of the Mesopotamian Semitic world, Judaic or Arabic, requires constant reference to the underlying Black reality. If certain Biblical passages, especially in the Old Testament, seem absurd, this is because specialists, puffed up with prejudices, are unable to accept documentary evidence.

3. The triumph of the monogenetic thesis of humanity (Leakey), even at the stage of "Homo sapiens-sapiens," compels one to admit that all races descended from the Black race, according to a filiation process that science will one day explain.*

4. In *L'Afrique Noire précoloniale* (1960), I had two objectives: (1) to demonstrate the possibility of writing a history of Black Africa free of mere chronology of events, as the preface to that volume clearly indicates; (2) to define the laws governing the evolution of African sociopolitical structures, in order to explain the direction that historical evolution has taken in Black Africa; therefore, to try henceforth to dominate and master that historical process by knowledge, rather than simply to submit to it.

These last questions, like those about origins (Egypt), are among

---

*Cf. Cheikh Anta Diop, "L'Apparition de l'homo-sapiens," *Bulletin de l'IFAN*, XXXII, Series II, number 3, 1970.

———, "La Pigmentation des anciens Egyptiens. Test par la mélanine," *Bulletin de l'IFAN*, 1973 (in press).

the key problems; once they are solved, a scholar can proceed to write the history of Africa. Consequently, it is evident why we are paying particular attention to the solution of such problems and of so many others which transcend the field of history.

The research pattern inaugurated by *L'Afrique Noire précoloniale* on the sociohistorical, not on the ethnographic, plane has since been utilized by many researchers. That, I suppose, is what has led them to describing the daily life of the Congolese or enlarging upon the various forms of political, economic, social, military, and judicial organization in Africa.

5. To define the image of a modern Africa reconciled with its past and preparing for its future.*

6. Once the perspectives accepted until now by official science have been reversed, the history of humanity will become clear and the history of Africa can be written. But any undertaking in this field that adopts compromise as its point of departure as if it were possible to split the difference, or the truth, in half, would run the risk of producing nothing but alienation. Only a loyal, determined struggle to destroy cultural aggression and bring out the truth, whatever it may be, is revolutionary and consonant with real progress; it is the only approach which opens on to the universal. Humanitarian declarations are not called for and add nothing to real progress.

Similarly, it is not a matter of looking for the Negro under a magnifying glass as one scans the past; a great people has nothing to do with petty history, nor with ethnographic reflections sorely in need of renovation. It matters little that some brilliant Black individuals may have existed elsewhere. The essential factor is to retrace the history of the entire nation. The contrary is tantamount to thinking that to be or not to be depends on whether or not one is known in Europe. The effort is corrupted at the base by the presence of the very complex one hopes to eradicate. Why not study the acculturation of the white man in a Black milieu, in ancient Egypt, for example?

7. How does it happen that all modern Black literature has remained minor, in the sense that no Negro African author or artist, to my knowledge, has yet posed the problem of man's fate, the major theme of human letters?

8. In *L'Unité culturelle de l'Afrique Noire,* we tried to pinpoint the features common to Negro African civilization.

---

*Cf. Cheikh Anta Diop, *Les Fondements culturels et industriels d'un futur Etat fédéral d'Afrique Noire.*

9. In the second part of *Nations nègres,* we demonstrated that African languages could express philosophic and scientific thought (mathematics, physics, and so forth)* and that African culture will not be taken seriously until their utilization in education becomes a reality. The events of the past few years prove that UNESCO has accepted those ideas.†

10. I am delighted to learn that one idea proposed in *L'Afrique Noire précoloniale*—the possibilities of pre-Columbian relations between Africa and America—has been taken up by an American scholar. Professor Harold G. Lawrence, of Oakland University, is in fact demonstrating with an abundance of proof the reality of those relationships which were merely hypothetical in my work. If the sum total of his impressive arguments stands up to the test of chronology, if it can be proved in the final analysis that all the facts noted existed prior to the period of slavery, his research will have surely contributed solid material to the edifice of historical knowledge.

I should like to conclude by urging young American scholars of good will, both Blacks and Whites, to form university teams and to become involved, like Professor Lawrence, in the effort to confirm various ideas that I have advanced, instead of limiting themselves to a negative, sterile skepticism. They would soon be dazzled, it not blinded, by the bright light of their future discoveries. In fact, our conception of African history, as exposed here, has practically triumphed, and those who write on African history now, whether willingly or not, base themselves upon it. But the American contribution to this final phase could be decisive.

Cheikh Anta Diop
July 1973

---

*In *Nations nègres,* Dr. Diop translates a page of Einstein's Theory of Relativity into Wolof, the principal language of Senegal.
†Bamako 1964 colloquium on the transcription of African languages, various measures taken to promote African languages, and so forth.

CHAPTER I

What Were the Egyptians?

In contemporary descriptions of the ancient Egyptians, this question is never raised. Eyewitnesses of that period formally affirm that the Egyptians were Blacks. On several occasions Herodotus insists on the Negro character of the Egyptians and even uses this for indirect demonstrations. For example, to prove that the flooding of the Nile cannot be caused by melting snow, he cites, among other reasons he deems valid, the following observation: "It is certain that the natives of the country are black with the heat. . . ."[1]

To demonstrate that the Greek oracle is of Egyptian origin, Herodotus advances another argument: "Lastly, by calling the dove black, they [the Dodonaeans] indicated that the woman was Egyptian. . . ."[2] The doves in question symbolize two Egyptian women allegedly kidnapped from Thebes to found the oracles of Dodona and Libya.

To show that the inhabitants of Colchis were of Egyptian origin and had to be considered a part of Sesostris' army who had settled in that region, Herodotus says: "The Egyptians said that they believed the Colchians to be descended from the army of Sesostris. My own conjectures were founded, first, on the fact that they are black-skinned and have woolly hair. . . ."[3]

Finally, concerning the population of India, Herodotus distinguishes between the Padaeans and other Indians, describing them as follows: "They all also have the same tint of skin, which approaches that of the Ethiopians."[4]

Diodorus of Sicily writes:

> The Ethiopians say that the Egyptians are one of their colonies which was brought into Egypt by Osiris. They even allege that this country was originally under water, but that the Nile, dragging much mud as it flowed from Ethiopia, had finally filled it in and made it a part of the continent. . . . They add that from them, as from their authors and ancestors, the Egyptians get most of their laws. It is from them that the Egyptians have learned to honor

I

kings as gods and bury them with such pomp; sculpture and writing were invented by the Ethiopians. The Ethiopians cite evidence that they are more ancient than the Egyptians, but it is useless to report that here.[5]

If the Egyptians and Ethiopians were not of the same race, Diodorus would have emphasized the impossibility of considering the former as a colony (i.e., a fraction) of the latter and the impossibility of viewing them as forebears of the Egyptians.

In his *Geography*, Strabo mentioned the importance of migrations in history and, believing that this particular migration had proceeded from Egypt to Ethiopia, remarks: "Egyptians settled Ethiopia and Colchis."[6] Once again, it is a Greek, despite his chauvinism, who informs us that the Egyptians, Ethiopians, and Colchians belong to the same race, thereby confirming what Herodotus had said about the Colchians.[7]

The opinion of all the ancient writers on the Egyptian race is more or less summed up by Gaston Maspero (1846–1916): "By the almost unanimous testimony of ancient historians, they belonged to an African race [read: Negro] which first settled in Ethiopia, on the Middle Nile; following the course of the river, they gradually reached the sea. . . . Moreover, the Bible states that Mesraim, son of Ham, brother of Chus (Kush) the Ethiopian, and of Canaan, came from Mesopotamia to settle with his children on the banks of the Nile."[8]

According to the Bible, Egypt was peopled by the offspring of Ham, ancestor of the Blacks: "The descendants of Ham are Chus, Mesraim, Phut and Canaan. The descendants of Chus are Saba, Hevila, Sabatha, Regma and Sabathacha. . . . Chus was the father of Nemrod; he was the first to be conqueror on the earth. . . . Mesraim became the father of Ludim, Anamim, Laabim, Nephthuhim, Phethrusim, Chasluhim. . . . Canaan became the father of Sid, his first-born, and Heth. . . ."[9]

For the peoples of the Near East, Mesraim still designates Egypt; Canaan, the entire coast of Palestine and Phoenicia; Sennar, which was probably the site from which Nemrod left for Western Asia, still indicates the kingdom of Nubia.

What is the value of these statements? Coming from eyewitnesses, they could hardly be false. Herodotus may be mistaken when he reports the customs of a people, when he reasons more or less cleverly to explain a phenomenon incomprehensible in his day, but one must grant that he was at least capable of recognizing the skin color of the inhabitants of countries he has visited. Besides, Herodotus was not a credulous historian who recorded everything without checking; he knew how to weigh things. When he relates an opinion that he does not share, he always takes care to note his disagreement. Thus, referring to the mores of the Scythians and Neurians, he writes apropos the latter: "It seems that these people are conjurers; for both the Scythians and the Greeks who dwell in Scythia say that every Neurian once a year becomes a wolf for a few days, at the end of which time he is restored to his proper shape. Not that I believe this, but they constantly affirm it to be true, and are even ready to back up their assertion with an oath."[10]

He always distinguishes carefully between what he has seen and what he has been told. After his visit to the Labyrinth, he writes:

There are two different sorts of chambers throughout—half under ground, half above ground, the latter built upon the former; the whole number of these chambers is three thousand, fifteen hundred of each kind. The upper chambers I myself passed through and saw, and what I say concerning them is from my own observation; of the underground chambers I can only speak from report, for the keepers of the building could not be got to show them, since they contained, as they said, the sepulchers of the kings who built the Labyrinth, and also those of the sacred crocodiles. Thus it is from hearsay only that I can speak of the lower chambers. The upper chambers, however, I saw with my own eyes and found them to excel all other human productions.[11]

Was Herodotus a historian deprived of logic, unable to penetrate complex phenomena? On the contrary, his explanation of the inundations of the Nile reveals a rational mind seeking scientific reasons for natural phenomena:

Perhaps, after censuring all the opinions that have been put forward on this obscure subject, one ought to propose some theory of one's own. I will therefore proceed to explain what I think to be the reason of the Nile's swelling in the summertime. During the winter, the sun is driven out of his usual course by the storms, and removes to the upper parts of Libya. This is the whole secret in the fewest possible words; for it stands to reason that the country to which the Sun-god approaches the nearest, and which he passes most directly over, will be scantest of water, and that here streams which feed the rivers will shrink the most.

To explain, however, more at length, the case is this. The sun, in his passage across the upper parts of Libya, affects them in the following way. As the air in these regions is constantly clear, and the country warm through the absence of cold winds, the sun in his passage across them acts upon them exactly as he is wont to act elsewhere in summer, when his path is in the middle of heaven— that is, he attracts the water. After attracting it, he again repels it into the upper regions, where the winds lay hold of it, scatter it, and reduce it into a vapor, whence it naturally enough comes to pass that the winds which blow from this quarter—the south and southwest—are of all winds the most rainy. And my own opinion is that the sun does not get rid of all the water which he draws year by year from the Nile, but retains some about him.[12]

These three examples reveal that Herodotus was not a passive reporter of incredible tales and rubbish, "a liar." On the contrary, he was quite scrupulous, objective, scientific for his time. Why should one seek to discredit such a historian, to make him seem naive? Why "refabricate" history despite his explicit evidence?

Undoubtedly the basic reason for this is that Herodotus, after relating his eyewitness account informing us that the Egyptians were Blacks, then demonstrated, with rare honesty (for a Greek), that Greece borrowed from Egypt all the elements of her civilization, even the cult of the gods, and that Egypt was the cradle of civilization. Moreover, archeological discoveries continually justify Herodotus against his detractors. Thus, Christiane Desroches-Noblecourt writes about recent excavations in Tanis*: "Herodotus had seen the outer buildings of these sepulchers and had described them. [This was the Labyrinth discussed above.] Pierre Montet has just proved once again that 'The Father of History did not lie.' "[13] It could be objected that, in the fifth century B.C. when Herodotus visited Egypt, its civilization was already more than 10,000 years old and that the race which had created it was not necessarily the Negro race that Herodotus found there.

But the whole history of Egypt, as we shall see, shows that the

---

*Tanis, the Biblical Zoan, at the mouth of the eastern branch of the Nile Delta.

mixture of the early population with white nomadic elements, conquerors or merchants, became increasingly important as the end of Egyptian history approached. According to Cornelius de Pauw, in the low epoch Egypt was almost saturated with foreign white colonies: Arabs in Coptos, Libyans on the future site of Alexandria, Jews around the city of Hercules (Avaris?), Babylonians (or Persians) below Memphis, "fugitive Trojans" in the area of the great stone quarries east of the Nile, Carians and Ionians over by the Pelusiac branch. Psammetichus (end of seventh century) capped this peaceful invasion by entrusting the defense of Egypt to Greek mercenaries. "An enormous mistake of Pharaoh Psammetichus was to commit the defense of Egypt to foreign troops and to introduce various colonies made up of the dregs of the nations."[14] Under the last Saite dynasty, the Greeks were officially established at Naucratis, the only port where foreigners were authorized to engage in trading.

After the conquest of Egypt by Alexander, under the Ptolemies, crossbreeding between white Greeks and black Egyptians flourished, thanks to a policy of assimilation: "Nowhere was Dionysus more favored, nowhere was he worshiped more adoringly and more elaborately than by the Ptolemies, who recognized his cult as an especially effective means of promoting the assimilation of the conquering Greeks and their fusion with the native Egyptians."[15]

These facts prove that if the Egyptian people had originally been white, it might well have remained so. If Herodotus found it still black after so much crossbreeding, it must have been basic black at the start.

Insofar as Biblical evidence is concerned, a few details are in order. To determine the worth of Biblical evidence, we must examine the genesis of the Jewish people. What, then, was the Jewish people? How was it born? How did it create the Bible, in which descendants of Ham, ancestors of Negroes and Egyptians, would thus be accursed; what might be the historical reason for that curse? Those who would become the Jews entered Egypt numbering 70 rough, fearful shepherds, chased from Palestine by famine and attracted by that earthly paradise, the Nile Valley.

Although the Egyptians had a peculiar horror of nomadic life and shepherds, these newcomers were first warmly welcomed, thanks to Joseph. According to the Bible, they settled in the land of Goshen and became shepherds of the Pharaoh's flocks. After the death of Joseph and the Pharaoh "Protector," and facing the proliferation of the Jews, the Egyptians grew hostile, in circumstances still ill-defined. The condition of the Jews became more and more difficult. If we are to believe the Bible, they were employed on construction work, serving as laborers in building the city of Ramses. The Egyptians took steps to limit the number of births and eliminate male babies, lest the ethnic minority develop into a national danger which, in time of war, might increase enemy ranks.[16]

So began the initial persecutions by which the Jewish people was to remain marked throughout its history. Henceforth the Jewish minority, withdrawn within itself, would become Messianic by suffering and humiliation. Such a moral terrain of wretchedness and hope favored the birth and development of religious sentiment. The circumstances were the more favorable because this race of shepherds, without industry or social organization (the only social cell was the patriarchal family), armed with nothing but sticks, could envisage no positive reaction to the technical superiority of the Egyptian people.

It was to meet this crisis that Moses appeared, the first of the Jewish prophets, who, after minutely working out the history of the Jewish people from its origins, presented it in retrospect under a religious perspective. Thus he caused Abraham to say many things that the latter could not possibly have foreseen: for example, the 400 years in Egypt. Moses lived at the time of Tell el Amarna*, when Amenophis IV (Akhnaton, circa 1400) was trying to revive the early monotheism which had by then been discredited by sacerdotal ostentation and the corruptness of the priests. Akhnaton seems to have attempted to bolster political centralism in his recently conquered immense empire through religious centralism; the empire needed a universal religion.

Moses was probably influenced by this reform. From that time on, he championed monotheism among the Jews. Monotheism, with all its abstraction, already existed in Egypt, which had borrowed it from the Meroitic Sudan, the Ethiopia of the Ancients. "Although the Supreme Deity, viewed in the purest of monotheistic visions as the 'only generator in the sky and on earth who was not engendered . . . the only living god in truth . . .' Amon, whose name signifies mystery, adoration, one day finds himself rejected, overtaken by Ra, the Sun, or converted into Osiris or Horus."[17]

Given the insecure atmosphere in which the Jewish people found

---

*Tell el Amarna, a city built 190 miles above Cairo in 1396, as the new capital of Akhnaton's empire.

itself in Egypt, a God promising sure tomorrows was an irreplaceable moral support. After some reticence at the outset, this people which apparently had not known monotheism previously—contrary to the opinion of those who would credit it as the inventor [of monotheism] —would nonetheless carry it to a rather remarkable degree of development. Aided by faith, Moses led the Hebrew people out of Egypt. However, the Israelites quickly tired of this religion and only gradually returned to monotheism. (The Golden Calf of Aaron at the foot of Mount Sinai.)

Having entered Egypt as 70 shepherds grouped in 12 patriarchal families, nomads without industry or culture, the Jewish people left there 400 years later, 600,000 strong, after acquiring from it all the elements of its future tradition, including monotheism.

If the Egyptians persecuted the Israelites as the Bible says, and if the Egyptians were Negroes, sons of Ham, as the same Bible says, we can no longer ignore the historical causes of the curse upon Ham— despite the legend of Noah's drunkenness. The curse entered Jewish literature considerably later than the period of persecution. Accordingly, Moses, in the Book of Genesis, attributed the following words to the Eternal God, addressed to Abraham in a dream: "Know for certain that your posterity will be strangers in a land not their own; they shall be subjected to slavery and shall be oppressed four hundred years."[18]

Here we have reached the historical background of the curse upon Ham. It is not by chance that this curse on the father of Mesraim, Phut, Kush, and Canaan, fell only on Canaan, who dwelt in a land that the Jews have coveted throughout their history.

Whence came this name Ham (Cham, Kam)? Where could Moses have found it? Right in Egypt where Moses was born, grew up, and lived until the Exodus. In fact, we know that the Egyptians called their country *Kemit,* which means "black" in their language. The interpretation according to which *Kemit* designates the black soil of Egypt, rather than the black man and, by extension, the black race of the country of the Blacks, stems from a gratuitous distortion by minds aware of what an exact interpretation of this word would imply. Hence, it is natural to find *Kam* in Hebrew, meaning heat, black, burned.[19]

That being so, all apparent contradictions disappear and the logic of facts appears in all its nudity. The inhabitants of Egypt, symbolized by their black color, Kemit or Ham of the Bible, would be ac-

2. Handsome East African Hamitic Type (from Nelle Puccioni, "Ricerche antropometriche sui Somali," *Archivio per l'antropologia,* 1911; cited by Seligman in *Egypt and Negro Africa*). Fully to appreciate the joke, replace Seligman's wording above by the "official" interpretation: Handsome type of the paleo-Mediterranean white race to which we owe all black civilizations, including that of Egypt.

cursed in the literature of the people they had oppressed. We can see that this Biblical curse on Ham's offspring had an origin quite different from that generally given it today without the slightest historical foundation. What we cannot understand however, is how it has been possible to make a white race of *Kemit*: Hamite, black, ebony, etc. (even in Egyptian). Obviously, according to the needs of the cause, Ham is cursed, blackened, and made into the ancestor of the Negroes. This is what happens whenever one refers to contemporary social relations.

On the other hand, he is whitened whenever one seeks the origin of civilization, because there he is inhabiting the first civilized country in the world. So, the idea of Eastern and Western Hamites is conceived—nothing more than a convenient invention to deprive Blacks of the moral advantage of Egyptian civilization and of other African civilizations, as we shall see. Figure 2 enables us to perceive the biased nature of these theories.

It is impossible to link the notion of Hamite, as we labor to understand it in official textbooks, with the slightest historical, geographical, linguistic, or ethnic reality. No specialist is able to pinpoint the birthplace of the Hamites (scientifically speaking), the language they spoke, the migratory route they followed, the countries they settled, or the form of civilization they may have left. On the contrary, all the experts agree that this term has no serious content, and yet not one of them fails to use it as a kind of master-key to explain the slightest evidence of civilization in Black Africa.

CHAPTER II

Birth of the Negro Myth

When Herodotus visited it, Egypt had already lost its independence a century earlier. Conquered by the Persians in 525, from then on it was continually dominated by the foreigner: after the Persians came the Macedonians under Alexander (333 B.C.), the Romans under Julius Caesar (50 B.C.), the Arabs in the seventh century, the Turks in the sixteenth century, the French with Napoleon, then the English at the end of the nineteenth century.

Ruined by all these successive invasions, Egypt, the cradle of civilization for 10,000 years while the rest of the world was steeped in barbarism, would no longer play a political role. Nevertheless, it would long continue to initiate the younger Mediterranean peoples (Greeks and Romans, among others) into the enlightenment of civilization. Throughout Antiquity it would remain the classic land where the Mediterranean peoples went on pilgrimages to drink at the fount of scientific, religious, moral, and social knowledge, the most ancient such knowledge that mankind had acquired.

Thus, all around the periphery of the Mediterranean, new civilizations have been built, one after the other, benefiting from the many advantages of the Mediterranean, a veritable crossroads in the world's best location. These new civilizations have evolved mainly toward materialistic and technical development. As the origin of that evolution, we must cite the materialistic genius of the Indo-Europeans: Greeks and Romans.

The pagan élan, which animated Greco-Roman civilization, died out about the fourth century. Two new factors, Christianity and the barbarian invasions, intruded on the old terrain of Western Europe and gave birth to a new civilization which today, in its turn, presents symptoms of exhaustion. Thanks to uninterrupted contacts between peoples, this latter civilization, which inherited all the technical progress of humanity, was already sufficiently equipped by the fifteenth century to plunge into the discovery and conquest of the world.

And so, as early as the fifteenth century, the Portuguese landed in

3. The God Osiris. (The Metropolitan Museum of Art, Rogers Fund, 1910.)

4. Protohistorical Figure of Lord Tera Neter, of the Negro Anu race, first inhabitants of Egypt. (Cf. Petrie, *The Making of Ancient Egypt.*)

5. Narmer (or Menes), typical Negro, first Pharaoh of Egypt, who unified Upper and Lower Egypt for the first time. He is assuredly neither Aryan, Indo-European, nor Semitic, but unquestionably Black.

6. Zoser. A typical Negro, this Pharaoh of the Third Dynasty inaugurated large architecture in hewn stone: step pyramid and tomb at Saqqara. With him, all the technological elements of Egyptian civilization were already in place and would be perpetuated from then on. (The Metropolitan Museum of Art, Rogers Fund, 1911.)

7. Cheops, Fourth Dynasty Pharaoh, builder of the Great Pyramid: a Black man resembling the present-day Cameroonian type.

8. Mycerinus (Fourth Dynasty), who built the third Giza pyramid. Next to him, the goddess Hathor.

9.   Pharaoh Mentuhotep I, a typical Negro, founder
of the Eleventh Dynasty (circa 2100 B.C.).

10. Pharaoh Sesostris I (Twelfth Dynasty).

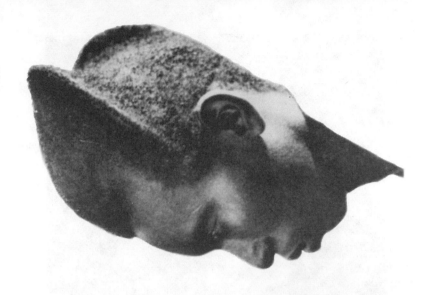

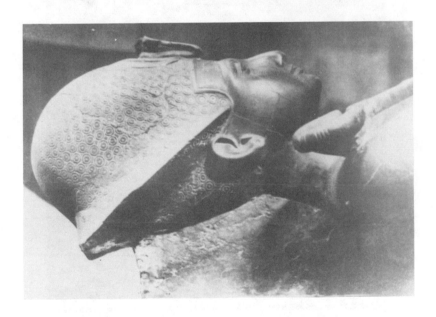

11. Pharaoh Ramses II (top), and a modern Watusi. The Watusi hair-do can be conceived only for woolly hair. The small circles on the Pharaoh's helmet represent frizzy hair (as noted by Denise Cappart in her article in *Reflet du Monde*, 1956).

12.   Pharaoh Tuthmosis III, son of a Sudanese woman, founded the Eighteenth Dynasty and inaugurated the era of Egyptian imperialism. He is sometimes referred to as the "Napoleon of Antiquity."

13.   The Sudanese Pharaoh Taharqa.

Africa via the Atlantic; they established the first modern contacts, henceforth unbroken, with the West. What did they find then in Africa? Which peoples did they encounter? Had these been there since early Antiquity or had they just migrated? What was their cultural level, the degree of their social and political organization? What impression could the Portuguese have had of these populations? What idea could they get of their intellectual capacity and technical aptitude? What kind of social relations were to exist between Europe and Africa from that time on? The answer to these different questions will fully explain the current legend of the primitive Negro.

To answer those queries, it is necessary to go back to Egypt at the time it fell under the yoke of the foreigner. The distribution of Blacks on the African continent probably went through two principal phases. It is generally agreed that by 7000 B.C., the Sahara had dried up. Equatorial Africa was probably still a forest zone too dense to attract men. Consequently, the last Blacks who had lived in the Sahara now presumably left it to migrate toward the Upper Nile, with the possible exception of a few small isolated groups on the rest of the continent, who either had migrated toward the south or had headed north.[1] Perhaps the first group found an indigenous Black population in the region of the Upper Nile. Whatever the case, it was from the gradual adaptation to the new living conditions which nature assigned to these various Black populations that the oldest phenomenon of civilization, came about. This civilization, called Egyptian in our period, developed for a long time in its early cradle; then it slowly descended the Nile Valley to spread out around the Mediterranean basin. This cycle of civilization, the longest in history, presumably lasted 10,000 years. This is a reasonable compromise between the long chronology (based on data provided by Egyptian priests, Herodotus and Manetho* place the beginning at 17,000 B.C.) and the short chronology of the moderns—for the latter are obliged to admit that by 4245 B.C. the Egyptians had already invented the calendar (which necessarily requires the passage of thousands of years).

Obviously, during that long period, the Blacks could have penetrated deeper and deeper into the interior of the continent to form nuclei which would become centers of the continental civilization analyzed in Chapter VIII. These African civilizations would be cut off from the rest of the world. They would tend to live in isolation, as a

---

*Manetho of Sebennytos, an Egyptian priest (third century B.C.), who wrote a chronicle on Egypt in Greek.

result of the enormous distance separating them from access routes to the Mediterranean. When Egypt lost its independence, their isolation was complete.

From then on, separated from the mother country which was invaded by the foreigner, and withdrawn in a geographical setting requiring a minimum effort of adjustment, the Blacks were oriented toward the development of their social, political, and moral organization, rather than toward speculative scientific research that their circumstances failed to justify, and even rendered impossible. Adaptation to the narrow, fertile Nile Valley required expert technique in irrigation and dams, precise calculations to foresee the inundations of the Nile and to deduce their economic and social consequences. It also required the invention of geometry to delimit property after the floods obliterated boundary lines. By the same token, the terrain in long flat strips required the transformation of the paleo-Negritic hoe into a plow, first drawn by men, subsequently by animals. Indispensable as all that was for the Negro's material existence in the Nile Valley, it became equally superfluous in the new living conditions in the interior.

Since history had disrupted his former equilibrium with the environment, the Black now found a new equilibrium, differing from the first in the absence of a technique no longer vital to the social, political, and moral organization. With economic resources assured by means that did not require perpetual inventions, the Negro became progressively indifferent to material progress.

It was under these new conditions that the encounter with Europe took place. In the fifteenth century, when the first Portuguese, Dutch, English, French, Danes, and Brandenburgers began to set up trading posts on the West African coast, the political organization of the African States was equal, and often superior, to that of their own respective States. Monarchies were already constitutional, with a People's Council on which the various social strata were represented. Contrary to the legend, the Negro king was not, and had never been, a despot with unlimited powers. In some places, he was invested by the people, with the Prime Minister an intermediary representing the free men. His mission was to serve the people wisely and his authority depended on his respect for the established constitution (cf. Chapter VIII).

The social and moral order was on the same level of perfection. Nowhere did any pre-logical mentality reign, in the sense that Lévy-Bruhl understood it, but there is no need to refute here an idea that its author rejected before his death. On the other hand, for all the reasons cited above, technical development was less stressed than in Europe. Although the Negro had been the first to discover iron, he had built no cannon; the secret of gunpowder was known only to the Egyptian priests, who used it solely for religious purposes at rites such as the Mysteries of Osiris (cf. Cornelius de Pauw's *Recherches sur les Egyptiens et les Chinois*).

Africa was therefore quite vulnerable from the technical standpoint. It became tempting, irresistible prey for the West, provided with firearms and far-ranging navies. So the economic progress of Renaissance Europe spurred on the conquest of Africa, which was rapidly accomplished. It passed from the stage of coastal trading-posts to that of annexation by Western international agreements, followed by armed conquest called "pacification."

At the beginning of this period America was discovered by Christopher Columbus and the overflow of the old continent was dumped on the new. The development of virgin lands required cheap labor. Defenseless Africa then became the readymade reservoir from which to draw that labor force with minimum expense and risk. The modern Negro slave trade was considered an economic necessity prior to the advent of the machine. This would last until the mid-nineteenth century.

Such a reversal of roles, the result of new technical relations, brought with it master-slave relationships between Whites and Blacks on the social level. Already during the Middle Ages, the memory of a Negro Egypt that had civilized the world had been blurred by ignorance of the antique tradition hidden in libraries or buried under ruins. It would become even more obscure during those four centuries of slavery.

Inflated by their recent technical superiority, the Europeans looked down on the Black world and condescended to touch nothing but its riches. Ignorance of the Black's ancient history, differences of mores and customs, ethnic prejudices between two races that believed themselves to be facing each other for the first time, combined with the economic necessity to exploit—so many factors predisposed the mind of the European to distort the moral personality of the Black and his intellectual aptitudes.

Henceforth "Negro" became a synonym for primitive being, "inferior," endowed with a pre-logical mentality. As the human being is always eager to justify his conduct, they went even further. The desire to legitimize colonization and the slave trade—in other words, the social condition of the Negro in the modern world—engendered an entire literature to describe the so-called inferior traits of the Black. The mind of several generations of Europeans would thus be gradually indoctrinated, Western opinion would crystallize and instinctively accept as revealed truth the equation: Negro=inferior humanity.[2] To crown this cynicism, colonization would be depicted as a duty of humanity. They invoked "the civilizing mission" of the West charged with the responsibility to raise the African to the level of other men [known to us as "the white man's burden"]. From then on, capitalism had clear sailing to practice the most ferocious exploitation under the cloak of moral pretexts.

At most they recognize that the Negro has artistic gifts linked to his sensitivity as an inferior animal. Such is the opinion of the Frenchman Joseph de Gobineau, precursor of Nazi philosophy, who in his famous book *On the Inequality of Human Races* decrees that the artistic sense is inseparable from Negro blood; but he reduces art to an inferior manifestation of human nature: in particular, the sense of rhythm is related to the Black's emotional aptitudes.

This climate of alienation finally deeply affected the personality of the Negro, especially the educated Black who had had an opportunity to become conscious of world opinion about him and his people. It often happens that the Negro intellectual loses confidence in his own possibilities and in those of his race to such an extent that, despite the validity of the evidence presented in this book, it will not be astonishing if some of us are still unable to believe that Blacks really played the earliest civilizing role in the world.

Frequently Blacks of high intellectual attainments remain so victimized by this alienation that they seek in all good faith to codify those Nazi ideas in an alleged duality of the sensitive, emotional Negro, creator of art, and the White Man, especially endowed with rationality.[3] So it is in good faith that a Black African poet expressed himself in a verse of admirable beauty:

"L'émotion est nègre et la raison hellène."[4] (Emotion is Negro and reason Greek.)

Little by little, a "complementary" Negro literature appeared, intentionally puerile, good humored, passive, resigned, whimpering. A mass of current Negro artistic creations, greatly appreciated by Westerners, forms a mirror in which these Westerners can look with pride, while wallowing in paternalistic sentimentality as they contemplate what they believe to be their superiority. The reaction would be quite different if the same judges were confronted by a perfectly composed Negro work which abandoned that pattern and broke with any reflexes of subordination as well as inferiority complexes to assume a natural place on a level of equality. Such a work would certainly risk appearing pretentious and at least exasperating to some people.

The memory of the recent slavery to which the Black race has been subjected, cleverly kept alive in men's minds and especially in Black minds, often affects Black consciousness negatively. From that recent slavery an attempt has been made to construct—despite all historical truth—a legend that the Black has always been reduced to slavery by the superior White race with which he has lived, wherever it may have been. This enables Whites easily to justify the presence of Negroes in Egypt or in Mesopotamia or Arabia, by decreeing that they were enslaved. Although such an affirmation is nothing but dogma designed to falsify history—those who advance it are fully aware that it is erroneous—it nonetheless contributes to alienating Black consciousness. Thus, another great Negro poet, perhaps the greatest of our time, Aimé Césaire, writes, in a poem entitled, "Since Akkad, since Elam, since Sumer":

> Master of the three roads, before you stands a man who has walked much.
> Master of the three roads, before you stands a man who has walked on his hands, walked on his feet, walked on his belly, walked on his backside,
> Since Elam, since Akkad, since Sumer.[5]

Elsewhere he writes:

> Those who invented neither gunpowder nor compass
> those who tamed neither steam nor electricity
> those who explored neither the sea nor the sky . . .[6]

Throughout these transformations in the Negro's relations with the rest of the world, it became increasingly difficult each day and even inadmissible, for those unaware of his past glory—and for Blacks themselves—to believe that they could have originated the first civilization which flowered on earth, a civilization to which humanity owes most of its progress.

Henceforth, even when the proofs are piled high before their eyes, the experts will not see them except through blinkers and will always interpret them falsely. They will build the most improbable theories, since any improbability seems more logical to them than the truth of the most important historical document attesting the early civilizing role of Blacks. Before examining the contradictions circulating in the modern era and resulting from attempts to prove at any price that the Egyptians were Whites, let us note the astonishment of a scholar of good faith, Count Constantin de Volney (1757–1820). After being imbued with all the prejudices we have just mentioned with regard to the Negro, Volney had gone to Egypt between 1783 and 1785, while Negro slavery flourished. He reported as follows on the Egyptian race, the very race that had produced the Pharaohs: the Copts.

> . . . all have a bloated face, puffed up eyes, flat nose, thick lips; in a word, the true face of the mulatto. I was tempted to attribute it to the climate, but when I visited the Sphinx, its appearance gave me the key to the riddle. On seeing that head, typically Negro in all its features, I remembered the remarkable passage where Herodotus says: "As for me, I judge the Colchians to be a colony of the Egyptians because, like them, they are black with woolly hair. . . ." In other words, the ancient Egyptians were true Negroes of the same type as all native-born Africans. That being so, we can see how their blood, mixed for several centuries with that of the Romans and Greeks, must have lost the intensity of its original color, while retaining nonetheless the imprint of its original mold. We can even state as a general principle that the face is a kind of monument able, in many cases, to attest or shed light on historical evidence on the origins of peoples.

After illustrating this proposition by citing the case of Normans who still resembled the Danes 900 years after the conquest of Normandy, Volney adds:

> But returning to Egypt, the lesson she teaches history contains many reflections for philosophy. What a subject for meditation, to see the present barbarism and ignorance of the Copts, descendants of the alliance between the profound genius of the Egyptians and

the brilliant mind of the Greeks! Just think that this race of black men, today our slave and the object of our scorn, is the very race to which we owe our arts, sciences, and even the use of speech! Just imagine, finally, that it is in the midst of peoples who call themselves the greatest friends of liberty and humanity that one has approved the most barbarous slavery and questioned whether black men have the same kind of intelligence as Whites![7]

14.   Egyptian Woman.

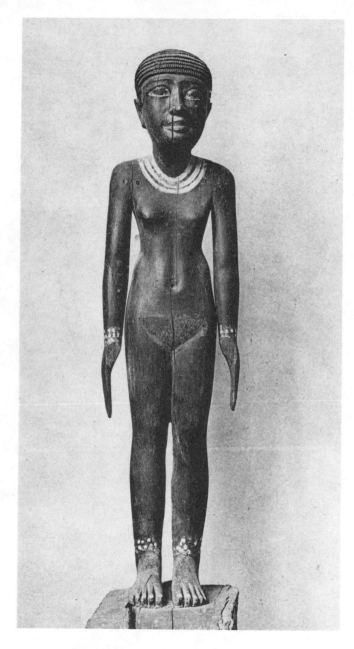

15.   Egyptian Woman (The Lady with Thumbs).

16.   Egyptian Women Making Perfume.

17.   Vintage Time (on the estate of an Egyptian priest).

18. Egyptian Sculpture: Battalion of 40 Armed Sudanese (from Tomb of Prince Masathi of Assiout, Twelfth Dynasty). (Cairo Museum. Photo by Federico Borromeo/Scala.)

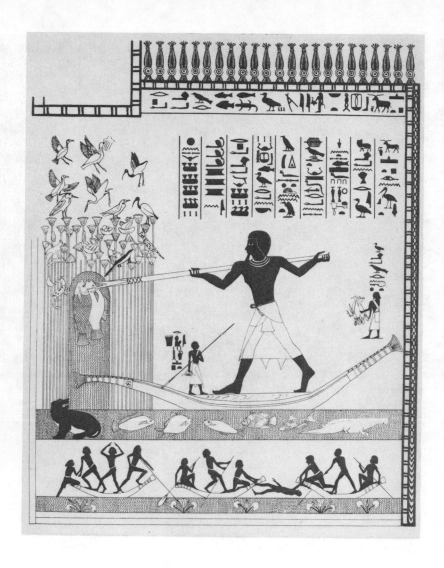

19. Egyptians Fishing (Twelfth Dynasty). The slender
bodies and rhythmic movements remind one of any work
scene in Black Africa today.

20. Egyptian Heads (Middle Kingdom?). These have been called "heads of foreigners," because they are too Negroid. (Photo by Tel.)

21.   A Cook (Fifth Dynasty), with "reddish-brown body."

22.   Nok Terra Cotta (Nigeria). The Negro depicted by himself. Compare this with Egyptian statuary: the same physical features; but note contrast with peasant-prisoners in Fig. 23. This is a difference of class, not of race. (Photo by W. Fagg, from *Nigerian Images, The Splendor of African Sculpture.*)

23.   Black Peasant Prisoners on the Tomb of Pharaoh Horemheb. Note the differences from the urban type in previous figure. This peasant type appears in African urban centers only after transplantation of rural elements bearing the signs of hard country life. So, what has been misinterpreted as a racial difference is in reality only class distinction between the city aristocrat and the wrinkled peasant with rough hands, who had become less common in Egypt where farming was not so difficult as in Nubia.

24. Egyptian Princess and Three Senegalese Girls. The coiffures of the Princess (upper left) and the three post-pubescent girls (prior to 1946) reflect a constant effort (from Egyptian Antiquity to the present) to adapt frizzy hair to feminine grace. The whole aspect of the world would be changed if Black girls had long hair.

25.   Djimbi and Djéré. Egyptian wigs corresponding
to the djimbi and djéré of Senegalese married women
(until about 1933).

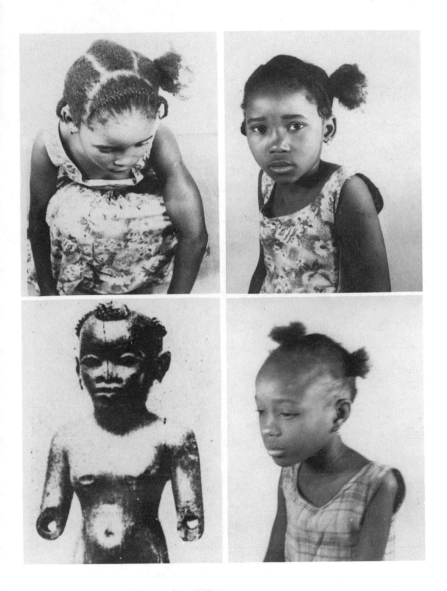

26. Totemic Coiffures. These hair-dos of pre-pubescent Senegalese girls (prior to World War II) correspond to that of the Eighteenth Dynasty Egyptian girl in the statuette (lower left), more than 3,500 years earlier—before Moses.

27.   A Negroid of Mesopotamia: Patesi, king of Lagash, more generally known as Gudea (2300 B.C.). (The
Metropolitan Museum of Art, Purchase, Dick Fund, 1959.)

CHAPTER III

Modern Falsification of History

The problem of the most monstrous falsification in the history of humanity by modern historians could not have been posed better than Volney did. No one could have been abler than he to render justice to the black race by recognizing its role as mankind's pioneer guide on the road to civilization. His conclusions should have ruled out the subsequent invention of a hypothetical white Pharaonic race that allegedly imported Egyptian civilization from Asia at the start of the historical period. In fact, that hypothesis is difficult to reconcile with the reality of the Sphinx, which is the image of a Pharaoh having the head of a Black. That image is there for all to see; it can hardly be discounted as an atypical document, nor relegated to the storeroom of a museum to remove it from the dangerous meditation of those susceptible of accepting factual evidence.

After Volney, another traveler, Domeny de Rienzi, early in the nineteenth century, reaches somewhat similar conclusions concerning the Egyptians: "It is true that back in the distant past, the dark red Hindu and Egyptian race dominated culturally the yellow and black races, and even our own white race then inhabiting western Asia. At that time our race was rather savage and sometimes tattooed, as I have seen it depicted on the tomb of Sesostris I in the valley of Biban-el-Moluk at Thebes, the city of the gods."[1]

As far as the dark red race is concerned, we shall see that it is simply a subgroup of the Black race as presented on the monuments of that time. In reality, there is no dark red race; only three well-defined races exist: the white, the black, and the yellow. The so-called intermediate races probably result solely from crossbreeding.[2]

Figure 28 shows that the dark red color of the Egyptians is nothing but the natural skin color of the Negro. If Rienzi speaks of a dark red race, instead of a black race, this is because he could not possibly rid himself of the prejudices of his day. In any event, his observations on the condition of the white race, then savage and tattooed, while the "dark red" races were already civilized, should have precluded any

43

28. The Famous Dark Red Color. This is the color that has caused so much ink to flow; it is the leitmotif of most works on the Egyptian race. The reader will judge whether it is anything other than the color of all African Negroes. Reference to this figure is often required to confront the tendentious writings of authors who base their arguments on that ethnic feature. (Reproduction British Museum.)

attempt to explain the origin of Egyptian civilization as due to Whites. Champollion expanded with humiliation on the backward condition of the latter at a time when Egyptian civilization was already several millennia old.

In 1799 Bonaparte undertook his campaign in Egypt. Thanks to the Rosetta stone, hieroglyphics were deciphered in 1822 by Champollion the Younger, who died in 1832. He left as his "calling card" an Egyptian grammar and a series of letters to his brother, Champollion-Figeac, letters written during his visit to Egypt (1828–1829). These were published in 1833 by Champollion-Figeac. From then on the wall of the hieroglyphics was breached, unveiling surprising riches in their most minute details.

Egyptologists were dumbfounded with admiration for the past grandeur and perfection then discovered. They gradually recognized it as the most ancient civilization that had engendered all others. But, imperialism being what it is, it became increasingly "inadmissible" to continue to accept the theory—evident until then—of a Negro Egypt. The birth of Egyptology was thus marked by the need to destroy the memory of a Negro Egypt at any cost and in all minds. Henceforth, the common denominator of all the theses of the Egyptologists, their close relationship and profound affinity, can be characterized as a desperate attempt to refute that opinion. Almost all Egyptologists stress its falsity as a matter of course. Usually these attempted refutations take the following form:

Unable to detect any contradiction in the formal statements of the Ancients after an objective confrontation with total Egyptian reality, and consequently unable to disprove them, they either give them the silent treatment or reject them dogmatically and indignantly. They express regret that people as normal as the ancient Egyptians could have made so grievous an error and thus create so many difficulties and delicate problems for modern specialists. Next they try in vain to find a White origin for Egyptian civilization. They finally become mired down in their own contradictions, sliding over the difficulties of the problem after performing intellectual acrobatics as learned as they are unwarranted. They then repeat the initial dogma, judging that they have demonstrated to all honorable folk the White origin of Egyptian civilization.

It is the whole body of these theses that I propose to expose one after the other. In the interest of objectivity, I feel compelled to examine each point of view thoroughly, so as to be fair to the author involved and to enable the reader to become directly familiar with whatever contradictions and other facts I may point out.

Let us start with the oldest of these theses, that of Champollion the Younger, set forth in the thirteenth letter to his brother. It concerns bas-reliefs on the tomb of Sesostris I, also visited by Rienzi. These date back to the sixteenth century B.C. (Eighteenth Dynasty) and represent the races of man known to the Egyptians. This monument is the oldest complete ethnological document available. Here is what Champollion says about it:

> Right in the valley of Biban-el-Moluk, we admired, like all previous visitors, the astonishing freshness of the paintings and the fine sculptures on several tombs. I had a copy made of the *peoples* represented on the bas-reliefs. At first I had thought, from copies of these bas-reliefs published in England, that these peoples of different races led by the god Horus holding his shepherd's staff, were indeed nations subject to the rule of the Pharaohs. A study of the legends informed me that this tableau has a more general meaning. It portrays the third hour of the day, when the sun is beginning to turn on its burning rays, warming all the inhabited countries of our hemisphere. According to the legend itself, they wished to represent the inhabitants of Egypt and those of foreign lands. Thus we have before our eyes the image of the various races of man known to the Egyptians and we learn at the same time the great geographical or ethnographical divisions established during that early epoch. Men led by Horus, the shepherd of the peoples, belong to four distinct families. *The first, the one closest to the god, has a dark red color,* a well-proportioned body, kind face, nose slightly aquiline, long braided hair, and is dressed in white. The legends designate this species as *Rôt-en-ne-Rôme,* the race of men par excellence, i.e., the Egyptians.
>
> There can be no uncertainty about the racial identity of the man who comes next: he belongs to the Black race, designated under the general term *Nahasi.* The third presents a very different aspect; his skin color borders on yellow or tan; he has a strongly aquiline nose, thick, black pointed beard, and wears a short garment of varied colors; these are called *Namou.*
>
> Finally, the last one is what we call flesh-colored, a white skin of the most delicate shade, a nose straight or slightly arched, blue eyes, blond or reddish beard, tall stature and very slender, clad in a

hairy ox-skin, a veritable savage tattooed on various parts of his body; he is called *Tamhou*.

I hastened to seek the tableau corresponding to this one in the other royal tombs and, as a matter of fact, I found it in several. The variations I observed fully convinced me that they had tried to represent here the inhabitants of the four corners of the earth, according to the Egyptian system, namely: 1. the inhabitants of Egypt which, by itself, formed one part of the world . . . ; 2. the inhabitants of Africa proper: Blacks; 3. Asians; 4. finally (and I am ashamed to say so, since our race is the last and the most savage in the series), Europeans who, in those remote epochs, frankly did not cut too fine a figure in the world. In this category we must include all blonds and white-skinned people living not only in Europe, but Asia as well, their starting point. This manner of viewing the tableau is all the more accurate because, on the other tombs, the same generic names reappear, always in the same order. We find there *Egyptians and Africans represented in the same way**, which could not be otherwise; but the Namou (the Asians) and the Tamhou (Europeans) present significant and curious variants. Instead of the Arab or the Jew, dressed simply and represented on one tomb, Asia's representatives on other tombs (those of Ramses II, etc.) are three individuals, tanned complexion, aquiline nose, black eyes, and thick beard, but clad in rare splendor. In one, they are evidently *Assyrians;* their costume, down to the smallest detail, is identical with that of personages engraved on Assyrian cylinders. In the other, are *Medes* or early inhabitants of some part of Persia. Their physiognomy and dress resemble, feature for feature, those found on monuments called *Persepolitan*. Thus, Asia was represented indiscriminately by any one of the peoples who inhabited it. *The same is true of our good old ancestors*, the Tamhou. Their attire is sometimes different; their heads are more or less hairy and adorned with various ornaments; their savage dress varies somewhat in form, but their white complexion, their eyes and beard all preserve the character of a race apart. I had this strange ethnographical series copied and colored. I certainly did not expect, on arriving at Biban-el-Moluk, to find sculptures that could serve as vignettes for the history of the primitive Europeans, if ever one has the courage to attempt it. Nevertheless, there is something flat-

---

*Italics Dr. Diop's.

tering and consoling in seeing them, since they make us appreciate the progress we have subsequently achieved.[3]

For a very good reason, I have reproduced this extract as Champollion-Figeac published it, rather than take it from the "new edition" of the *Letters* published in 1867 by the son of Champollion the Younger (Chéronnet-Champollion). The originals were addressed to Champollion-Figeac; therefore his edition is more authentic.

What is the value of this document for information on the Egyptian race? By its antiquity, it constitutes a major piece of evidence, which should have rendered all conjecture unnecessary. As early as that very ancient epoch, the Eighteenth Dynasty (between Abraham and Moses), the Egyptians habitually represented, in a manner that could not possibly be confused by the white and yellow races of Europe and Asia, the two groups of their own race: civilized Blacks of the valley, and Blacks from certain areas in the interior. The order in which the four races are consistently arranged in relation to the god Horus, confers upon it the character of a social hierarchy. As Champollion finally recognized, it also brushes aside any idea of a conventional portrayal that might blur the two distinct levels and place Horus on the same plane as the personages, whereas in reality he should rightfully be in front of them all.

It is typical for the Egyptians to be represented in a color officially called "dark red." Scientifically speaking, there really is no dark red race. The term was launched only to create confusion. There is no really black man in the exact sense of the word. The Negro's color in actual fact verges on brown; but it is impossible to apply an exact descriptive term to it, the more so because it varies from region to region. Thus it has been noted that Blacks in limestone areas are lighter than those elsewhere.

Consequently, it is very hard to capture the Negro's color in painting, and one settles for approximations. The color of the two men closest to the god Horus is merely the expression of two Negro shades. If today a Wolof portrayed a Bambara, a Mossi, a Yoruba, a Toucouleur, a Fang, a Mangbetu, or a Baulé, he would need as many if not more hues than there are on the two Blacks of the bas-relief. Would not the Wolof, Bambara, Mossi, Yoruba, Toucouleur, Fang, Mangbetu, and Baulé still be Negroes? This is how the color difference between the first two men on the bas-reliefs should be interpreted. On Egyptian bas-reliefs, it is impossible to find a single painting which depicts Egyptians in a color different from those of such Negro peoples as the Bambara, Agni, Yoruba, Mossi, Fang, Batutsi, Toucouleur, etc.

If Egyptians were White, then all these forementioned Negro peoples and so many others in Africa are also Whites. Thus we reach the absurd conclusion that Blacks are basically Whites.

On these numerous bas-reliefs, we see that, under the Eighteenth Dynasty, all the specimens of the White race were placed behind the Blacks; in particular, the "blond beast" of Gobineau and the Nazis, a tattooed savage, dressed in animal skin, instead of being at the start of all civilization, was still essentially untouched by it and occupied the last echelon of humanity.

Champollion's conclusion is typical. After stating that these sculptures can serve as vignettes for the history of the early inhabitants of Europe, he adds, "if ever one has the courage to attempt it." Finally, after those comments, he presents his opinion on the Egyptian race:

> The first tribes that inhabited Egypt, that is, the Nile Valley between the Syene cataract and the sea, came from Abyssinia to Sennar. The ancient Egyptians belonged to a race quite similar to the Kennous or Barabras, present inhabitants of Nubia. In the Copts of Egypt, we do not find any of the characteristic features of the ancient Egyptian population. The Copts are the result of crossbreeding with all the nations that have successively dominated Egypt. It is wrong to seek in them the principal features of the old race.[4]

Here we see the first attempts to link the Egyptians with a stock different from that of the Copts, as confirmed by Volney's observations. The new origin that Champollion the Younger thought he discovered was not a happier choice; on both sides the difficulty remains the same. Fleeing from one Negro source (the Copts) only leads to another, equally Negro (Nubians and Abyssinians).

As a matter of fact, the Negro characters of the Ethiopian or Abyssinian race have been sufficiently affirmed by Herodotus and all the Ancients; there is no need to reopen the subject. The Nubians are the accepted ancestors of most African Blacks, to the point that the words Nubian and Negro are synonymous. Ethiopians and Copts are two Negro groups subsequently mixed with different white elements in various regions. Negroes of the Delta interbred gradually with Mediterranean Whites who continually filtered into Egypt. This formed the Coptic branch, composed mostly of stocky individuals inhabiting a rather swampy region. On the Negro Ethiopian substratum a White element was grafted, consisting of emigrants from Western Asia, whom we shall consider shortly. This mixture, in a plateau region, produced a more athletic type.

Despite this constant and very ancient crossbreeding, the Negro characteristics of the early Egyptian race have not yet disappeared; their skin color is still obviously black and quite different from that of a mixed breed with 50 percent white blood. In most cases, the color does not differ from that of other Black Africans. Thus we can understand why the Copts, and especially the Ethiopians, have features slightly deviant from those of Blacks free of any admixture with white races. It often happens that their hair is less frizzy. Although they have remained essentially prognathous, an effort has been made to present them both as pseudo-Whites, on the strength of their relatively fine features. They are pseudo-Whites when they are our contemporaries and when their ethnic reality prevents us from considering them as authentic Whites. But the skeletons of their forebears, found in the tombs, emerge completely whitened by the measurements of the anthropologists. We shall see how, thanks to these so-called scientific measurements, it is no longer possible to distinguish an Ethiopian, that is to say, a Negro skeleton, from that of a German. In view of the gap separating those two races, we realize how gratuitous and confusing such measurements are.

Champollion's opinion on the Egyptian race was recorded in a memoir prepared for the Pasha of Egypt, to whom he delivered it in 1829.

Now let us see whether the research of the brother of Champollion the Younger, Father of Egyptology, has shed any light on the subject. This is how he introduces the topic:

The opinion that the ancient population of Egypt belonged to the Negro African race, is an error long accepted as the truth. Since the Renaissance, travelers in the East, barely capable of fully appreciating the ideas provided by Egyptian monuments on this important question, have helped to spread that false notion and geographers have not failed to reproduce it, even in our day. A serious authority declared himself in favor of this view and popularized the error. Such was the effect of what the celebrated Volney published on the various races of men that he had observed in Egypt. In his

Voyage, which is in all libraries, he reports that the Copts are descended from the ancient Egyptians; that the Copts have a bloated face, puffed up eyes, flat nose, and thick lips, like a mulatto; that they resemble the Sphinx of the Pyramids, a distinctly Negro head. He concludes that the ancient Egyptians were true Negroes of the same species as all indigenous Africans. To support his opinion, Volney invokes that of Herodotus who, apropos the Colchians, recalls that the Egyptians had black skin and woolly hair. Yet these two physical qualities do not suffice to characterize the Negro race and Volney's conclusion as to the Negro origin of the ancient Egyptian civilization is evidently forced and inadmissible.[5]

After indirectly expressing regret that Volney's book is found in all libraries, Champollion-Figeac advances, as a decisive argument to refute the thesis of that scholar and all his predecessors, that black skin and woolly hair "do not suffice to characterize the Negro race." It is at the price of such alterations in basic definitions that it has been possible to whiten the Egyptian race. Lo and behold! It is no longer enough to be black from head to foot and to have woolly hair to be a Negro! One would imagine oneself in a world where physical laws are turned upside down; in any case, one is certainly far removed from the analytical Cartesian mind. These, however, were the definitions and alterations of the initial data that were to become cornerstones on which "Egyptological science" would be built.

The advent of Egyptology, through the interpretation of scientific erudition, is thus marked by the crude, conscious falsifications that we have just indicated. That is why Egyptologists so carefully avoided discussing the origin of the Egyptian race. To treat this question today, we have been obliged to unearth old texts by authors once famous, but later almost anonymous. Champollion's alterations show how hard it is to prove the contrary of reality and still remain intelligible. Where we were expecting a logical, objective refutation, we meet the typical word, "inadmissible," which is hardly synonymous with demonstration.

Champollion-Figeac continues:

It is recognized today that the inhabitants of Africa belong to three races, quite distinct from each other for all time: 1. Negroes proper, in Central and West Africa; 2. Kaffirs on the east coast, who have a less obtuse facial angle than Blacks and a high nose, but thick lips and woolly hair; 3. Moors, similar in stature, physiognomy and hair to the best-formed nations of Europe and western Asia, and differing only in skin color which is tanned by the climate. The ancient population of Egypt belonged to this latter race, that is, to the white race. To be convinced of this, we need only examine the human figures representing Egyptians on the monuments and above all the great number of mummies that have been opened. Except for the color of the skin, blackened by the hot climate, they are the same men as those of Europe and western Asia: frizzy, woolly hair is the true characteristic of the Negro race; the Egyptians, however, had long hair, identical with that of the white race of the West.[6]

Let us analyze Champollion-Figeac's statements, point by point. Contrary to his opinion, the Kaffirs do not constitute a race: the word Kaffir comes from an Arab word meaning pagan, the opposite of Moslem. When the Arabs entered Africa via Zanzibar, this was the word that designated the populations they found there who practiced a religion different from their own. As for the Moors, they descend directly from post-Islamic invaders who, starting from Yemen, conquered Egypt, North Africa, and Spain between the seventh and fifteenth centuries. From Spain they fell back on Africa. Thus, the Moors are basically Arab Moslems whose installation in Africa is quite recent. Numerous manuscripts preserved by the principal Moorish families in Mauritania today, manuscripts in which their genealogy is minutely traced since their departure from Yemen, testify to their origin. Moors are therefore a branch of those whom it is customary to call Semites, What will be said about the Semites later in this volume will dispel any possibility of making them the creators of Egyptian civilization. Like the Berbers, the Moors are hostile to sculpture, whereas Egyptian culture attaches great importance to that artistic manifestation. In the same chapter, the racial admixture of the Semite will be stressed; to this, rather than to climate, the color of the Moors should be attributed. Moreover, whether it be a question of mummies or living persons, there is no possible comparison between the skin color of the Moors, even tanned by the sun, and the black, Negro complexion of the Egyptians.

Yet to convince us, Champollion asks us to examine the human figures representing Egyptians on the monuments. The whole reality of Egyptian art contradicts him. Apparently he paid little attention to

Volney's typical remarks about the Sphinx, although he has just referred to them. On the strength of these same illustrations of which he speaks, we can say that in general, contrary to Champollion-Figeac, as one proceeds from Menes to the end of the Egyptian Empire and from the common people to the Pharaoh, passing in review the dignitaries of the Court and the high officials, it is impossible to find —and still keep a straight face—a single representative of the white race or of the Semitic race. It is impossible to find anyone there except Negroes of the same species as all indigenous Africans. The illustrations in this volume reproduce a series of monuments representing the various social strata of the Egyptian population, including especially the Pharaohs. And they forcibly lead us to note, strangely enough, that Egyptian art is often more Negro than Negro art proper. On examining these pictures, contrasting them one with the other, we wonder how they could possibly inspire the notion of a white Egyptian race.

Finally, after stating that black skin and woolly hair do not suffice to characterize the Negro race, Champollion-Figeac contradicts himself 36 lines later by writing, "frizzy, woolly hair is the true characteristic of the Negro race."[7] He goes so far as to say that the Egyptians had long hair and that, consequently, they belonged to the white race. It would appear from that text that the Egyptians were Whites with black skin and long hair. Though we may be unaware of the existence of such Whites, we can try to see how the author reached that conclusion. What has been said about Ethiopians and Copts shows that their hair may be less frizzy than that of other Negroes. Moreover, a black, completely black, race with long hair exists: the Dravidians, considered Negroes in India and Whites in Africa.

On the monuments the Egyptians are portrayed with artificial coiffures identical with those worn everywhere in Black Africa. We shall return to these in our analysis of Narmer's Tablet. The author concludes by describing the Egyptian's hair as being similar to that of Western Whites. We cannot accept that remark. Even when the hair of the Egyptian is less woolly than that of other Blacks, it is so thick and black as to rule out any possible comparison with the thin, light hair of Westerners. Lastly, it is curious to read about long-haired Egyptians when we know that Herodotus described their hair as woolly. Furthermore, as early as the Eleventh Dynasty, Blacks, Whites, and yellow-skinned men lived in Thebes, just as there are foreigners residing today in Paris.

When the Theban wants a luxurious coffin for his mummy, a tree-trunk is hollowed out and cut into human shape, with the cover representing the front of the corpse. The face is hidden under a yellow, white or black color. The choice of coloring shows that in Thebes, under the Eleventh Dynasty, yellow, white and black men lived, were accepted as fellow-citizens, and admitted into the Egyptian necropolis.[8]

We may wonder then why only long-haired mummies have survived and why the Negro mummies cited by Fontanes are neither shown nor mentioned. What has become of them? Statements by Herodotus leave no doubt about their existence. Were they considered foreign types irrelevant to the history of Egypt? Were they destroyed or hidden in the attics of museums? This is an extremely grave subject.

Champollion-Figeac's text continues:

Dr. Larrey investigated this problem in Egypt; he examined a large number of mummies, studied their skulls, recognized the principal characteristics, tried to identify them in the various races living in Egypt, and succeeded in doing so. The Abyssinians seemed to him to combine them all, except for the Black race. The Abyssinian has large eyes, an agreeable glance, . . . prominent cheekbones; the cheeks form a regular triangle with the prominent angles of the jawbone and mouth; the lips are thick without being everted as in Blacks; the teeth are fine, just slightly protruding; finally, the complexion is merely copper-colored: such are the Abyssinians observed by Dr. Larrey and generally known as Berbers or Barabras, present-day inhabitants of Nubia.[9]

Champollion adds that Frédéric Cailliaud, who had seen the Barabras, describes them as "industrious, sober, with dry humor . . . their hair is half-frizzy, short and curly, or braided like the Ancient Egyptian's and slightly oiled." This description, once again, sounds familiar. Thick lips, teeth slightly protruding—in clearer terms, prognathism—semi-frizzy hair, copper skin, are basic characteristics of the Negro race.

It is curious to note here that Champollion-Figeac speaks of the Abyssinian complexion as being "merely copper-colored." Yet, two pages later in the same chapter, he refers as follows to the many color nuances of the Negro:

> Lengthy wars had brought Egypt into contact with the African interior; thus, one distinguishes on Egyptian monuments several species of Blacks, differing among themselves in the principal features that modern travelers have listed as dissimilarities either with respect to complexion, which makes Negroes black or copper-colored, or with respect to other features no less typical.[10]

This new contradiction from the same pen confirms what we have said about the two men placed next to the god Horus, namely, the Egyptian and the Negro. These two men belong to the same race; there is no more color difference between them than between a Bambara and a Wolof, who are both Negroes. The so-called "dark red" color of the first, the "merely copper-colored" of the Abyssinian, and the "copper color" of the Negro are one and the same. We note in passing that the author's description tarries over insignificant details, such as an "agreeable glance," and so on.

The confusion over the term Berber must be pointed out. This too is a word improperly applied to populations of the Nile Valley that have nothing in common with those properly called Berber and Tuareg. There are no Berber in Egypt. On the contrary, we know that North Africa was called Barbary, the Barbary States; this area is the only real habitat of the Berber. Subsequently, the term was incorrectly applied to other populations. The root of this word, used during Antiquity, was probably of Negro rather than Indo-European origin. In reality, it is an onomatopoeic repetition of the root *Ber*. This kind of intensification of a root is general in African languages, especially in Egyptian.

Moreover, the root *Bar,* in Wolof, means to speak rapidly, and *Bar-Bar* would designate a people that speaks an unknown language, therefore a foreign people. In Wolof, especially, an adjective indicating nationality is formed by doubling the root: for example, Djoloff-Djoloff, inhabitants of Djoloff.*

Reproducing the bas-relief of Biban-el-Moluk, according to the drawing of Champollion the Younger, Champollion-Figeac did not re-

---

*Djoloff: one of the seven regions of Senegal.

spect the colors of the original. He completely shaded in the Negro's body, to remind us of his color, but avoided doing the same for the Egyptian, whom he left untinted. This is perhaps one way to whiten the latter, but it is not consistent with the document.

Chérubini, Champollion's travel companion, utilizes the same Biban-el-Moluk document to characterize the Egyptian race. He insists beforehand on the anteriority of Ethiopia to Egypt and cites the unanimous opinion of the Ancients that Egypt is merely a colony of Ethiopia, that is, Sudanese Meroitic. Throughout Antiquity, the Meroitic Sudan was even believed to be the birthplace of humanity:

> The human race must have been considered there as spontaneous, having been born in the upper areas of Ethiopia where the two sources of life—heat and humidity—are ever present. It is also in this region that the first glimmerings of history reveal the origin of societies and the primitive home of civilization. In the earliest Antiquity, before the ordinary calculations of history, a social organization appears, fully structured, with its religion, laws and institutions. The Ethiopians boasted of having been the first to establish worship of the divinity and the use of sacrifices. There, too, the torch of science and the arts was probably first lighted. To this people we must attribute the origin of sculpture, the use of written symbols, in short, the start of all the developments that make up an advanced civilization.[11]
>
> . . . They boasted of having preceded the other peoples on earth and about the real or relative superiority of their civilization while most societies were still in their infancy, and they seemed to justify their claims. No evidence attributed to any other source the beginnings of the Ethiopian family. On the contrary, a combination of very important facts tended to assign it a purely local origin at an early date.[12]
>
> Ethiopia was considered as a country apart. From this more or less paradisiacal source, the beginnings of life, the origin of living beings, seemed to emanate. . . .
>
> Except for some particulars furnished by the Father of History on those Ethiopians known as Macrobians, there was a rather hazy idea that Ethiopia produced men who surpassed the rest of humanity in height, beauty and longevity. One nevertheless recognized two great indigenous nations in Africa: the Libyans and the Ethiopians. The latter included the southernmost peoples of the

Black race; they were thus distinguished from the Libyans who, occupying the north of Africa, were less tanned by the sun. Such is the information that the Ancients have provided. . . .[13]

It is reasonable to assume that nowhere else on earth could we find a civilization whose progress would seem more certain and present such unquestionable evidences of priority . . .

Consistent with the original monuments, the writings of scholarly philosophical Antiquity authentically testify to this anteriority. In the history of primitive societies, perhaps no fact is supported by more complete and more decisive unanimity.[14]

Once again a modern reminds us that the Ancients, the very scientists and philosophers who have transmitted present-day civilization to us, from Herodotus to Diodorus, from Greece to Rome, unanimously recognized that they borrowed that civilization from Blacks on the banks of the Nile: Ethiopians or Egyptians. This text clearly indicates that the Ancients never questioned the Negro's role as an initiator of civilization.

Yet Chérubini nonetheless interprets the facts as he wishes. On the strength of the Biban-el-Moluk bas-relief, after Champollion the Younger and Champollion-Figeac, he supplies no new element concerning the Egyptian race, except a wrong interpretation of its complexion. He reports that if the *Rôt-en-ne-Rôme* (man par excellence) is depicted in a reddish-brown color (!), it is in order that he may be distinguished from the rest of mankind; thus it is a purely conventional choice:

In this classification of men of Antiquity that they themselves have bequeathed to us, we see the African population of the Nile Valley constituting by itself alone one of the four divisions of humanity and invariably occupying the first rank next to the god. This order is observed in several other places and does not appear to be due to chance. . . .

To make the distance separating them from other men more readily discernible, they attributed to themselves, as well as to the god incarnate in human form, a reddish-brown color perhaps a bit exaggerated or even somewhat conventional, which left no doubt about the originality of their race. They characterized it, moreover, on the monuments of their ancient civilization, by special features which would disclose an unquestionable African origin.[15]

The "reddish-brown" color that Champollion called "dark red" and which is quite simply "Negro colored," could not be a conventional color as Chérubini suggests. If it were, it would be the only conventional color on that bas-relief, whereas all the others are natural. There is no doubt about the reality of the white clothes worn by the first man, or the "flesh-colored bordering on yellow" complexion or tanned tint of the third, or the "white skin of the most delicate shade," the blond beard, and eyes of the fourth. Among so many natural colors, why should only one be conventional? Even less understandable is that it should be a Negro color rather than any other. According to Chérubini:

> The Egyptians carried their classification, or more precisely, their racial pride so far as to establish the most clear-cut distinction between themselves and their native African neighbors, such as the Negro populations with whom they were loath to be confused, and whom they placed in a separate category.[16]

The Egyptians went even further and represented their god in a Negro color, i.e., in their own image: coal black. The idea of anything conventional is thus to be rejected purely and simply. So, after Champollion-Figeac, it is Chérubini who sees the same Biban-el-Moluk document through blinkers. In this connection, we may appropriately repeat what was said earlier: By running away from the evidence of a Negro origin, the specialists fall into improbabilities and dead-end contradictions. Only such blindness can explain how Chérubini found it reasonable to resort to a conventional representation which contradicts his own opinion on the Egyptians and which they, too, would have found inadmissible. The author invokes the bas-reliefs of the Abu Simbel Temple (Lower Nubia), where prisoners captured by Sesostris after an expedition toward the south are portrayed. Chérubini reproduces these in an attempt to demonstrate that Egyptians and Blacks belonged to two different races:

> We see King Sesostris returning from an expedition against these Southerners; several captives precede his chariot. Farther on, the monarch offers the local gods two groups of prisoners evidently belonging to these savage tribes, an offering consecrated to the powerful protectors of civilization, who have smiled on the punishment of its enemies . . . these men, roped together, almost stark naked

except for a panther skin about their loins, are distinguished by their color, some entirely black, others dark brown. The long facial angle, the top of the head quite flat, the combination of coarse features and a generally frail body, characterize a special type, a race on the lowest rung of the human ladder (fig. 29). The hideous grimaces and contortions that contract the faces and limbs of these men reveal savage habits; the strangeness of that race, in which the moral sense seems almost nonexistent, would tend to place it on a plane more or less intermediate between man and brute. These facts are all the more striking when compared with the noble, serious attitude of their Egyptian captors.

This impressive contrast demonstrates sufficiently that the ancient population on the banks of the Nile was as far removed from the species of southern Africans as from that of Asian peoples. It refutes the theories which, until now, had tried to establish a purely Negro origin for it.[17]

Disregarding Chérubini's pejorative epithets, let us try to see how the prisoners he describes differ ethnically from the Egyptian. His account does not contain a single scientific term likely to attract our attention. On the contrary, the excessive nature of the insults that form the greater part of this description—written by a representative of a people whose sense of proportion is reputed to be a national virtue —indicates the irritation of a person unable to establish what he would like to prove. He goes so far as to forget the objective order followed on the Biban-el-Moluk bas-relief, on which he dwells at length. In reality, if the Black race is "on the lowest rung of the human ladder," even so it stands ahead of Gobineau's "blond beast" on that bas-relief, in an order consistently observed on all the monuments. On which rung, then, would the latter be placed?

We reproduce here the drawing that Chérubini is discussing. How would one recognize on the faces any evidence of moral degradation? How do these features differ from those of the Egyptian? Chérubini himself tells us that the complexion is sometimes "dark brown," in other words, the same reddish-brown hue of the Egyptians on the monuments. Clearly, the one valid ethnic trait he cites is common to both races.

The color of these Abu Simbel prisoners refutes the claim that the Egyptians did not encounter Negroes until the Eighteenth Dynasty and depicted them in a color different from their own; this claim

29.   The Prisoners of Abu Simbel. The color of those
in the background shows that, contrary to general asser-
tions, the Egyptians did not paint themselves any differently from other Negroes. There are scenes at Abu Simbel
in which no difference can be detected between the Pharaoh and the other "Negroes," whereas in the scene where
he is holding a group of prisoners by the hair there can
be no comparison between the Pharaoh's color and that
of the members of the white race shown.

Captif de race blanche aryenne.
Gravé sur les murs du temple de Médinet Abou.
Type libyen ou peuple du Nord. Les Atlantes du Pasteur Jurgen Sparnüth.

Types de captifs sémites gravés sur les
rochers du Sinaï.

30. Aryan, Libyan, and Semitic Captives. (Reproduced from Lenormant's book on Egypt.) The two figures at the top, engraved on the temple of Medinet Abu, are a white Aryan and a Libyan; those below, on the rocks of Sinai, are Semitic.

stems from the imagination, not from documentary evidence. Are not these bodies basically athletic rather than frail? The facial "contortions" and "contractions" of the persons in the forefront, the disdainful resignation of those in back, suggest a high conception of dignity, rather than moral degradation, to the viewer strong enough to interpret them objectively.

It has also been insinuated that if Sesostris—and Pharaohs in general—fought the Black populations of southern Ethiopia, it was because they did not belong to the same race. This is tantamount to saying that since Caesar undertook expeditions in Gaul, the Gauls and Romans did not belong to the same white race or that, if the Romans were white, the Gauls must have been yellow or black. The Negroes who lived in the African interior were at times very warlike and often raided Egyptian territory. (Cf. our section on the Stela of Philae.) Sesostris' intervention, which the Abu Simbel bas-relief commemorates, fits into the context of these repressions. Furthermore, this expedition occurred during the later period of the Egyptian Empire (Eighteenth Dynasty). Thus it was that Shem's sons came to call their southern brothers: "wicked sons of Kush."[18]

But those most detested by the Egyptians were the Asian shepherds of all kinds, from the Semites to the Indo-Europeans. For these, no epithets were insulting enough. According to Manetho, they called them: "ignoble Asians." From Hyk=king, in the sacred language, and Sos=shepherd, in the popular tongue, came the name $Hyksos$ to designate the invaders. The Egyptians also called them "accursed" and "pestiferous," "pillagers," "thieves . . ."[19] They also called the Scythians "Scheto's plague" (cf. Chérubini, p. 34).

The bas-reliefs left by the Egyptians and commemorating Pharaonic expeditions against those mobile plagues from Asia portray personages whose ethnic contrast with the Egyptians is visible at first glance and without any possible doubt. To make the Semitic, Aryan, alien character of these enemies of Egypt more apparent, we have reproduced Asian and European captives, engraved on the rocks at Sinai and at the temple of Medinet-Habu. They contrast with the similarity of features observable between the Egyptians and the Abu Simbel prisoners.

Despite his efforts, Chérubini clearly failed dismally to destroy the thesis "which, until now, had tried to establish" the purely Negro origin of the Egyptians. By the incoherence and weakness of arguments he deems overwhelming, he confirmed that Negro origin better than anyone.

In *Les Egyptes,* a volume published around 1880, Marius Fontanes attacks the same problem:

> Since the Egyptians always painted themselves red on their monuments, partisans of the "southern origin" had to point out a great number of interesting peculiarities likely to help solve the ethnographical problem. Near the Upper Nile today, among the Fulbe, whose skin is quite yellow, those whom contemporaries consider as belonging to a pure race, are rather red; the Bisharin are exactly of the same brick-red shade used on Egyptian monuments. To other ethnographers, these "red men" would probably be Ethiopians modified by time and climate, or perhaps Negroes who have reached the halfway mark in the evolution from blackness to whiteness. It has been noted that, in limestone areas, the Negro is less black than in granitic and plutonic regions. It has even been thought that the hue changed with the season. Thus, Nubians were former Blacks, but only in skin color, while their osteology has remained absolutely Negritic.
>
> The Negroes represented on Pharaonic paintings, so clearly delineated by engravers and named Nahasou or Nahasiou in the hieroglyphics, are not related to the Ethiopians, the first people to come down into Egypt. Were the latter then attenuated Negroes, Nubians? Lepsius's canon* gives . . . the proportions of the perfect Egyptian body; it has short arms and is Negroid or Negritian. From the anthropological point of view, the Egyptian comes after the Polynesians, Samoyeds, Europeans, and is immediately followed by African Negroes and Tasmanians. Besides, there is a scientific tendency to find in Africa, after excluding foreign influences, from the Mediterranean to the Cape, from the Atlantic to the Indian Ocean, nothing but Negroes or Negroids of various colors. The ancient Egyptians were Negroes, but Negroes to the last degree.[20]

Fontanes's view, which needs no comment, confirms once again the

---

*Richard Lepsius, nineteenth-century German Egyptologist. For an explanation of his "canon of proportions", see p. 117 of his *Discoveries in Egypt, Ethiopia and the Peninsula of Sinai in the years 1842–1848*. London, 1852.

impossibility of escaping the reality of a Negro Egypt, however little one is willing to accept the facts. Limiting himself to objective measurements, Lepsius reaches the formal, major conclusion that the perfect Egyptian is Negritian. In other words, his bone structure is Negritic and that is why anthropologists say little about the osteology of the Egyptian.

Fontanes next considers the claim that Egypt was probably civilized by Berbers or Libyans coming from Europe, via the west:

> If it is shown that civilization moved from north to south, from the Mediterranean to Ethiopia, it does not necessarily follow that this civilization is Asiatic; it can still be African, but coming from the west instead of the south. In that case, North African Berbers could have "civilized" Egypt.
>
> A goodly number of present-day Berbers have an essentially Egyptian osteology. The ancient Berber was probably brown. It is to the influence of the European race, to the immigration of the "men of the north," that we should attribute this description of the Tamhou, Libyans of the Nineteenth Dynasty, "with pale face, white or russet, and blue eyes"! These Whites, hired as mercenaries by the Pharaohs, strongly hybridized the Egyptian and also the Libyan. It is therefore necessary to disregard this and go back to the brown Libyan, the true Berber, to find the people who probably civilized Ancient Egypt. This is a difficult task, for the African Berber has become increasingly rare in Algeria. In Egypt the Berber type is too mixed. According to this theory, the African Berber from the west, the brown Libyan, settled in the valley of the new Nile; but almost immediately, or shortly afterwards, an invasion of Europeans hybridized the North African Libyan. This Libyan mixed-blood "with white skin and blue eyes" may have modified the early Egyptian. By his European blood, this Egyptian could be related to the Indo-European race and to the Aryan.[21]

This thesis is the masterpiece of explanations based on pure imagination; it rests solely on emotion. I have cited it only for its ingenuity and determination to succeed at any cost in demonstrating that somehow or other the Egyptians had something Aryan about them. Aryan was the key word he had to reach. I have quoted the passage because, contrary to the previous theories, it is explicit. It is the fruit of unwarranted suppositions by specialists convinced that everything valuable in life can come only from their race and that, if we look carefully, we are sure to be able to prove it. An explanation is not complete until it attains that objective. From then on it matters little whether the demonstration is supported by facts. It is self-sufficient; its valid criterion merges with its aim.

We have already referred to the confused ideas about the Berber, so there is no need to return to that subject. The brown Libyan, the true Berber, prototype of the white race, is as real as the Sirens. Moreover, if one sticks to the archeological documents, North Africa has never been the starting point of a civilization. It began to count in history only with the Phoenician colony of Carthage, when Egyptian civilization was already several millennia old. If the Egyptian civilization had come from the south of Europe, as Maspero assumes, and if it had "slipped into the valley via the west or southwest,"[22] to introduce elements of civilization, we cannot understand why it should not have left traces in its birthplace or along its route. It is difficult to perceive how this white race, propagator of culture, could have left Europe, a milieu so conducive to the development of civilization, without having created it, how it crossed the rich plains of Tell and the enormous expanse that separates North Africa from Egypt—before that expanse became a desert—or why it would have crossed the swampy, unhealthy region of Lower Egypt, spanned the Nubian desert, climbed to the high plateaus of Ethiopia, traversed thousands and thousands of miles to create civilization on some caprice in so remote an area, so that this civilization might later return slowly down the Nile. Assuming this to be the case, how can we explain that a fraction of that race, which stayed at home, in an environment so favorable to the flowering of a civilization, remained unpolished until the centuries just preceding the Christian era?

Opposing the hypothesis that North Africa was inhabited from early Antiquity by a white race, we can invoke archeological and historical documents unanimously attesting that this region was always inhabited by Negroes. Furon tells us that, at the end of the Paleolithic, in the province of Constantine, Algeria, five layers of fossilized men were found. Among these, "several Negroids presenting affinities with the Nubians of Upper Egypt are mentioned."[23]

During the historical epoch, Latin documents testify to the existence of Blacks throughout North Africa: "Latin historians have given us information on the population, mostly names which mean little to us. We should remember that at least a sizable Negro population existed, Herodotus' Ethiopians, whose descendants were probably the Haratins of the Moroccan Upper Atlas."[24] This last quotation proves that, even now, there are Blacks in the area. The only prehistoric civilization which radiated from there, even in Egypt, was probably due to Blacks.

During that time, in Africa and the Orient, which are untouched by the Solutrean and Magdalenian, Aurignacian Negroids are directly continued by a civilization called Capsian, the center of which seems to have been Tunisia. From there it probably reached the rest of North Africa, Spain, Sicily, and southern Italy, on the one hand, competing with Caucasians and Mongoloids for the Mediterranean basin. On the other hand, Libya, Egypt, and Palestine. In short, its influence was felt to some extent in the Sahara, Central Africa, and even South Africa. This Capsian civilization leads to an artistic flowering comparable in its cave drawing to what the Magdalenian attained in Europe. But Capsian art tends to abstraction, to that schematic stylization of figures which was perhaps to become the origin of writing. True enough, everyone does not agree on the date of those drawings found in numerous places in the Sahara and even in Hoggar (Algeria). Some view them as the expression of a Capsian civilization, while others attribute them to a later period, in the Neolithic. . . .[25]

The appearance of the ram holding a disc or a sphere between his horns would link this Saharan civilization to predynastic Egyptian cults. This is Amon, the ram-god, whom we see created in the Sahara, then inhabited by shepherds leading their sheep and oxen to pasture where today there is only a desert.[26]

The examination of the documents therefore testifies, as early as prehistoric times, to the presence of a Negro civilization on the very spot claimed as the starting point of Egyptian civilization.

Previously, in the Capsian and Magdalenian, the facts noted would reveal instead an invasion of Eurasia by Blacks who supposedly conquered the world. So it is that Dumoulin de Laplante writes, referring to the beginning of the Pleistocene:

A migration of Hottentot-type Negroes, then leaving South and Central Africa, probably submerged North Africa, Algeria, Tunisia, Egypt, and forcibly brought a new civilization—the Aurignacian

—to Mediterranean Europe. These Bushmen were the first to engrave rough drawings on rocks and to carve limestone figurines representing monstrously fat pregnant women. Was it to these Africans that the inner Mediterranean basin owed the cult of fertility and of the Maternity Goddess? . . .

This hypothesis of an invasion by Negro Africans on both shores of the Mediterranean clashes, however, with several objections. Why, fleeing the sun, would these men have come to seek the cold? If we accept the assumption of a migration from Africa, it is not surprising to find Aurignacian tools in France, Italy, and Spain. But the presence of these tools in Bohemia, Germany, and Poland, makes the hypothesis more fragile. Finally, Aurignacian tools exist in Java, Siberia, and China. Either the Blacks had conquered the world or we would have to assume that there were "cultural exchanges" between the different peoples on the planet.[27]

Facing the same archeological evidence, Furon adopts the idea of a fertility cult, to avoid reaching the same conclusions.[28] To accept that theory is to favor the hypothesis of a Negro invasion, which, indeed, is supported by the Aurignacian skulls, the Grimaldi skeletons.

Africa's civilizing role, even in prehistoric times, is increasingly affirmed by the most distinguished scholars: "Moreover," writes Abbé Breuil, "it seems more and more probable that, even in the age-old days of ancient pebble tools, Africa not only knew stages of primitive civilization comparable to those of Europe and Asia Minor, but was perhaps the source of several such civilizations, whose swarms conquered those classic lands toward the North."[29] The opinion of that great scholar goes even further. It seems increasingly evident that humanity was born in Africa. In fact, the most important stock of human bones found up to now has been in South Africa. Although not the most extensively excavated location, it is the only place in the world where the bones found allow us to reconstitute the genealogical tree of mankind uninterruptedly from its beginnings until today.

Although it is not in the field of archeology, I shall first speak about the problem of the origin of the human type. Thanks to the finds of Dr. Raymond Dart in Taung and Makapan, and to those of Dr. Robert Broom in Sterkfontein, Kromdraai, and Swartkrans, great progress has been made in that country. Before man, two-legged anthropoids of many forms were there, but increasingly de-

veloping hominian traits, so much so that we can begin to believe
that the human type was created there. The attention of all the
specialists is more and more attracted to these magnificent discoveries which multiply almost every month.[30]

Practically everyone agrees that until the fourth glacial epoch, flat-
nosed Negroids were the only humans. A South African scientist has
recently declared that the first men were black, strongly pigmented,
according to the proofs at his disposal. It was probably not until the
fourth glaciation, which lasted 100,000 years, that the differentiation
of the Negroid race into distinct races occurred, following a long period of adaptation by the fraction isolated and imprisoned by the ice:
narrowing of the nostrils, depigmentation of the skin and of the pupils
of the eyes.

A single fact then remains vouched for by the documents in the
"Libyan" thesis (Aryan, cited by Fontanes): that is the utilization of
Whites, blue-eyed, tattooed blonds, as mercenaries by the Negro
Pharaohs. Those tribes, called Libyans, were savage hordes in the
western part of the Delta, where their presence, historically, is not
recognized until the Eighteenth Dynasty. The Egyptians, who always
considered them as veritable savages, took care not to be confused
with them. At most, they condescended to use them as mercenaries.
They never stopped holding them in check outside their borders by
constant expeditions. Not until the low epoch was Egypt gradually
permeated by domesticated Libyans who settled in the Delta area.

Herodotus' description shows that, until the end of Egyptian history, the Libyans remained on the lowest rung of civilization. The
word "civilized," however broadly defined, could not be applied to
them. Concerning the Libyan tribe of the Adrymachidae, the Father
of History wrote: "Their women wear on each leg a ring made of
bronze; they let their hair grow long, and when they catch vermin on
their person, bite it and throw it away."[31] Consequently, we may well
be puzzled by the attempts to attribute Egyptian civilization to the
Libyans.

As a result of this hypothesis, efforts have been made to relate the
Berber and Egyptian languages by claiming that the Berber is the
descendant of the Libyan. But Berber is a strange tongue that can be
related to all kinds of languages:

On the one hand, similarities have been noted between Berber,

Gaelic, Celtic, and Cymric. But the Berber use as many Egyptian as African words and, depending on one's point of view, the basis of their language becomes Indo-European, Asian, or African. The Libyan languages are, in fact, African. Through these languages the Ligurians and Siculans, on arriving in Europe from North Africa, probably imported an African tongue, of which Basque could be one example.[32]

The same applies to Berber grammar. Specialists in Berber are careful not to insist on the relationship between Berber and Egyptian. Professor André Basset, for example, felt that more convincing facts should be presented before he could accept the Hamitic-Semitic hypothesis (Berber-Egyptian kinship, in particular). Both form the feminine by adding *t* to the noun, but the same is true of Arabic. Given what is known about the Arab and Berber peoples, we can wonder with Amélineau (*Prolégomènes*) why the influence should not be assumed to come from the opposite direction, which would conform to the historical relationship between those two peoples.

That is not the whole story. Careful search reveals that German feminine nouns also end in *t* and *st*. Should we consider that Berbers were influenced by Germans or the reverse? This hypothesis could not be rejected *a priori,* for German tribes in the fifth century overran North Africa via Spain, and established an empire that they ruled for 400 years.[33] After that conquest, the Vandals who remained there mixed with the population. Only one segment, led by Genseric, tried unsuccessfully to conquer Rome by crossing through Sicily, and probably returned to North Africa. Furthermore, the plural of 50 percent of Berber nouns is formed by adding *en,* as is the case with feminine nouns in German, while 40 percent form their plural in *a,* like neuter nouns in Latin.[34]

Since we know that the Vandals conquered the country from the Romans, why should we not be more inclined to seek explanations for the Berbers in that direction, both linguistically and in physical appearance: blond hair, blue eyes, etc.? But no! Disregarding all these facts, historians decree that there was no Vandal influence and that it would be impossible to attribute anything in Barbary to their occupation.

However barbarous they were, however imperfect their administration, we cannot believe, in view of their number and their position as conquerors, that they spontaneously abandoned their language to adopt that of the Berbers; no Latin text indicates this. Usually, social relations are much more complex and that complexity is reflected in linguistics. Even when a language disappears, it reacts on the victorious tongue by transforming it and the latter no longer remains exactly what it was before. Thus, it is hard to understand how modern Berber can be free from any Vandal influence. Even harder to understand is that the modern Berber is not a descendant of the Vandals, especially when he has blue eyes and blond hair.

Ibn Khaldun's treatise on the Berber is merely a series of undocumented quotations.[35] The fact that there are no Berber in Egypt, except imaginary ones, that there are scarcely any in Tunisia, and that their number increases from east to west to reach its maximum in Morocco, seems to confirm the hypothesis of a Vandal origin. Historians pay little attention to these facts because it is absolutely necessary to make the Berber ancient enough to justify Egyptian civilization. Yet the 20 Berber sentences found in Arab texts scarcely date back to the twelfth century, whereas "Tifinagh" writing and the still undeciphered symbols called "Libyan" seem due to the influence of the indigenous element of the Negroid Phoenician colony of Carthage, prior to the arrival of the Vandals.

To recapitulate, the stratification of the North African population, from prehistoric times to our day, would be as follows:

Negroes and Cro-Magnons (a race extinct for 10,000 years);
Negroes in the Capsian;
Negroes during the Phoenician epoch;
Indo-Europeans, starting in 1500 B.C. and probably mixed with Negroes;
Negroes at the time of the Romans, with a large percentage of mixed-bloods;
Vandals; and
Arabs.

What then is more natural than that the basis of Berber vocabulary should be in turn Indo-European, Semitic, or African, depending on one's point of view?

Continuing with the development of Egyptology, we reach Maspero who, in the first chapter of his *Histoire ancienne des peuples de l'Orient,* describes the origins of the Egyptians:

The Egyptians seem quite early to have lost the memory of their beginnings. Did they come from Central Africa or from the interior of Asia? According to the almost unanimous testimony of the ancient historians, they belonged to an African race which, first established in Ethiopia on the Middle Nile, gradually came down toward the sea, following the course of the river. To demonstrate this, one relied on the evident analogies between the customs and religion of the kingdom of Meroë and the customs and religion of the Egyptians proper. Today we know beyond the shadow of a doubt that Ethiopia, at least the Ethiopia known by the Greeks, far from having colonized Egypt, was itself colonized by Egypt, starting with the Twelfth Dynasty, and was for centuries included in the kingdom of the Pharaohs.[36]

Before continuing with Maspero's thesis, we should note what seems already to have been altered in those few introductory sentences. It is unlikely that the Egyptians ever forgot their origin. Maspero apparently confuses two distinct notions: the primitive birthplace from which a people started and the ethnic origin responsible for the color of the race. The Egyptians never forgot the latter, any more than they forgot the former.[37] It is expressed in all their art, throughout all their literature, in all their cultural manifestations, in their traditions and language. So much so that even their country was designated—by analogy with their own color, not by analogy with the color of the soil—by the name *Kemit,* which coincides with Ham (Cham), Biblical ancestor of Blacks. To say that *Kemit* refers to the color of the Egyptian earth, rather than designating the country through the color of the race, could inspire similar reasoning to explain the present-day expressions: "Black Africa" and "White Africa."

Maspero refers to the unanimous testimony of ancient historians on the Egyptian race, but he intentionally omits their precision. What we already know about the testimony of the Ancients proves that they did not use the vague term, "African race." From Herodotus to Diodorus, whom Maspero quotes, whenever they mentioned the Egyptian people, they specified that a Negro race was involved.

Here we can trace the evolution of the gradual alteration of facts in textbooks that will mold the opinion of high school and university students. This is all the more serious because the great mass of knowledge to be acquired, in the modern world, leaves the younger generation, with the exception of professionals, no time to consult original sources and to appreciate the gap between the truth and what they have been taught. On the contrary, a certain tendency to laziness encourages them to be satisfied with the textbooks and to accept stereotyped notions of "infallible authority" from them, as if from a catechism. If we applied Maspero's reasoning to refute the ideas of Diodorus on Ethiopia's Antiquity, we would be able to conclude that, since Napoleon conquered and annexed Italy in the nineteenth century, Rome never civilized Gaul—which would be an obvious historical error.

"Moreover, the Bible states that Mesraim, son of Ham, brother of Kush and of Canaan, came from Mesopotamia to settle, along with his children, on the banks of the Nile."[38] Maspero fails to add that Ham, Canaan, and Kush are Negroes, according to that same Bible he is quoting. This means once again that Egypt (Ham, Mesraim), Ethiopia (Kush), Palestine and Phoenicia before the Jews and Syrians (Canaan), Arabia Felix before the Arabs (Pout, Hevila, Saba), were all occupied by Negroes who had created civilizations thousands of years old in those regions and had maintained family relationships. But then he continues:

Loudim, the eldest among them, personifies the Egyptian proper, the Rotou or Romitou of the hieroglyphic inscriptions. Anamim represents the great tribe of the Anu, who founded On of the north (Heliopolis) and On of the south (Hermonthis) in prehistoric times.

Lehabim is the Libyan people living west of the Nile, Naphtouhim settled in the Delta, south of Memphis; finally, Pathrousim (Patorosi, land of the south) inhabits present-day Said, between Memphis and the first cataract.

This tradition which brings the Egyptians from Asia, through the Isthmus of Suez was not unknown to classical authors. Pliny the Elder attributes the founding of Heliopolis to Arabs; but it was never so popular as the opinion that they came from the high plateaus of Ethiopia.[39]

This identification* is more or less unfounded. It becomes contra-

---

*Borrowed by Maspero from Rougé's *Recherches sur les monuments qu'on peut attribuer aux six premières dynasties de Manéthon.*

dictory when it links Libyans, said to have blue eyes and blond hair, with Lehabim, son of Mesraim, both of them Negroes. Another contradiction: Maspero seems at times to accept the theory of an Asiatic origin for the Egyptians and recalls the opinion of Pliny the Elder, who attributes the founding of Heliopolis to Arabs. In the same text, Maspero credits the settlement of that city to the Anu, whom he identifies with Anamim, son of Mesraim, a Negro. Our comments on the Arabs in a later chapter will eliminate any possibility of placing them at the founding of Heliopolis, especially if it occurred in "prehistoric" times, as the author affirms. We can see why Pliny's opinion did not enjoy the popularity among the Ancients that Maspero would have wished. To return to Maspero's account:

> In our day the origin and ethnographic affinities of the population have inspired lengthy debate. First, the seventeenth- and eighteenth-century travelers, misled by the appearance of certain mongrelized Copts, certified that their predecessors in the Pharaonic age had a puffed up face, bug eyes, flat nose, fleshy lips. And that they presented certain characteristic features of the Negro race. This error, common at the start of the century, vanished once and for all as soon as the French Commission had published its great work.[40]

Anyone reading that statement without first consulting Volney's testimony and explanatory note on climatic effects on racial appearance . . . might easily be persuaded that those travelers in centuries past could have let themselves be easily deceived by appearances. Bearing in mind what has been said about the gradual infiltration of Whites into Egypt—especially during the low epoch—in the Delta, if there was mongrelization, it could only have resulted in whitening the population, not in any Negrification that would make former Whites unrecognizable by unprejudiced observers.

Let us see how, if we are to believe Maspero, that "common error" vanished once and for all after the publication of the "great work" by the French Commission:

> On examining innumerable reproductions of statues and bas-reliefs, we recognized that the people represented on the monuments, instead of presenting peculiarities and the general appearance of the Negro, really resembled the fine white races of Europe and Western

Asia. Today, after a century of research and excavation, we no longer find it difficult to imagine, I shall not say Psammetichus and Sesostris, but Cheops, who helped to build the Pyramids. It suffices to enter a museum and examine the old-style statues assembled there. At first glance, we feel that the artist has sought to reproduce an exact likeness, in the accurate portrayal of head and limbs. Then, brushing aside the nuances proper to each individual, we easily detect the general character and principal types of the race. One of them, thick-set and heavy, corresponds quite well to one of the prevalent types among the modern fellahs. Another, depicting members of the upper class, shows us a man tall and slender, with broad, muscular shoulders, well-developed chest, sinewy arms, small hands, slim hips, thin legs. The anatomical details of his knee and calf muscle stand out, as is the case with most people who walk a lot. His feet are long, narrow, flattened at the end by habitually walking without shoes. His head, often too heavy for his body, expresses kindness and instinctive sadness. His brow is square, perhaps somewhat low; his nose short and fleshy; his eyes are large and opened wide; his cheeks round; his lips thick but not everted; his mouth, stretched a bit too far, retains a resigned and almost painful smile. These features, common to most of the statues of the Old and Middle Empire, persist through all the epochs. The monuments of the Eighteenth Dynasty, so inferior in artistic beauty to those of the old dynasties, transmit the primitive type without appreciable alteration. Today, although the upper classes have been disfigured by repeated miscegenation with the foreigner, ordinary peasants almost everywhere have retained the appearance of their ancestors. Any fellah can contemplate with astonishment the statues of Chephren or the colossi of Sanuasrit transporting across Cairo, after more than 4,000 years of existence, the physiognomy of those old Pharaohs.[41]

Such is the hub of Maspero's demonstration. We have not omitted a single word. What does it prove? What does the "great work" teach us? The author informs us that Egyptology is already a very old science; for a century specialists have excavated and searched; now we know the prototype of the ancient Egyptian down to the most minor ethnic detail. The artist has depicted his "exact likeness." Thanks to this realistic art, we can reconstitute ethnically the members of the upper class. According to Maspero's observations, they had a "nose

short and fleshy," a "mouth stretched a bit too far," "thick lips,"
"large eyes opened wide," "round cheeks," a brow "perhaps somewhat low," "broad, muscular shoulders," "small hands," "slim hips,"
"thin legs." These common features, perpetuated throughout the Old
and Middle Kingdoms, "instead of presenting peculiarities and the
general appearance of the Negro, really resembled the fine white
races of Europe and Western Asia." That conclusion needs no com-
mentary.

After so solemn a confirmation of the Negro origin by an author
whose intent was to destroy it, we see once again the impossibility of
proving the opposite of the truth. Gaston Maspero, who became in
1889 the Director of the Cairo Museum, was a scholar to whom we
are indebted for several translations of Egyptian texts. He had the
technical preparation necessary for establishing all that was demonstrable. His failure, despite that knowledge, like the failure of
scholars who tackled this problem before or after him, constitutes, as
it were, the most solid, if unintentional, proof of the Negro origin.

Next we come to the thesis of Abbé Emile Amélineau (1850–
1916), a great Egyptologist seldom mentioned. He excavated at
Om El'Gaab, near Abydos, and discovered a royal necropolis where
he was able to identify the names of 16 kings more ancient perhaps than Menes. He found tombs of four kings: Ka, Den, the Serpent King Djet (whose stela is at the Louvre), and another whose
name has not been deciphered. As Amélineau reports, attempts have
been made to include these monarchs in the historical period: "At
the meeting of the Academy of Inscriptions and Belles-Lettres, Mr.
Maspero tried to place these kings in the Twelfth Dynasty . . . then
. . . he attributed them to the Eighteenth . . . next to the Fifth . . .
then to the Fourth. . . ."[42] After refuting his detractors, Amélineau
concludes: "Those are reasons which seem to me not to deserve
scorn, but rather to merit serious consideration by scholars of good
will, for the others do not count in my opinion."[43]

To Amélineau we owe the discovery of Osiris' tomb at Abydos,
thanks to which Osiris could no longer be considered a mythical hero
but an historic personage, an initial ancestor of the Pharaohs, a Black
ancestor, as was his sister, Isis. Thus we can understand why the
Egyptians always painted their gods black as coal, in the image of
their race, from the beginning to the end of their history. It would be
paradoxical and quite incomprehensible for a white people never to
have painted its gods white, but to choose, on the contrary, to depict

its most sacred beings in the black color of Isis and Osiris on Egyptian monuments. This fact reveals one of the contradictions of the moderns who assert dogmatically that the White race created Egyptian civilization with an enslaved Black race living by its side. The choice of the slaves' color, rather than that of the masters and civilizers, to represent the deities, is, to say the least, inadmissible and should shock a logical, objective mind. . . .

So it is that Amélineau, after his tremendous finds and his in-depth study of Egyptian society, reaches the following conclusion of major importance for the history of mankind:

> From various Egyptian legends, I have been able to conclude that the populations settled in the Nile Valley were Negroes, since the goddess Isis was said to have been a reddish-black woman. In other words, as I have explained, her complexion is *café au lait* (coffee with milk), the same as that of certain other Blacks whose skin seems to cast metallic reflections of copper.[44]

Amélineau designates the first Black race to occupy Egypt by the name *Anu*. He shows that it came slowly down the Nile and founded the cities of Esneh, Erment, Qouch, and Heliopolis, for, as he says:

> All those cities have the characteristic symbol which serves to denote the name *Anu*.[45] It is also in an ethnic sense that we must read the term *Anu* applied to Osiris. As a matter of fact, in a chapter in-troducing hymns in honor of Ra and containing Chapter XV of *The Book of the Dead,* we read: "Hail to thee, O God Ani in the mountainous land of Antem! O great God, falcon of the double solar mountain!"
> If Osiris was of Nubian origin, although born at Thebes, it would be easy to understand why the struggle between Set and Horus took place in Nubia. In any case, it is striking that the goddess Isis, according to the legend, has precisely the same skin color that Nubians always have, and that the god Osiris has what seems to me an ethnic epithet indicating his Nubian origin. Apparently this observation has never before been made.[46]

If we accept the evidence of their own creations, *The Book of the Dead* among others, these Anu, whom Maspero tried to transform into Arabs . . . appear essentially as Blacks. In support of Amélineau's theory, it may be pointed out that *An* means man (in Diola). Thus *Anu* originally may have meant men. (For other similarities, see Chapter X.)

According to Amélineau, this Black race, the Anu, probably created in prehistoric times all the elements of Egyptian civilization which persist without significant change throughout its long existence. These Blacks were probably the first to practice agriculture, to irrigate the valley of the Nile, build dams, invent sciences, arts, writing, the calendar. They created the cosmogony contained in *The Book of the Dead*, texts which leave no doubt about the Negroness of the race that conceived the ideas.

These Anu . . . were an agricultural people, raising cattle on a large scale along the Nile, shutting themselves up in walled cities for defensive purposes. To this people we can attribute, without fear of error, the most ancient Egyptian books, *The Book of the Dead* and the *Texts of the Pyramids,* consequently, all the myths or religious teachings. I would add almost all the philosophical systems then known and still called Egyptian. They evidently knew the crafts necessary for any civilization and were familiar with the tools those trades required. They knew how to use metals, at least elementary metals. They made the earliest attempts at writing, for the whole Egyptian tradition attributes this art to Thoth, the great Hermes, an Anu like Osiris, who is called the Onian in Chapter XV of *The Book of the Dead* and in the *Texts of the Pyramids.* Certainly the people already knew the principal arts; it left proof of this in the architecture of the tombs at Abydos, especially the tomb of Osiris, and in those sepulchers objects have been found bearing the unmistakable stamp of their origin—such as carved ivory, or the little head of a Nubian girl found in a tomb near that of Osiris, or the small wooden or ivory receptacles in the form of a feline head—all documents published in the first volume of my *Fouilles d'Abydos.*[47]

Formulating his theory, Amélineau continues:

The conclusion to be drawn from these considerations is that the conquered Anu people guided its conquerors at least along some of the paths to civilization and the arts. This conclusion, as can readily be seen, is most important for the history of human civilization and the history of religion. It clearly follows from what has been stated earlier: Egyptian civilization is not of Asiatic, but of African origin, of Negroid origin, however paradoxical this may seem. We are not accustomed, in fact, to endow the Black or related races with too much intelligence, or even with enough intelligence to make the first discoveries necessary for civilization. Yet, there is not a single tribe inhabiting the African interior that has not possessed and does not still possess at least one of those first discoveries.[48]

Amélineau supposes that a Negro Egypt, already civilized by the Anu, may have been invaded by a coarse white race from the African interior. Gradually conquering the valley as far as Lower Egypt, this uncultivated white race was probably civilized by the Black Anu, large numbers of whom it nonetheless destroyed. The author bases this theory on an analysis of scenes depicted on Narmer's Tablet, discovered at Hierakonpolis by James Edward Quibbell (1867–1935) (fig. 31). Current opinion unanimously recognizes that the prisoners portrayed on that tablet, with their aquiline noses, represent Asian invaders conquered and punished by the Pharaoh who, in that remote epoch, had his capital in Upper Egypt.

This interpretation is confirmed by the fact that the persons walking ahead of the Pharaoh and belonging to his victorious army are Nubians, wearing Nubian insignia, such as the symbol of the Jackal and that of the Sparrow-hawk, which we would call Nubian totems. Besides, archeological data do not support the hypothesis of a white race originating in the heart of Africa.

The ox-tail carried by the Pharaoh on this tablet, and that Egyptian Pharaohs and priests always carried, is still borne at ceremonies and official functions by Nigerian religious leaders. The same is true of the garment worn by the Pharaoh; the amulet-filled sachet on his chest is always present throughout Egyptian history. It is found on the chest of any Negro chief who holds a responsible position; in Wolof, it is called *dakk*.

The servant is holding the Pharaoh's sandals, identical with the Negroes' *voganti*. Walking behind the king and carrying a kettle, he has the typical attitude of the modern Negro servant, or *bek-neg* (compare with *bak*, which means servant in Egyptian). The fact that the king has taken off his sandals suggests that he is about to perform a sacrifice in a holy place, and that he must first purify his limbs with the water in the kettle. The Egyptians are known to have practiced ablutions thousands of years before the advent of Islam. Thus, Narmer's Tablet probably portrays a ritual sacrificial scene after a victory. Similar human sacrifices were still practiced in Black Africa until very recent times; in Dahomey, for example.

Above the victim, the scene depicting Horus holding what seems to be a cord passing through the nostrils of an amputated head, perhaps symbolizes these very lives sacrificed to the god, escaping through the nose of the victims and being accepted by Horus. This idea conforms to the Negro belief that life escapes through the nostrils. *Life* and *nose* are synonyms in Wolof and often used interchangeably.

What is the racial identity of the persons represented on this side of the tablet, which I consider the front rather than the back, as is generally thought? I contend that they all belong to the same Black race. The king has thick lips, even everted. His profile cannot conceal the fact that his nose is fleshy. This is also true of all the persons on this side, even the captives in the scene underneath, who are running away. The latter, like the victims about to be immolated, have artificial hair, arranged in layers or tiers, a style still seen in Black Africa. A similar hair-do, worn by girls, is called *djimbi*; slightly modified and worn by married women, it is called the *djéré,* which disappeared from the Senegalese scene some 15 years ago. Quite recently, Islam has caused the men to discontinue the custom. Such hair-dos are no longer seen except among the non-Islamic Serer prior to circumcision, and among the Peul. A special form of these coiffures is called *Ndjumbal.* The king's hair and that of his servant is hidden by their bonnets; in Egypt, the use of such wigs was popular with all social classes. The king's bonnet is still worn in Senegal by those about to be circumcized, although this usage tends to disappear under the influence of Islam. It is made by sewing together two elliptical pieces of white cloth, with one end left open for the head to pass through. A bamboo frame gives it the form of the crown worn by the Pharaoh of Upper Egypt. When this bonnet is worn by mature men, the bamboo frame is omitted and the oblong part is generally smaller. This produces what has been called the form of the Phrygian bonnet that the Greeks were to transmit to the Western world. In *Dieu d'eau,* Marcel Griaule has published photographs of these bonnets worn by the Dogon.

It can be noted here that the king carries only a mace in his right hand; his left hand, weaponless, holds the head of the victim. The

31. Narmer's Tablet. The invention and introduction
of writing mark the dividing line between prehistory and

the historical period of humanity. Narmer's Tablet bears written signs: it would be of great import to be able to date it precisely.

mace may thus be considered as an attribute of Upper Egypt, as was the white crown. The king was probably beginning the conquest of the Nile Valley in this first scene. This was perhaps the moment when he was subjecting men of his own race to his domination.

The back of the tablet begins with a typical scene: the conquered victim belongs to the city of the "abominables," as indicated by the hieroglyph pointed out by Amélineau. The fortified city was probably a town in Lower Egypt, inhabited by a race clearly different from the Black race on the other side: a white Asiatic race. The hair of the captives is long and natural, without layers; the noses exceptionally long and aquiline; the lips quite indistinct. In short, all the ethnic features of the race on the back are diametrically opposite to those of the race on the front. We cannot overemphasize the fact that only the race on the back has Semitic features.

After this second victory, the unification of Upper and Lower Egypt was probably achieved. It was symbolized by the scene in the middle of the reverse side: the symmetry of the two felines with menacing leonine heads, indicating that they would be fighting if they were free. But they will henceforth be held in check and unable to injure each other, thanks to the ropes tied around their necks and held by the two symmetrical personages. This would symbolize unification, in line with a characteristic representation common to Egyptians and Blacks in general.

In the scene at the top, the king is wearing the crown of Lower Egypt, which shows that he has just conquered it. The second stage of the conquest of the Nile Valley is thus ended by the Pharaoh. He now holds in both hands what can be considered as the attributes of Lower and Upper Egypt. Here, once again, the king has removed his sandals. These are held by his servant who, carrying the same receptacle, walks behind him as in the scene on the front side. We may therefore assume that the site is sacred and that the victims were immolated ritually, not massacred.

Before the king stand five persons, four of them hold banners bearing totems. The first two—Hawk and Jackal—are clearly from Upper Egypt. The last one represents not an animal, but an unidentified object which may well be the emblem of Lower Egypt just conquered.

For all these reasons, Amélineau's interpretation seems unacceptable. The opinion that all the captives depicted are Asiatics is apparently a generalization that overlooks the detail of the tablet. To the same extent, Amélineau's explanation, which considers all the conquered people as Nubians, seems erroneous. The fact that the captives on the obverse are really Nubians may have led him to miss the ethnic difference between the latter and the victim crushed by the bull on the reverse. According to Amélineau's own reproduction, the latter does not wear his hair in layers as do the Nubians on the other side. Furthermore, he does not have their other ethnic features. Only by disregarding these details, in good faith, could he have reached the conclusion that an uncultivated white race from Central Africa probably conquered the valley from the Negro Anu population.

As a matter of fact, even if there were infiltration by Asians or early Europeans during that prehistoric period, the Egyptian Negroes had never lost control of the situation. This is also indicated by the numerous Amratian statuettes portraying a conquered race of foreigners. In his *Les Débuts de l'art en Egypte,* the Belgian Egyptologist Jean Capart reproduces a statuette of a white captive kneeling, hands bound behind his back, hair in a long braid hanging down his back.[49]

From the same period proto-caryatids are also found, in the form of furniture pedestals, depicting the type of the conquered white race.[50] By contrast, we see Blacks shown as citizens freely strolling around in their own country:

> Here we see four women in long skirts, quite similar to Black women represented on Eighteenth Dynasty tombs, including the tomb of Rekhmara*. Although indistinct, the object they seem to be carrying has been assumed to be a cow's ear! I should be inclined to view it as the earliest appearance of the ansate cross, a symbol that soon thereafter entered Egyptian semeiology and never left it. This indicates that Negro women were quite at home in the midst of animals from their own land. The question again arises: How could the Egyptians of that epoch know animals from Central Africa, as well as the inhabitants of Central Africa, if these people were Asians or Semites entering the Nile Valley through the Isthmus of Suez? Is not the recorded presence of the aforementioned animals and Blacks on the ivory pieces just described conclusive evidence that Egypt's conquerors came from Central Africa? (*Prolégomènes,* pp. 425–426.)

---

*Vizier of Pharaohs Tuthmosis III and Amenhotep II (circa 1471–1448 B.C.)

Contrary to generally accepted notions, it is clear that the most ancient documents available on Egyptian and world history portray Blacks as free citizens, masters of the country and of nature. Near them, the several white prototypes then known, the result of early European or Asian infiltration, are depicted as captives, with hands tied behind their backs, or else crushed by the load of a piece of furniture. (This, incidentally, could be the origin of the caryatids of the fifth-century Erechtheum, imitated by the Greeks thousands of years later.)

CHAPTER IV

Could Egyptian Civilization Have Originated in the Delta?

To explain the settlement and civilization of Egypt, specialists invoke four hypotheses, corresponding to the four points of the compass. The most natural of all—a local origin—is the one most often challenged. This latter hypothesis, in turn, could be localized in two different places: Upper or Lower Egypt. In the case of Lower Egypt, it would be a question of what is now called the "preponderance of the Delta." Why would an Egyptologist, supporting the local-origin theory, try so hard to prove the "preponderance of the Delta," despite the absence of any historical evidence, if this were not a roundabout way to establish a White, Mediterranean origin for Egyptian civilization?

This view, which is generally that of all who place the start of Egyptian civilization outside of Egypt—whether in Asia or in Europe—is shared by Alexandre Moret who, nevertheless, apparently favors a local. but White, origin. To the former, the idea seems logical to some extent; in their eagerness for a reasonable explanation, this is one affirmation added to another equally devoid of historical foundation. In fact, if the pioneers of civilization came from abroad, and if they were forced by geography to cross the Delta, it is logical to assume that the Delta was civilized before Upper Egypt, and that civilization radiated from there. If the supporters of an external origin had been able to demonstrate the Delta's prior claim with the aid of valid arguments, their thesis would obviously have been advanced immeasurably. At least this would have provided a semblance of truth for the contradictory notions they propose.

In actual fact, it is impossible, not only to demonstrate that theory, but even to find valid historical documents to support it. No document suggests that priority. It is in Upper Egypt, from the Paleolithic to the present, that material evidence has been found to attest the successive stages of civilization: Tasian, Badarian (circa 7471 B.C.?),

Amratian (circa 6500 B.C.?), protodynastic. In contrast to Upper Egypt, no traces of continuous evolution exist in the Delta. The Merimde* center disappeared at the end of the Tasian; there is nothing north of Badari.[1] The ivory statuettes with triangular heads, found in the epoch called Gerzean (circa 5500 B.C.?), correspond to those found in Crete at the time of Menes.[2] These statuettes cannot date back earlier than the epoch of Hierakonpolis, which Capart attributes to the Amratian period.

Between S.D. 39 and S.D. 79, a Gerzean civilization allegedly existed in Lower Egypt:

> In any case, Lower Egypt eventually became the seat of a higher civilization with definitely Asiatic, as opposed to African, affinities, and this civilization ultimately dominated Upper Egypt as well. In fact, it is only known directly from the latter region, though its presence in the North may be inferred with confidence. In Upper Egypt there is no sharp break between the Amratian civilization and the Gerzean; the latter gradually trickled in, mixing with, but dominating, the older elements. New types of vases, weapons with ornaments intrude in ever greater number until they predominate or even oust the old entirely. . . .[3]
>
> It is universally agreed that the new elements which distinguish the culture of Upper Egypt in the Middle Predynastic phase are derived from the north or northeast. And it is almost certain that the authors of these innovations had been living in touch with the Upper Nile for a considerable time prior to S.D. 39, since before that date isolated Decorated Vases had occasionally found their way into Upper Egypt.[4]

This Gerzean civilization, said to be Asiatic, is known only through vestiges found in Upper Egypt. How paradoxical, inasmuch as it is supposed to have originated in Lower Egypt! (Moreover, these vestiges are identical with those of Amratian civilization, evolved from the Badarian which, in turn, resulted from the Tasian.)

Nevertheless, although no traces of Gerzean civilization have been found and although it is known "directly" only by vestiges in Upper Egypt, "its presence in the North may be inferred with confidence," meaning its presence in the Delta. In clearer terms, this is

---

*V. Go·don Childe calls Merimde a typical example of "Neolithic culture" and places this site two kilometers west of the Rosetta branch of the Nile.

equivalent to saying: "All that I find here in Upper Egypt comes from where I find nothing or almost nothing (Lower Egypt). Though I cannot prove this and have no hope of ever seeing it proved, and though I find nothing here, I judge that it is so." This is hardly the way to write history.

It is alleged that the Delta is a humid region and preserves documents poorly. It could not have preserved them so poorly as to have left no sign of them, not even shapeless lumps resulting from chemical decomposition through humidity. In reality, the soil of Lower Egypt has yielded up, after a fashion, all that was entrusted to it: for example, all those works, even in wood, of the Old Kingdom after the Third Dynasty. If it has not produced more ancient documents, we must more logically assume that it never contained any.

Had the Delta really played the role they try so hard to ascribe to it in Egyptian history, it would be possible to recognize this in other ways. The history of Upper Egypt, considered independently of the Delta, would present gaps; however, this is not the case. The history of Upper Egypt (i.e., Egyptian history) presents no unsurmountable difficulties. Historical explanation does not become impossible except when one struggles, in the absence of historical evidence, to assign to the Delta a role it never played. This seems to be the case with Moret when he writes:

> We know nothing of the history of those early kingdoms. Yet, tradition alleges that the kings of the north had a pre-eminence over the rest of Egypt at the beginning of time. No text enables us to delimit their zone of influence, but the religion of later days indicates that such influence was profound. This is explained by the exceptional fertility of the Delta.
>
> As soon as it could be made fit for cultivation by dint of embanking and draining and irrigating, this stretch of earth, repeatedly renewed by the Nile silt, offered a wider area, a more productive soil, and a more favorable habitat for the growth of a prolific race than the narrow valley of Upper Egypt. The result was a precocious material prosperity and intellectual development, attested by the fact that the great gods of the Delta later imposed authority on the rest of Egypt; the sun, Ra, was first worshiped at Heliopolis; Osiris, Isis, and Horus are the gods of Busiris, Mendes, and Buto. The extension of the worship over the whole valley in very early times indicates a corresponding political influence from the Delta.[5]

Up to this point, Moret has agreed with Maspero. He disagrees, however, apropos the route followed by the Shemsu-Hor, in order to be entirely consistent in defending the preeminence of the Delta. In his book, *Le Nil et la civilisation égyptienne* (p. 118), contrary to Maspero who suggests that the Shemsu-Hor (predecessors of Menes) are "Negro blacksmiths" who conquered the valley and built forges as far as the Delta, Moret claims that the "Shemsu-Hor and their forebears . . . came from the Delta."

He reports a great transformation during the epoch preceding Menes, marked by the appearance of gold, copper, and especially writing. As this transformation is evident only in Egypt, Moret poses the question: "By whom was Upper Egypt influenced, if not by Lower Egypt . . . ?" He cites the invention of the calendar as probably occurring in the region of Memphis. Elsewhere Moret had claimed that the Egyptian gods, Osiris, Isis, and Horus, were originally from the Delta. So he uses this argument, which he assumes to be correct, to press his point:

Another fact will support this argument. Throughout Antiquity, the intercalary days were consecrated to those gods born on the five additional days placed at the start of the year (cf. Plutarch). Egyptian and Greek texts agree in calling these gods Osiris and Isis, Set, Nephthys, and Horus. At the start of the year opening with the simultaneous rising of Sothis, Ra, and the Nile, Osiris, god of the Nile and of vegetation, is chosen as patron. He is thought to have been born on the first of the five additional days. We can conclude that the worshipers of Osiris were powerful in Heliopolis even at the time its astronomers established the calendar.[6]

Thus, with the calendar, Lower Egypt imposed the authority of Osiris and Ra, the supremacy of the Nile and the sun, upon Upper Egypt. The "civilized of the Delta" had conquered Upper Egypt.[7]

When one finds such important ideas expressed by such an authority, one tends to believe that they are supported by conclusive documents. This, however, is not true when we examine these statements thoroughly. The author poses the Nordic origin of Egyptian gods as consistent with Egyptian tradition. In other words, Osiris, Isis, and Horus were all gods of the Delta. From this, he draws the important consequences noted above, relative to the invention of the calendar and the origin of Egyptian civilization in general.

What precisely are we taught by Egyptian tradition, if we consider it from the most ancient epoch to which one can refer? This tradition, expressed in *The Book of the Dead,* whose doctrine is earlier than any written history of Egypt, teaches us that Isis is a Negro woman, Osiris a Negro man, an Anu. Thus, in the oldest Egyptian texts his name is accompanied by an ethnic designation to indicate his Nubian origin. This we have known since Amélineau.

Amélineau informs us, moreover, that no Egyptian text lists Osiris and Isis as having been born in the Delta. Consequently, when Moret affirms this, he does not draw it from any document. We may even add that the legend pinpoints the birth of Osiris and Isis in Upper Egypt: Osiris born at Thebes and Isis at Denderah. The legend also places in Nubia the first site of the struggle between Set and Horus*. In Amélineau's opinion:

The parts of the legend which relate to the Delta have obviously been added to the original version, except for the sojourn of Isis in Buto. In fact, the episode of Isis in Byblos hardly fits in with the stay of this goddess in Buto. In my view, it is merely an interpretation of Greek or quasi-Greek origin to explain the adoption of the Osiris cult in Byblos, or rather the myths resembling some local deity. This, moreover, is one of the points to which Egyptian documents never refer. Likewise, the coffin of Osiris, brought by the Nile to the sea, and from the sea to Byblos, seems to me to be one of those obvious impossibilities. I doubt seriously that the Egyptians accepted it . . . because Egyptian documents never mention it. We must not forget that, with the exception of the portions concerning the Delta and Asia Minor, the Osiris legend was firmly established in Egypt before the time of Menes. Hence, it is indeed difficult to see how a legend born in the Delta was almost localized in Upper Egypt and made no apparent reference to the Delta except in certain passages that are clearly later additions.[8]

Similarly, if Osiris and Isis were born in Lower Egypt, it would be hard to understand how their relics were all appropriated by Upper Egypt. The whole skeleton of Osiris was taken over by cities in

---

*In the legend, Set murdered his brother Osiris. When Horus, son of Isis and Osiris, grew up, his father's ghost appeared to demand vengeance. Thereupon Horus and Set fought for many days; both were severely injured. Later Set attacked Horus in the courts as a bastard son of Osiris. Thoth decided the case in favor of Horus.

Upper Egypt, so completely that nothing was left for the towns of Lower Egypt. On this point, Amélineau refers to Brugsch's *Geographical Dictionary*. Rivalry between the cities over the attribution of the relics caused so much confusion that at first it was difficult to determine which city possessed such and such a relic now claimed by several other towns. Amélineau suggests it be decided generally in favor of Upper Egypt whenever this rivalry opposes cities of Lower and Upper Egypt: "I believe that one fact tilts the scales in favor of Upper Egypt: the attribution of Osiris' head to Upper Egypt, to the city of Abydos."[9]

That fact would not be important if Amélineau had not discovered the tomb of Osiris and the head of the divine ancestor in a jar. We may doubt the authenticity of that discovery; nevertheless, Amélineau writes: "I myself have found other shrines during the preliminary excavations which culminated in the royal necropolis, before unearthing the shrine where the skull of the god I believed I had found was preserved."[10]

He then refers to the papyrus in the Museum of Leiden, cited by Brugsch. It expressly states that the god's head was preserved at Abydos, in a place designated on the papyrus by a name signifying "the necropolis of Abydos." Amélineau sought confirmation from Eugène Revillout on the validity of this document written in demotic. He received confirmation that the head of Osiris was indeed mentioned as being located at Abydos. Further assurance came in 1898, in the geographical text on Edfu in Brugsch's *Dictionary:* "It is stated there that the god's head was in the Abydos reliquary."[11]

But Amélineau observes: "Since Brugsch copied it, the text has disappeared, if one can believe the publication on the Edfu temple begun in the *Memoirs* of the Cairo Mission. . . . It would be interesting to ascertain whether that inscription has completely disappeared."[12] Finally, Amélineau records another important fact: In the *Texts of the Pyramids,* Osiris' throne is described just as Amélineau "found it in the funeral bed placed in the tomb at Abydos."[13] Quite justifiably, Amélineau wonders: "Why would the cities of Upper Egypt have claimed the most important parts of Osiris' body if he was born in the Delta, reigned in the Delta, died in the Delta, and had been the local god of a tiny district in the Delta? I see no reason for it."[14] Whether or not Amélineau really discovered the tomb and head of Osiris is unimportant. The essential fact is that the texts state that these are to be found at Abydos.

Thus, contrary to Moret's affirmation, authentic Egyptian tradition, as old as recorded time and written into the *Texts of the Pyramids* and *The Book of the Dead,* teaches us in unequivocal terms that the Egyptian deities belonged to the Black race and were born in the south. Furthermore, the myth of Osiris and Isis points out a cultural trait characteristic of Black Africa: the cult of ancestors, the foundation of Negro religious life and of Egyptian religious life, just as Amélineau reports.

Each dead ancestor becomes the object of a cult. The most remote forebears, whose teachings in the realm of social life, that is to say, in the realm of civilization, have proved effective, gradually become veritable gods (the mythical ancestors referred to by Lévy-Bruhl). They are totally detached from the human level, which does not mean that they never existed. Transformed into gods, they are placed on a plane different from that of the Greek hero; this is what made Herodotus think that the Egyptians had no heroes.[15]

It is apparent that Moret's argument concerning the invention of the calendar in Memphis is jarred seriously awry upon close examination. The author specifies that only in Memphis can one observe the heliacal rising of Sothis. He concludes that the Egyptian calendar, based on the cycle of that star (Sirius), whose rise coincides with that of the sun every 1,461 years, was invented at Memphis.[16] But the calendar was in use in 4236, the oldest date known with certainty in the history of man. Herodotus informs us, moreover, that Memphis was created by Menes, after the latter had turned the course of the river and made the muddy region of Lower Egypt more habitable: Menes, "the first king, having thus, by turning the river, made the tract where it used to run dry land, proceeded in the first place to build the city now called Memphis." (*Op. cit.,* p. 113.) Consequently, the site of Memphis was under water prior to the advent of Menes. If we accept 3200 as the year of his advent, that city did not even exist when the calendar was invented.

Besides, it would help the supporters of the Delta's priority if the heliacal rising of Sothis could be observed, not from the region of Memphis, but from that of Heliopolis, the city of Ra, where for these same theoreticians all Egyptian astronomy and astrology were allegedly born. Even so, it seems that Heliopolis, or Northern On, was founded by the Anu, whose name it bears.

Similar comments could be made about the argument that Egypt was civilized by invaders from the north. In Egyptian the west was designated by the right, the east by the left; from this fact one could deduce proof of a march toward the south. First of all, there are several ways to designate the east and west in Egyptian. . . . Furthermore, the divining art led to a division of the heavens into regions, for purposes of observation. As a result, a special orientation made a given cardinal point coincide with the right or left. This was practiced in Egypt and throughout the Aegean Mediterranean which had come under Egyptian influence, especially in Etruria.

Edouard Naville's explanation is even more edifying:

From which country did the conquerors come? It seems to me that they undoubtedly came from the south. If we consult the legend as it is preserved in a series of large paintings that adorn one of the corridors of the Edfu temple, and which date from the Ptolemaic epoch, we can see that the god Harmachis reigned in Nubia, upriver from Egypt. He left there with his son Horus, a warrior god, who conquered the whole country for him, as far as the city of Zar, now Kantarah, a fortress built on the easternmost branch of the Nile. This was the Pelusiac branch, which blocked any arrival from the direction of the Sinai peninsula and Palestine. In the principal Egyptian cities, the conquerors ruled whatever had to do with religion. In several localities, Horus settled his companions, who were called blacksmiths. Thus the introduction of metal work is connected with the conquest in the legend. . . .

This legend, which must belong to an ancient tradition, seems to me to merit attention. It agrees completely with what Greek historians tell us, namely, that Egypt was a colony of Ethiopia. Thus the Egyptians, at least those who became the Pharaonic Egyptians, probably followed the course of the great river. This is confirmed by certain features of their religion or customs. The Egyptian gets his bearings by looking toward the south; the west is on the right, the east on the left. I cannot believe that this means he is headed toward the south. On the contrary, he turns toward his country of origin; he looks in the direction from which he came and from which he may expect help. From there the conquering forces emerged; from there too the beneficial waters of the Nile bring fertility and riches. Besides, the south has always taken precedence over the north. The word king first meant king of Upper Egypt. Their god shows us the road they followed. The deity that walks before them has the form of a jackal or a dog: this is the god Oup-ouatou, he who shows the way.[17]

In the final analysis, to counter the attempts to present the Delta as a region more favorable than Upper Egypt for the flowering of a civilization, it is important to answer with what is really known about the Delta. The Delta is universally recognized as the permanent home of the plague in the Near East. It has been the point of departure for all the epidemics of the plague that have raged in that region throughout the course of history. Without exaggerating, we can go farther and affirm that the Delta, as such, did not exist, even at the time of Menes, since Memphis was at the edge of the sea. The region of Lower Egypt was at that time completely unhealthy and almost uninhabitable. One became mired in the mud. After the public works initiated by Menes, it became less unhealthy.

As for the western Delta, one can wonder what it was like before Menes, since we know that the course of the river was not the same as it is today and that the first Pharaoh gave it its present direction by having dams built and the earth filled in. Earlier the river had flowed westward:

> . . . the river flowed entirely along the sandy ridge of hills which skirts Egypt on the side of Libya. Menes, however, by banking up the river at the bend which it forms about a hundred furlongs south of Memphis, laid the ancient channel dry, while he dug a new course for the stream halfway between the two lines of hills. To this day, the elbow which the Nile forms at the point where it is forced aside into the new channel is guarded with the greatest care by the Persians, and strengthened every year; for if the river were to burst out at this place, and pour over the mound, there would be danger of Memphis being completely overwhelmed by the flood.[18]

If the dams broke, Memphis would be submerged by the waters of the Nile. This proves that the site of the city was really won from the waters, somewhat like polders. The capital of the first Egyptian king was in the south, at Thebes, and Memphis was founded, above all, for military purposes. It was a fortified place at the junction of infiltration routes for Asian shepherds from the east and nomads from the west, whom the Egyptians called *Rebou* or *Lebou*, whence the name Libyans (Eighteenth Dynasty).

More than once these barbarians tried to penetrate Egypt by force, attracted by its wealth, but almost every time they were defeated and pushed back across the border after heavy fighting. The nature of these coalitions between peoples of the north and east in the Delta area, the fierce battles waged there, justified the foundation of Memphis as an advanced fortress. Nevertheless, we should not confuse the races that faced one another there. As this passage from Moret indicates, it was a veritable confederation of Whites against the Negro race of Egypt:

About the month of April, 1229 B.C., Merneptah at Memphis learned that the King of the Libyans, Merirey, was coming from the land of Tehenu with his archers and a coalition of "Peoples of the North," composed of Shardana, Siculans, Achaeans, Lycians, and Etruscans, the warrior elite of each country. His aim was to attack the western frontier of Egypt in the plains of Perir. The danger was all the graver since the province of Palestine itself was affected by the disturbance. Indeed, it seems that the Hittites had also been embroiled in the turmoil, although Merneptah had continued his good offices in their behalf, sending them wheat by his ships at the time of a drought, to help the land of Khatti to survive.[19]

After a furious battle lasting six hours, the Egyptians had completely routed that coalition of barbarian hordes. Survivors long remembered their panic and passed that memory on for generations.

Merirey fled at top speed, abandoning his arms, his treasures, and his harem. The artist reported among the slain 6,359 Libyans, 222 Siculans, 742 Etruscans, and Shardana and Achaeans by thousands. More than 9,000 swords and pieces of armor, and a great booty were captured on the battlefield. Merneptah engraved a hymn of victory on the walls of his mortuary temple at Thebes, in which he described the panic among his enemies. The young Libyan men said of the victories: "We have had none since the days of Ra," and the old man said to his son: "Alas! poor Libya!" The Tehenu have been consumed in a single year. And the other provinces outside Egypt were also reduced to obedience. Tehenu is laid waste,

Khatti is pacified, Canaan is pillaged, Ascalon is despoiled, Gezer is captured, Yenoam is annihilated, Israel is made desolate and no longer has any crops, Kharu has become like a widow (without support) against Egypt. All the countries are unified and pacified.[20]

Significantly, in this quotation the victory, though won at Memphis, was commemorated at Thebes in Merneptah's mortuary temple. This confirms what was said earlier: The Pharaoh Merneptah resided in Memphis by military necessity but, like almost all Egyptian Pharoahs, he was to be buried at Thebes. Even when a Pharaoh died at Memphis, in Lower Egypt, they took the trouble to transport the corpse to Upper Egypt and bury it in the sacred Theban cities: Abydos, Thebes, Karnak. In those towns of Upper Egypt, the Pharaohs had their tombs next to those of the ancestors; there they always sent offerings, even if they resided in Memphis.

After the revolution that terminated the Old Kingdom, when the people gained access to the privilege of the Osirian death—in other words, the possibility of enjoying eternal life in heaven (after judgment by the Osiris Tribunal)—all social classes were symbolically interred in the Thebaid, by the erection of a stela in the name of the deceased. Thus, for all Egyptians without exception, the sacred region par excellence was the Thebaid in Upper Egypt. This would have been sacrilege on the part of the Egyptians, if their civilization and religious tradition had been born in the Delta. In that case, the sacred cities, ancestral tombs and principal sites for worship and pilgrimages would have been located in the Delta. These examples should suffice to discourage support in any form for the primacy of an alleged civilization in the Delta.

The coalition of peoples from the North and East at the time of Merneptah was but one episode in Egyptian history. Throughout that history, there were similar wars, more or less important, in that region. But, except during the low period, the Negroes of the Nile Valley always got the upper hand over the barbarians. As evidence, one can cite the numerous bas-reliefs depicting captives, from the cliffs of Sinai as far as the temple of Medinet-Habu and Thebes (cf. Narmer's Tablet); in other words, from the predynastic period until the Nineteenth Dynasty. By the admission of the Libyans themselves, if we are to believe the Egyptian texts, they never scored a victory from the beginning of time, since the days of the god Ra. No fact, no evidence,

32. A Black Queen of Ancient Sudan. Possibly a descendant of Candace, whose name was often adopted by later Sudanese queens in memory of her glorious resistance. (Discovered by Lepsius, this figure was published by Lenormant in his history of Egypt.)

no text has come to light to refute that statement. Moret himself writes:

> Against the background of the fertile loams of the valley, these Libyans and Troglodytes assume the mien of starveling pillagers, always on the lookout for a chance to raid the Egyptian fellah, peaceful and absorbed in the tasks of farming. They were never a source of real danger to the Egyptians, for they had as yet no swift mount capable of bearing loads; the ass, their only draught animal, cannot travel very fast nor carry heavy loads; the camel, which will give mobility and power to the desert tribes in the days of Islam, though not unknown, was but little used. Confronted with these nomads, Egypt was ever watchful and on guard and kept up police operations, on which she employed the Libyans themselves. Several tribes, like that of the Mashauasha, entered her service as mercenaries. In the same way she recruited excellent troops among the Mazoi. The Pharaoh found it expedient thus to insure himself against theft by paying a premium to these incorrigible freebooters, in the guise of wages. It was only in the last days of the Theban Empire that the Libyans, grouped in a sort of federation and set in motion by a migration of peoples, became a serious menace to Egypt which was not to be conjured away by extemporized expedients.[21]

That statement sums up everything concrete and tangible known about the Libyans. History teaches that they were half-starved pilferers, living on the periphery of Egypt, in the western part of the Delta; that they served as mercenaries; that they settled in the Delta during the low period; that they were Whites, with the exception of the Tehenu,[22] and basically refractory to civilization at a time when the Black world was already civilized. That is what historical documents teach us about the Libyans, along with their geographical distribution on the northern coast of Africa, as reported by Herodotus.

We may well wonder what sort of fabrication led to attributing to such peoples, different in every respect from the Egyptians, the origin of Egyptian civilizaton. As a crowning contradiction, they have even been presented as the Egyptian's so-called savage or less-cultured cousins. These Libyans were to come to the Delta as mercenaries during the low period and receive plots of land from the Pharaoh. Egypt would then be saturated with foreigners. From this intermingling comes the relatively lighter complexion of the Copts.

Thus the Delta never really mattered in Egyptian history until the low period. If Egypt was never a maritime power, that can perhaps by explained by the fact that its civilization was born in the interior of the continent, contrary to that of other peoples on the periphery of the Mediterranean. According to Plutarch, in "Isis and Osiris," the Egyptians considered the sea "a tainted secretion." This conception is incompatible with the notion of a riparian origin.

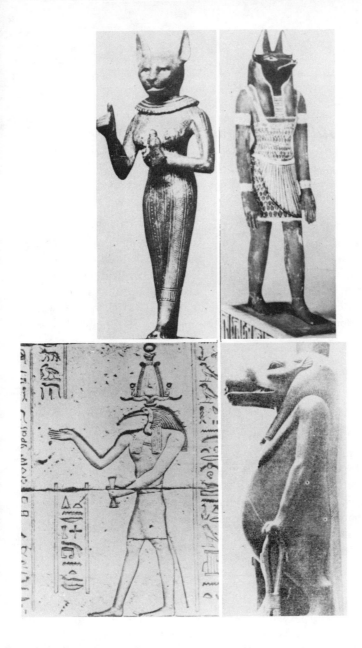

33. Egyptian Totemic Deities. *To Notir,* land of the gods, was also especially that of the Cynocephalus, the breed of sacred (dog-headed) monkeys, emblems of the god Thoth, the father of science (cf. the scene at bottom left).

CHAPTER V

Could Egyptian Civilization Be of Asian Origin?

Here, as in all that has preceded, it is important to distinguish between what can be deduced from a strict examination of historical documents and what is claimed over and beyond those documents—contrary to their testimony. To assign Egyptian civilization an Asiatic or any foreign origin whatsoever, we must be able to demonstrate the prior existence of a cradle of civilization outside of Egypt. However, we cannot overemphasize the fact that this basic, indispensable condition has never been met.

> Nowhere else had natural conditions favored the development of a human society to the same extent as in Egypt. Nowhere else do we find a Chalcolithic industry comparable in its technical perfection. Moreover, apart from some stations of uncertain age in Palestine, no trace of man earlier than 4000 B.C. exists in Syria or Mesopotamia. By that date the Egyptians had their feet on the threshold of their history proper. It is, then, reasonable to attribute this precocious development of Egypt's first inhabitants to their own genius and to the exceptional conditions in the Nile Valley. Nothing proves that it was due to the incursion of more civilized strangers. The very existence of such, or at least of their civilization, remains to be proved.[1]

By and large, these observations by Moret are still irrefutable today. The author alludes to the date 4241 B.C. [4236 after a slight correction of the first calculations], when the calendar was definitely in use in Egypt. . . . Thus, it is in Egypt that we encounter, with mathematical certainty, humanity's most ancient historical date. What do we find in Mesopotamia? Nothing susceptible of being dated with certainty. Mesopotamia was still building with sun-dried bricks made of clay that rain transformed into a mass of mud.

Egypt's pyramids, temples, and obelisks, its abundance of columns at Luxor and Karnak, its avenues of Sphinxes, the colossi of Memnon, its rock carvings, its underground temples with proto-Doric columns (Deir-el-Bahari) at Thebes, are an architectural reality still palpable today, historical evidence that no dogma can blow into thin air. In contrast, what did Iran (Elam) and Mesopotamia produce prior to the eighth century (epoch of the Assyrians)? Only shapeless clay mounds.

These mounds have been heralded as ruins of crumbling temples and towers that it is hoped to restore. Thus a British archeologist, Seton Lloyd, is restoring the interior of a hypothetical Babylonian temple of the second or third millennium, reproduced by Breasted.[2] This restoration is to be carried out with excavations undertaken by the Oriental Institute of the University of Chicago. Such restorations, including that of the Tower of Babel, are extremely serious for the history of mankind because of the illusion they can create. "The remains of these Babylonian tower buildings are very scanty, and there has been much difference of opinion regarding the proper form of restoration."[3]

In Egypt, the study of history rests largely on such written documents as the *Palermo Stone,* the *Royal Tablets of Abydos,* the *Royal Papyrus of Turin,* and Manetho's *Chronicle.* To those authentic documents, we must add the whole body of evidence reported by ancient writers, from Herodotus to Diodorus, not to mention the *Texts of the Pyramids, The Book of the Dead,* and thousands of inscriptions on the monuments.

In Mesopotamia, it was fruitless to seek anything similar. The cuneiform tablets generally carry nothing but merchants' accounts, tersely written receipts and bills. The Ancients remained silent about the alleged Mesopotamian culture prior to the Chaldeans. They considered the latter a caste of Egyptian astronomer-priests, that is to say, Negroes.[4] According to the Egyptians, Diodorus reports, the Chaldeans were "a colony of their priests that Belus had transported on the Euphrates and organized on the model of the mother-caste, and this colony continues to cultivate the knowledge of the stars, knowledge that it brought from the homeland."[5] So it is that "Chaldean" formed the root of the Greek word for astrologer. The Tower of Babel, a step pyramid similar to the tower of Saqqara, also known as "Birs-Nimroud" and "Temple of Baal," was probably the astronomical observatory of the Chaldeans.

This fits in, for Nimrod (Nemrod), son of Kush, grandson of Ham, the Biblical ancestor of the Blacks, is the symbol of worldly power: "He was a mighty hunter before the Lord. Hence the saying, 'Like Nemrod, a mighty hunter before the Lord.' The beginning of his kingdom was Babylon, Arach and Akkad, all of them in the land of Sennar. From that region Assur went forth."[6] What, then, would be more normal than the existence of step pyramids in Saqqara, in Babylon (Kushite city of Bel), in the Ivory Coast (in the form of bronze weights), and in Mexico where Negro emigration across the Atlantic is attested by Mexican authors and archeologists themselves?

Since Western Asia was the cradle of the Indo-Europeans, if a civilization comparable to that of Egypt had flowered there, prior to the Chaldean period, its memory, no matter how vague, would have been transmitted to us by the Ancients, who form one branch of the Indo-Europeans, the very ones who furnished so many corroborative testimonials on the Negro-Egyptian culture.

According to the short chronology, 3,200 years before Christ Egypt was unified into a kingdom under Menes. In Western Asia, nothing similar occurred. Instead of a powerful, unified kingdom, we find only cities: Susa, Ur, Lagash, Mari, Sumer, attested sometimes by anonymous tombs that are dubbed "royal tombs" without any proof. Thus elevated to kingly rank are persons who were either fictitious or merely village or town patriarchs. Today in every Senegalese village, one can find a family who claims to be its founder. The oldest member of such a family is often the patriarch of the village in question and the object of a certain deference on the part of its inhabitants. Nevertheless, two thousand years hence it would be absurd to give him the title of king and speak of the king of Koki Jad, Koki Guy, Koki Dahar, and so on.

On the significance of the so-called royal tombs of Ur, Dr. Georges Contenau writes:

> In the presence of the royal sepulchers, we may wonder whether kings were really involved and whether we should not connect these tombs with the fertility cult. As a matter of fact, what strikes us is that the occupants of these tombs are, so to speak, anonymous. . . .
> M.S. Smith thinks that these tombs may contain not real kings, but actors in the sacred drama presented at festivals where the principal protagonist was sacrificed. . . .

The inventor (of the tombs), Sir Leonard Woolley, denies this categorically. . . .
Describing this sensational discovery of the royal tombs, I pointed out, quite naturally, that the Scythians much later practiced similar rites. . . .
Though we have never had the good fortune to find a Mesopotamian tomb intact, beyond the royal tombs of Ur, and though we have never encountered explicit documents on the continuity of the funeral ritual revealed by the excavations at Ur, a few tablets nonetheless throw a bit of light on the somewhat weakened persistence of that practice.
A letter dating from the Assyrian epoch of the Sargonites informs us that the son of the Governor of Akkad and other places "has gone to his destiny," as has the lady of the palace, and that both have been buried.[7]

It is regrettable that the vague documents available date from so recent a period (eighth century B.C.). It is no less regrettable that the comparison which comes "quite naturally" to mind is with Scythian customs as described by Herodotus in the fifth century. In fact, on referring to the same descriptions quoted by Dr. Contenau (III, 1556), we realize that it is impossible to be more savage and barbarous than the Scythians. Consequently, we are far from the traces of a civilization that could be claimed as the mother of Egyptian civilization.

The term "inventor," applied to Sir Leonard Woolley who discovered these tombs, proves that the word "royal" could not be justified except as a working hypothesis. On the contrary, the most ancient kings of Elam were Blacks, without the slightest doubt, as attested by monuments exhumed by Dieulafoy:

Many other marvels were about to be revealed and we went from one surprise to another. In the demolition of a Sassanid wall made of the most ancient materials available locally, monuments were found dating back to the Elamite period of Susa's history, in other words, earlier than the capture of this fortress by Ashurbanipal. But here we must yield the floor to Dieulafoy:
"On removing a tomb placed across a raw-brick wall which was part of the fortifications of the Elamite gate, the workers uncovered a funeral urn. The urn was encased in a masonry covering

composed of enamelled bricks. These came from a panel depicting a personage superbly dressed in a green robe with yellow, blue, and white embroidery. He wore a tiger skin and carried a cane or a golden spear. Most surprising of all, the personage whose lower jaw, beard, neck, and hand I found was black. His lips were thin, his beard thick; the embroidery, of archaic style, seemed to be the work of Babylonian artisans."

In other Sassanid walls built of earlier materials, were found glazed bricks revealing two feet shod in gold, a very well-shaped hand, a wrist covered with bracelets; the fingers held one of those long canes that became the emblem of the sovereign power under the Achaemenides. A piece of the robe bore the coat-of-arms of Susa, partly hidden under a tiger skin. Finally, a flowered fringe on a brown background. His head and feet were black. It was even evident that the whole decoration had been designed to blend with the dark complexion of the face. Only powerful personages had the right to carry long canes and wear bracelets. Only the governor of a fortified post could have his image embroidered on his tunic. Yet, the owner of the cane, the master of the citadel was black. It is therefore highly probable that Elam was ruled by a black dynasty and, judging by the features of the face already described, an Ethiopian dynasty. . . .[8]

Half a century later, the findings of Dr. Contenau confirmed Dieulafoy's conclusions on the role played by the Black race in Western Asia. First he recalled the opinion of Quatrefages and Hamy on the ethnic types represented on Assyrian monuments. The Susian, in particular, "a probable product of some mixture of Kushite and Negro with his relatively flat nose, dilated nostrils, prominent cheekbones, and thick lips, is a racial type well observed and well depicted."[9]

Next he reports Houssaye's classification of the present population, probably composed of three strata, one of which is thus described:

Aryano-Negroids corresponding to the ancient Susians who for the most part were Blacks, a race of short Negroes, with slight cranial capacity. The Aryano-Negroids are brachycephalic, not dolichocephalic like large Negroes; they are found in Japan, islands of Malaysia, the Philippines, and New Guinea.

Although this classification may be slightly modified, the place it assigns to the Negroes is to be retained. By their existence we can explain the presence, among the Persian archers portrayed in colored brick, of black warriors who, however, do not have the ethnic characteristics of Negroes. Without exaggerating the importance of this element, it does not seem their presence in Ancient Elam can be doubted.[10]

The early Negro background of ancient Elam sheds new light on certain verses of the Gilgamesh Epic, a Babylonian (Kushite) poem:

> Father Enlil, Lord of the countries,
> Father Enlil, Lord of the true word,
> Father Enlil, Pastor of the Blacks . . .[11]

In this epic, Anu, the primitive god, father of Ishtar, has the same Negro name as Osiris the Onian: "The goddess Ishtar took the floor and spoke thus to the god Anu, her father . . ." (verses 92–93). We have already seen that, according to Amélineau, the Anu were the first Blacks to inhabit Egypt. A number of them remained in Arabia Petraea throughout Egyptian history. The Negro Anu is thus an historical fact, not a mental concept or a working hypothesis. We can also report the existence, even today, of an Ani (Agni) people in the Ivory Coast; the names of their kings are preceded by the title Amon, as has been noted earlier.

The chronology of Viktor Christian, who relies on Kugler's astronomical calculations, dates the start of the first Ur dynasty between 2600 and 2580, which would thus also be the period of the so-called "royal" tombs. The official date, adopted until now for no special reason, wavers between 3100 and 3000. In actual fact, the choice of 3100 results from no necessity but that of synchronizing Egyptian and Mesopotamian chronology. Since Egyptian history, according to the most moderate estimates, starts in 3200, it becomes indispensable, "out of solidarity," to make Mesopotamian history begin at about the same time, even if all known historical facts about that region can fit into a much shorter period. Alluding to Christian's estimate, Contenau writes: "What must we think of these new figures? In themselves, they seem to allow sufficient time for the historical events." Nevertheless, he is careful not to adopt that chronology for two reasons:

The first is that the aforementioned calculation of astronomical phenomena, which ought to be a fixed standard, is subject to variations; . . .

The second reason is that the extra-short chronology does not take neighboring civilizations into account; it is difficult to explain how Egyptian civilization which Egyptologists, in the most moderate estimates, start about 3100 B.C., could have preceded Mesopotamian history by 600 years. The relationships existing between Asia and Egypt, in the proto-historical epoch, are an established fact; they become inexplicable, as the advance of Minoan (Cretan) civilization would be, if these new figures were adopted. The proposal seems hardly acceptable. I believe that Mr. Christian's very interesting study leads to an admissible conclusion only if a parallel study can cause a similar reduction in the starting date of Egyptian and Aegean civilizations.[12]

In another work, published in 1934, Dr. Contenau insists: "A general solidarity exists that must be taken into account. The historical period opens at approximately the same time in Egypt and Mesopotamia; nevertheless, Egyptologists generally refuse to fix the date of Menes, founder of the First Dynasty, at later than 3200 B.C."[13]

From these texts it is clear that the synchronization of Egyptian and Mesopotamian history is a necessity resulting from ideas, not from facts. The motivating idea is to succeed in explaining Egypt by Mesopotamia, that is, by Western Asia, the original habitat of Indo-Europeans. The foregoing demonstrates that, if we remain within the realm of authentic facts, we are forced to view Mesopotamia as a belatedly born daughter of Egypt. The relationships of protohistory do not necessarily imply the synchronization of history in the two countries.

To conclude this section, we can ponder this passage from Lovat Dickson, quoted by Marcel Brion: "Thirty years ago, the name Sumer meant nothing to the public. Today there is something called the *Sumerian problem,* a subject for controversy and constant speculation among archeologists."[14] Referring to Persian monuments, Diodorus writes that they were built by Egyptian workers forcibly carried off by Cambyses, "the Vandal." "Cambyses set fire to all the temples in Egypt; that was when the Persians, transporting all the treasures to Asia and even kidnapping some Egyptian workmen, built the famous palaces of Persepolis, Susa, and several other cities in Media."[15]

According to Strabo, Susa had been founded by a Negro, Tithonus,

King of Ethiopia and father of Memnon: "In fact, it is claimed that
Susa was founded by Tithonus, Memnon's father, and that his citadel
bore the name Memnonium. The Susians are also called Cissians and
Aeschylus calls Memnon's mother Cissia."[16] Cissia reminds us of
Cissé, an African family name. . . .

Phoenicia

The man found in Canaan in prehistoric times, the Natufian, was a
Negroid. The Capsian tool industry, which doubtless came from
North Africa to that region, was also of Negroid origin. In the Bible,
when the first white races reached the place, they found a black race
there, the Canaanites, descendants of Canaan, brother of Mesraim,
the Egyptian, and Kush, the Ethiopian, sons of Ham.

> The Lord said to Abram: "Leave your country, your kinsfolk and
> your father's house, for the land which I will show you. . . ."
> Abram went away as the Lord had commanded him, and Lot went
> with him. . . . Abram took Sarai his wife, Lot his brother's son, all
> the property they had acquired and the persons they had got in
> Haran and they departed for the land of Canaan. When they came
> to the land of Canaan, Abram passed through the land to the sa-
> cred place at Sichem, near the plain of More. At that time the Ca-
> naanities were in the land.[17]

After many ups and downs, the Canaanites and the white tribes,
symbolized by Abraham and his descendants (Isaac's lineage),
blended to become in time the Jewish people of today:

> So Hemor and his son Sichem went to the gate of their city and
> spoke to their fellow citizens. "These men," they said, "are friendly;
> let them dwell with us and trade in the land, since there is ample
> room for them. Let us marry their daughters and give them our
> daughters to marry."[18]

Those few lines, which seem to be a ruse, nonetheless reveal the economic imperatives which at that time were to govern relations between white invaders and black Canaanites. Phoenician history is
therefore incomprehensible only if we ignore the Biblical data according to which the Phoenicians, in other words, the Canaanites,

were originally Negroes, already civilized, with whom nomadic, un-cultured white tribes later mixed.

From that time on, the term Leuco-Syrians, applied to certain White populations of that region, is a confirmation of the Biblical data, not a contradiction, as Hoefer believes: "The name Syrian appears to have reached from Babylonia to the Gulf of Issus and even from that gulf to the Euxine Sea. The Cappadocians, those of Taurus as well as those of the Euxine Sea, are still called Leuco-Syrians (white Syrians), as if there were also black Syrians."[19] This is how the lasting alliance between Egyptians and Phoenicians can be explained. Even throughout the most troubled periods of great misfortune, Egypt could count on the Phoenicians as one can more or less count on a brother.

Among the monumental narratives engraved on the walls of Egyptian temples and referring to the great insurrections in Syria against Egyptian hegemony, never do we see on the lists of rebels and the vanquished the names of Sidonians, of their capital, or any of their cities. The most formidable of those uprisings, instigated by the Assyrians or else by northern Hittites, were put down by Tuthmosis III, Seti I, Ramses II, and Ramses III. . . .

An invaluable papyrus in the British Museum contains the fictional account of a visit to Syria by an Egyptian official at the end of the reign of Ramses II, after peace with the northern Hittites was finally restored. . . . Throughout Syria, the traveler was on Egyptian soil; he circulated as freely and safely as he would in the valley of the Nile and even, by virtue of his position, exercised some authority.[20]

To be sure, we should not minimize the role of economic relations between Egypt and Phoenicia in explaining that loyalty which seems to have existed. One can also understand that Phoenician religion and beliefs are to some extent mere replicas of Egypt's. Phoenician cosmogony is revealed in fragments of *Sanchoniation,* translated by Philo of Byblos and reported by Eusebius. According to these texts, in the beginning there was uncreated, chaotic matter, in perpetual disorder *(Bohu);* Breath *(Rouah)* hung over Chaos. The union of those two principles was called *Chephets,* Desire, which is at the origin of all creation.

What impresses us here is the similarity between this cosmic Trinity and that found in Egypt, as reported by Amélineau in his *Prolégomènes*: In Egyptian cosmogony also, at the beginning there was chaotic, uncreated matter, the primitive *Nun* (cf. *Nen*=nothingness, in Wolof). This primitive matter contained, in the form of principles, all possible beings. It also contained the god of potential development, Khepru. As soon as the primitive nothingness created Ra, the demiurge, its role ended. Henceforth the thread would be unbroken until the advent of Osiris, Isis, and Horus, ancestors of the Egyptians. The primitive Trinity then moved from the scale of the universe to that of man, as it did later in Christianity.

After successive generations in Phoenician cosmogony, we reach the ancestors of the Egyptians, Misor,* who will engender Taaut, inventor of sciences and letters (Taaut is none other than Thoth of the Egyptians). In the same cosmogony, we reach Osiris and Canaan, forebear of the Phoenicians (cf. Lenormant, *op.cit.,* p. 583).

Phoenician cosmogony reveals once again the kinship of Egyptians and Phoenicians, both of Kushite (Negro) origin. This kinship is confirmed by the revelations of the Ras Shamra (ancient Ugarit, on the Syrian coast) texts, which place the original habitat of Phoenicia's national heroes in the south, on Egypt's frontiers:

> The Ras Shamra texts give us an opportunity to reexamine the origin of the Phoenicians. While the tablets on everyday life take into account various foreign elements who participated in the city's daily routine, those that present myths and legends allude to a quite different past. Though they concern a city of the extreme Phoenician north, they adopt the far south, the Negeb, as the setting for events they describe. To the national heroes and ancestors, they assign a habitat located between the Mediterranean and the Red Sea. This tradition, moreover, has been noted by Herodotus (fifth century) and, before him, by Sophonias (seventh century).[21]

Geographically, the body of land between the Mediterranean and the Red Sea is, essentially, the Isthmus of Suez, that is to say, Arabia Petraea, land of the Anu, Blacks who founded Northern On (Heliopolis) in historical times.

Toward the middle of the second millennium (1450 B.C.), under the increasing pressure of white tribes who occupied the hinterland and drove the Phoenicians back toward the coast, the Sidonians

---

*And Egypt is today named *Misr* in Egyptian.

founded the first Phoenician colonies in Boeotia, where they installed the excess population. Thus, Thebes was created, as well as Abydos on the Hellespont. The name Thebes confirms, once again, the ethnic kinship of Egyptians and Phoenicians. We know, as a matter of fact, that Thebes was the holy city of Upper Egypt, from which the Phoenicians took the two Black women who founded the oracles of Dodona in Greece and Amon in Libya.[22]

During the same period the Libyans settled in Africa, around Lake Triton, as indicated by a study of the historical monuments of Seti I. Cadmus, the Phoenician, personifies the Sidonian period and the Phoenician contribution to Greece. The Greeks say that Cadmus introduced writing, as we would say today that Marianne [symbol of the French Republic] introduced railroads into French West Africa.

Greek traditions place the installation of Egyptian colonies in Greece at approximately the same time: Cecrops settled in Attica; Danaus, brother of Aegyptus, in Argolis; he taught the Greeks agriculture as well as metallurgy (iron). During this Sidonian epoch, elements of Egypto-Phoenician civilization crossed into Greece. At first the Phoenician colony held the upper hand, but soon the Greeks began to struggle for liberation from the Phoenicians who, at this period prior to the Argonauts, possessed mastery of the seas as well as technical superiority.

This conflict is symbolized by the fight between Cadmus (the Phoenician) and the serpent son of Mars (the Greek); it lasted about three centuries.

> The dissension thus aroused among the natives by the arrival of the Canaanite settlers is represented in mythical legend by the combat waged by Cadmus and the Spartans. From then on, those of the Spartans whom the fable allows to survive and become the companions of Cadmus, represent the principal Ionian families who accepted domination by the foreigner.
>
> Not for long does Cadmus rule his empire in peace; he is soon chased away and compelled to retire among the Enchelians. The indigenous element regains control, after having accepted the authority of the Phoenicians and receiving the benefits of civilization, it rises up against them and tries to expel them. . . .
>
> All that we can discern in this part of the narrative concerning the Cadmeans is the horror that their race and religion, still impregnated by barbarism and oriental obscenity, inspired in the

poor but virtuous Greeks whom, however, they had taught. And so, in Hellenic tradition, a superstitious terror is attached to the memory of the kings of Cadmus' race. They provided most of the subjects for antique tragedy.[23]

At this point we have indeed reached a period of demarcation when the Indo-European world was freeing itself from the domination of the Black Egypto-Phoenician world.

This economic and political struggle, similar in all respects to that which colonial countries are now waging against modern imperialism, was supported, as it is today, by a cultural reaction caused by the same reasons. To understand the *Orestes* of Aeschylus and Virgil's *Aeneid,* we must view them in the context of this cultural oppression. Instead of interpreting, as Bachofen and others believe, the universal transition from matriarchy to patriarchy, these works mark the encounter and conflict of two different conceptions: the one with deep roots in the Eurasian plains, the other embedded in the heart of Africa. At the outset the latter (matriarchy) dominated and spread throughout the Aegean Mediterranean thanks to Egypto-Phoenician colonization of populations, sometimes even White populations, but whose inconsistent culture permitted no positive reaction at the time. This was perhaps true of the Lycians and several other Aegean groups. Yet, the writers of Antiquity unanimously report that these ideas never really penetrated the White world of northern Europe, which rejected them as soon as it could, as notions alien to its own cultural conceptions. This is the meaning of the *Aeneid.* In its forms most foreign to the northern mentality, Egypto-Phoenician cultural imperialism hardly survived economic imperialism.[24]

The history of humanity will remain confused as long as we fail to distinguish between the two early cradles in which Nature fashioned the instincts, temperament, habits, and ethical concepts of the two subdivisions before they met each other after a long separation dating back to prehistoric times. The first of those cradles, as we shall see in the chapter on Egypt's contribution, is the valley of the Nile, from the Great Lakes to the Delta, across the so-called "Anglo-Egyptian" Sudan. The abundance of vital resources, its sedentary, agricultural character, the specific conditions of the valley, will engender in man, that is, in the Negro, a gentle, idealistic, peaceful nature, endowed with a spirit of justice and gaiety. All these virtues were more or less indispensable for daily coexistence.

Because of the requirements of agricultural life, concepts such as matriarchy and totemism, the most perfect social organization, and monotheistic religion were born. These engendered others: thus, circumcision resulted from monotheism; in fact, it was really the notion of a god, Amon, uncreated creator of all that exists, that led to the androgynous concept. Since Amon was not created and since he is the origin of all creation, there was a time when he was alone. To the archaic mentality, he must have contained within himself all the male and female principles necessary for procreation. That is why Amon, the Negro god par excellence of the "Anglo-Egyptian" Sudan (Nubia) and all the rest of Black Africa, was to appear in Sudanese mythology as androgynous. Belief in this hermaphroditic ontology would produce circumcision and excision in the Black world. One could go on to explain all the basic traits of the Negro soul and civilization by using the material conditions of the Nile Valley as the point of departure.

By contrast, the ferocity of nature in the Eurasian steppes, the barrenness of those regions, the overall circumstances of material conditions, were to create instincts necessary for survival in such an environment. Here, Nature left no illusion of kindliness: it was implacable and permitted no negligence; man must obtain his bread by the sweat of his brow. Above all, in the course of a long, painful existence, he must learn to rely on himself alone, on his own possibilities. He could not indulge in the luxury of believing in a beneficent God who would shower down abundant means of gaining a livelihood; instead, he would conjure up deities maleficent and cruel, jealous and spiteful: Zeus, Yahweh, among others.

In the unrewarding activity that the physical environment imposed on man, there was already implied materialism, anthropomorpnism (which is but one of its aspects), and the secular spirit. This is how the environment gradually molded these instincts in the men of that region, the Indo-Europeans in particular. All the peoples of the area, whether white or yellow, were instinctively to love conquest, because of a desire to escape from those hostile surroundings. The milieu chased them away; they had to leave it or succumb, try to conquer a place in the sun in a more clement nature. Invasions would not cease, once an initial contact with the Black world to the south had taught them the existence of a land where the living was easy, riches abundant, technique flourishing. Thus, from 1450 B.C. until Hitler, from the Barbarians of the fourth and fifth centuries to Genghis Khan and the Turks, those invasions from east to west or from north to south continued uninterrupted.

Man in those regions long remained a nomad. He was cruel.[25] The cold climate would engender the worship of fire, to remain burning from the fire of Mithras* to the flame on the tomb of the Unknown Soldier under the Arch of Triumph and the torches of the ancient and modern Olympics. Nomadism was responsible for cremation: thus the ashes of ancestors could be transported in small urns. This custom was perpetuated by the Greeks; the Aryans introduced it to India after 1450, and that explains the cremation of Caesar and of Gandhi in our own epoch.

Obviously, man was the pillar of that kind of life. Woman's economic role was much less significant than in Black agricultural societies. Consequently, the nomadic patriarchal family was the only embryo of social organization. The patriarchal principle would rule the whole life of the Indo-Europeans, from the Greeks and Romans to the Napoleonic Code, to our day. This was why woman's participation in public life would arrive later in European than in Negro societies.[26] If the opposite seems true today in certain parts of Black Africa, it can be attributed to Islamic influence.

These two types of social concepts clashed and were superimposed upon the Mediterranean. Throughout the entire Aegean epoch, the Negro influence preceded that of the Indo-European. All the populations on the periphery of the Mediterranean at the time were Negroes or Negroids: Egyptians, Phoenicians; what Whites there were came under the economic and cultural Egypto-Phoenician influence: Greece, epoch of the Boeotians; Asia Minor, Troy; Hittites, allies of Egypt; Etruscans in northern Italy, allies of the Phoenicians, with strong Egyptian influence; Gaul, crisscrossed by Phoenician caravans, under the direct influence of Egypt. This Negro pressure extended as far as certain German tribes who adored Isis, the Negro goddess:

In fact, inscriptions have been found in which Isis is associated with the city of Noreia; Noreia today is Neumarkt in Styria (Austria). Isis, Osiris, Serapis, Anubis have altars in Fréjus, Nîmes, Arles, Riez (Basses-Alpes), Parizet (Isère), Manduel (Gard), Boulogne (Haute-Garonne), Lyons, Besançon, Langres, Soissons.

---

*In Persian mythology, Mithras was the god of light and truth, later of the sun.

Isis was honored at Melun . . . at York and Brougham Castle, and also in Pannonia and Noricum.[27]

Worship of the "Black Madonnas" probably began during the same period. This cult still survives in France (Our Lady Underground, or the Black Madonna of Chartres). It remained so vivid that the Roman Catholic Church finally had to consecrate it.[28] The very name of the French capital might be explained by the Isis cult. "The term 'Parisii' could well mean 'Temple of Isis,' for there was a city with this name on the banks of the Nile, and the hieroglyph *per* represents the enclosure of a temple on the Oise."[29]

The author is referring to the fact that the first inhabitants of the present site of Paris, who fought against Caesar, bore the name Parisii, for some reason unknown today. The worship of Isis was evidently quite widespread in France, especially in the Parisian basin; temples of Isis, in Western parlance, were everywhere. But it would be more exact to say "Houses of Isis," for in Egyptian these so-called temples were called *Per,* the exact meaning of which in ancient Egyptian, as in present-day Wolof, is: the enclosure surrounding the house. The name "Paris" could have resulted from the juxtaposition of Per-Isis, a word that designated certain cities in Egypt, as Hubac observes (quoting Maspero). Accordingly, the root of the name of France's capital could be derived basically from Wolof. This would indicate to what extent the situation has been reversed.

Other common cultural features exist between the West and Black Africa: *Ker*=house, in Egyptian, Wolof, and Breton; *Dang*=taut, in Wolof and Irish; *Dun*=island, in Wolof=closed, isolated place (on ·land), in Celtic and Irish, whence we get names for such cities as Ver-Dun, Château-Dun, Lug-Dun-Um (Lyons), and so on.

It would be equally enlightening to study the relationships between the exchanges of consonants in the languages of Brittany and Africa. To this same influence we must attribute the existence of the god *Ani* among the Irish and Etruscans. The Egypto-Phoenician impact on the Etruscans is quite clear, as it is on the Sabines, whose name and customs suggest southern Negro civilizations.

The distinction just made between the two cradles of civilization enables us to avoid all confusion and mystery concerning the origins of the peoples who met on the Italian peninsula. Sabines and Etruscans buried their dead. The Etruscans knew and utilized the Egyptian sarcophagus. These populations were agricultural; their life was ruled by the matriarchal system. The Etruscans brought all the elements of Egyptian civilization to the Italian peninsula: farming, religion, arts, including the divining art. When they destroyed the Etruscans, the Romans assimilated the substance of that civilization, while eliminating those aspects most alien to their Eurasian patriarchal conception. In this way, after the transitional period of the Tarquins, the last Etruscan kings, the Black matriarchal system was completely rejected. . . .

The end of an ancient world, the beginning of the new! Black culture, in its forms most foreign to Eurasian conceptions, was evicted from the northern Mediterranean basin. It would not survive except as a substratum among the young tribes that it had introduced to civilization. This substratum was nonetheless so hardy that we can determine even today how far it extended. To all this we may add that the Roman she-wolf recalls the southern Negro practice of totemism, and that Sabine seems to contain the root of Saba (Sheba).

Consequently, if one wished, the history of humanity could be quite lucid. Despite the repeated acts of vandalism from the days of Cambyses, through the Romans, the Christians of the sixth century in Egypt, the Vandals, etc., we still have enough documents left to write a clear history of man. The West today is fully aware of this, but it lacks the intellectual and moral courage required, and this is why textbooks are deliberately muddled. It then devolves on us Africans to rewrite the entire history of mankind for our own edification and that of others.

The same Negro influence also accounts for a linguistic fact reported by von Wartburg, who stresses its breadth of usage:

The change of *ll* into *dd* (a cacuminal sound pronounced with the tip of the tongue curled back to touch the palate, sometimes with the lower part of the tongue), in Sardinia, Sicily, Apulia, Calabria, is not without importance and interest. According to Merlo, this particular mode of articulation was probably due to the Mediterranean people who lived in the country before its Romanization. Although cacuminal sounds also exist in other languages, the articulatory change here proceeded on so wide a base and in an area so vast, extending across the seas and is so clearly archaic that Merlo's conception certainly appears true. . . . Pott and Benfey have long since revealed that cacuminal articulation, introduced into Aryan languages spoken by the invaders of Deccan, came from the underlying Dravidian populations.[30]

Accordingly, the introduction of cacuminal sounds into the Aryan languages of India when that country was invaded by unpolished Nordic peoples is due to the influence of Dravidian Negroes. It can be assumed that the same thing happened in the Mediterranean basin, the more so since Egyptian and Negro languages are saturated with these cacuminal sounds.

Furthermore, in pre-Columbian Mexico the fact that the peasants were buried, whereas warriors were cremated, can be explained by the distinction outlined above of humanity's two cradles. Whites from the north and Blacks crossing the Atlantic from Africa probably met on the American continent and gradually blended to produce the more or less Yellow race of Indians.

A brief explanation is in order here. When I write that Arabs and Jews, the two ethnic branches known today as Semites, are mixtures of Black and White, that is a demonstrable, historical truth long dissembled. When I write that the Yellow races are mixtures of Black and White, this is only a working hypothesis, worthy of interest for all the reasons cited above.

Although scientifically attractive, the hypothesis that man existed everywhere at the same time will remain inadmissible so long as we fail to find fossilized man in America, a continent not submerged during the fourth quaternary when man appeared and on which we have all the climatic zones, from the South Pole to the North Pole.

As already indicated, it would be most helpful to have a systematic study of the roots that passed from Negro languages (Egyptian and others) to Indo-European languages throughout the period of their contact. Two principles could guide us in such a study: 1. The anteriority of civilization and forms of social organization in Negro countries, such as Egypt; 2. The fact that a word expressing an idea of social organization or some other cultural aspect, may be common to Egyptian and to Latin or Greek, without appearing in other languages of the Indo-European family. For example:

Maka : veteran, in Egyptian.
Mag : veteran, venerable, in Wolof.
Kay Mag : he who is great, venerable, in Wolof.

Kaya Magan : the great, the king. This term served to designate the Emperor of Ghana from the third century to approximately 1240. The language was Sarakole (or a neighboring tongue). In any event, it was obviously related to Wolof.

Magnus : great, in Latin; the Latins did not count in history before 500 B.C.

Carle Magnus : Charlemagne, Charles the Great, first emperor of the West.

Mega : great, in Greek. The root *Magnus* is not found in the vocabulary of Anglo-Saxon and Germanic languages except as an obvious borrowing from Latin.

Mac : Scottish proper name.

Kora : musical instrument in West Africa; *Choeur:* chant, in Greek.

Ra, Re : Egyptian god, symbolized by the sun, title of the Pharaoh.

Rog : celestial Serer god whose voice is the thunder.

Rex : king, in Latin; which, in the Romance languages, becomes *re, rey, roi,* whereas in the Anglo-Germanic we have only *king* or *König.*

In the same connection, we could study the word *hymen,* which may be related to Negro matriarchy. It suggests *men*: matrilineal descendant, in Wolof; it means breast, in Egyptian and Wolof; it designates the first king of Egypt, whose distorted name is Menes. Thus, in this name, the idea of a matrilineal transmission of political power is implied. It was not by chance that the Sudanese king who first codified the Sun cult in Nubia bore the name *Men-thiou;* he was either contemporary with or earlier than Menes.

All things considered, when the Nazis say that the French are Negroes, if we disregard the prejorative intention of that affirmation, it remains well-founded historically, insofar as it refers to those contacts between peoples in the Aegean epoch. But that is true not only of the French; it is even more applicable to the Spaniards, Italians, Greeks, etc., all those populations whose complexion, less white than that of other Europeans, has wishfully been attributed to their southern habitat. What is false in Nazi propaganda is the claim of racial superiority, but certainly the blue-eyed, blond Nordic race has been the least mixed since the fourth glaciation. These Nazi theories prove what I said about the insincerity of the specialists. They show, in fact, that the Black influence on the Mediterranean is no secret for any scholar: they pretend to be unaware of it, yet use it when they feel so inclined.

According to Lenormant, in the fourteenth century B.C. the white, Japhetic Philistines invaded the coasts of Canaan. They were conquered by Ramses III, who destroyed their fleet and thus removed any possibility of their return by sea. The Pharaoh was compelled to find a way to relocate an entire people deprived of any means of departing. He gave them land and the Philistines settled there. After two centuries of development, they destroyed Sidon in the twelfth century, during the period when Troy, aided by 10,000 Ethiopians sent by the king of Egypt, was overthrown by the Greeks. The Phoenicians founded Tyre, which welcomed the refugees from Sidon. This was the Tyrian epoch of relations with the Etruscans, first called Tyrrhenes, which gives us the name of the Tyrrhenian Sea.

Spain became a stop on the road to Brittany and the British Isles, where the Phoenicians went to pick up tin that they used in making bronze. The colonization of Spain was rapid; at that time crossbreeding was so widespread that the Iberian peninsula (Tarsis) was considered by the Greeks as being of Canaanite origin. If today the Spaniards are the brownest of Europeans, this should be ascribed to that crossbreeding, more so than to their later contact with the Arabs —apart from the ethnic effects that may have resulted from the presence of the Negro Grimaldi race in the south of Europe at the close of the Paleolithic (cf. Lenormant, op.cit., pp. 509–510).

Roman colonization merely supplanted Phoenician colonization, first in Italy, where all that could perpetuate the memory of the Etruscans (monuments, language) was obliterated, then in Spain and Africa, with the destruction of Carthage. Founded on the African coast circa 814 B.C., Carthage was one of the last Phoenician colonies.

Since 1450, white Libyans, people of the sea, or Rebou, had invaded North Africa west of Egypt. Before the founding of Carthage, they had time to scatter all along the coast, toward the west, as Herodotus reports. The hinterland of Carthage was then inhabited by indigenous Blacks who had been there throughout Antiquity, and by white Libyan tribes. Crossbreeding occurred gradually, as in Spain, and the Carthaginians, both common people and elite, were evidently Negroid. We need not insist on the fact that the Carthaginian general, Hannibal, who barely missed destroying Rome and who is considered one of the greatest military leaders of all time, was Negroid. It can be said that, with his defeat, the supremacy of the Negro or Negroid world ended. Henceforth the torch passed to the European populations of the northern Mediterranean. From then on its technical civilization would spread from the coast toward the interior of the continent (just the opposite of what happened in Africa). From then on the northern Mediterranean dominated the southern Mediterranean. Except for the Islamic breakthrough, Europe has ruled Africa down to the present day. With the Roman victory over Carthage, European penetration and control of Africa began; it reached its high point at the end of the nineteenth century.

When one studies the civilization that developed in the Mediterranean basin, it seems impossible to exaggerate the essential role played by Negroes and Negroids at a time when European races were still uncivilized:

The Phoenicians had trading-posts everywhere, and these posts exercised immense influence on the different countries where they were located. Each became the nucleus of a great city, for the savage natives, attracted by its advantages and by the lures of civilized life, quickly grouped themselves around the Phoenician trading-station. All were active centers for spreading industry and material civilization. A savage tribe does not begin active, prolonged commerce with a civilized people without borrowing something of its culture, especially when races as intelligent and as apt to progress as the Europeans are involved. New needs were awakened; the European eagerly sought the manufactured products brought to him and revealing more refinement than he had ever imagined. Soon, however, he desired to penetrate the secrets of their manufacture, to learn the arts that produced them, to begin himself to utilize the resources provided by his soil, instead of always handing them over to those strangers who knew how to put them to such good advantage.

This direct influence of civilization on barbarism is so inherent in human nature, that it appears almost unconsciously and despite misunderstandings, hatred, hostility, and even wars that may erupt between the merchants and the peoples they frequent. So it was with the Phoenicians and the Greeks, and yet their relations were far from friendly at the start.[31]

While the Phoenicians controlled the seas, the business of providing White women for the Black world took place. Its role in whitening the Egyptians should not be minimized. The following quotation leaves no doubt about the reality and importance of that trade, nor of the contrast in the color of Black Egyptians and the Whites from the northern coasts:

> Phoenician ships laden with merchandise from Egypt and Assyria dock in a Greek port. They display their cargo on the shore for five or six days to give the inhabitants of the interior time to come, to view, and to buy. The Peloponnesian women, curious and unsuspecting, approach the ships. Among them is Io, daughter of King Inachus. At a given signal, the corsairs seize the beautiful Greek women and carry them away. They lift anchor immediately and set sail for Egypt. The Pharaoh had to pay a high price for those white-skinned girls with such pure features, so different from the human cargo his armies brought back from Syria.[32]

In this context, we can also place the kidnapping by the Phoenicians of Eumea, daughter of a notable of Skyros, and the rape of Helen by Paris, son of Priam. This must have occurred under similar conditions, if we recall that the Pharaoh sent 10,000 Ethiopians to aid Troy.

The Canaanites were surely more rapidly mixed than the Egyptians, for they were less numerous and more directly located on the escape routes of the Whites who finally invaded the territory from all sides. The Jewish people, that is, the first branch called Semitic, descendants of Isaac, seem to have been the product of that crossbreeding. That is why a Latin historian wrote that the Jews are of Negro origin. As for the cynical, mercantile spirit which constitutes the very foundation of the Bible (Genesis, Exodus), it simply reflects the conditions in which the Jewish people were placed from the start.

The intellectual production of the Jews, from the beginning until now, is likewise explained by the conditions under which they perpetually lived. Forming clusters of stateless persons since their dispersion, they have constantly experienced a double anxiety: that of assuring their material existence, often in hostile surroundings, and the fear resulting from obsession with periodic pogroms. In the relatively recent past, in the Eurasian steppes, physical conditions had allowed for no illusion, no lethargy, and if man failed to create a marvelous civilization there, it was because the environment was too hostile. Now, it was political and social conditions that allowed the Jews no intellectual let-up. They did not begin to count in history until David and Solomon, or the beginning of the first millennium, the epoch of the Queen of Sheba. Egyptian civilization was already several millennia old, *a fortiori* Nubian-Sudanese civilization.

It is thus unthinkable to try to explain the latter by any Jewish contribution. Solomon was but a minor king, ruling a small strip of land; he never governed the world as the legends claim. He distinguished himself by his spirit of justice and his talents as a businessman. As a matter of fact, he had joined with the merchants of Tyre in building a merchant marine to exploit overseas markets. Thanks to that commercial activity, Palestine prospered under his reign. That was the only important reign in Jewish history down to the present. Later, the country was conquered by Nebuchadnezzar who transferred the Jewish population to Babylon: this was the period known as the Captivity. Gradually the Jews scattered. The Jewish State went rapidly into eclipse and did not reappear until modern Zionism under Ben-Gurion.

The meager anthropological research anyone has dared undertake clearly proves that the Phoenicians had nothing in common with the official Jewish type: brachycephaly, aquiline or Hittite nose, and so on. Since the Phoenicians went all over the Mediterranean, their remains have been sought in different locations in that basin. Thus, skulls, presumably Phoenician, have been found west of Syracuse; but these skulls are dolichocephalic and prognathous, with distinctly Negroid affinities. (Cf. Eugène Pittard, *Les Races et l'histoire*. Paris, 1924, p. 108.)

Pittard also quotes a description by Bertholon of the Carthaginians and the Basques, whom Bertholon considered a branch of the Carthaginians. This description is important because the author, without realizing it, is actually describing a Negro type:

He [Bertholon] has painted the following portrait of men he deemed the surviving descendants of the ancient Carthaginians: these people had very brown skin. This reflects the Phoenician's habit of coloring his statues reddish-brown in order to reproduce the tint of the skin. . . . The nose is straight, sometimes slightly concave. More often it is fleshy, occasionally flat at the end. The mouth is average, sometimes quite wide. The lips most often are thick, the cheekbones not very prominent.[33]

Despite these euphemisms, it is easy to sense that we have just read a description of a Negro or, at the very least, of a Negroid.

The same author also shows that the whole Carthaginian aristocracy had Negro affinities: "Other bones discovered in Punic Carthage, and housed in the Lavigerie Museum, come from personages found in special sarcophagi and probably belonging to the Carthaginian elite. Almost all the skulls are dolichocephalic . . . with a rather short face . . . "[34] Dolichocephaly and a short face are Negro characteristics.

Even more important is still another passage from Pittard, proving more conclusively that the upper class of Carthaginian society was Negro or Negroid:

Those who have recently visited the Lavigerie Museum in Carthage will recall that magnificent sarcophagus of the Priestess of Tanit, discovered by Father Delattre. That sarcophagus, the most ornate, the most artistic yet found, whose external image probably represents the goddess herself, must have been the sepulcher of a very high religious personage. Well, the woman buried there had Negro features. She belonged to the African race! (p. 410).

The conclusion that the author draws from this passage is that several races coexisted in Carthage. Obviously, we agree. Nevertheless, there is one conclusion that the author did not draw, but which is even more compelling: Among the various races in Carthage, the one most highly placed socially, the most respected, the one that held the levers of political command, the one to whom they owed that civilization, if we are to judge by the material proofs presented instead of interpreting them in line with prejudices we have been taught, was the Negro race.

If an atom bomb destroyed Paris but left the cemeteries intact, anthropologists opening the graves to determine what the French were like would similarly discover that Paris was inhabited not only by Frenchmen. On the other hand, it would be inconceivable that the corpse buried in the most beautiful tomb, as exceptional as that of Napoleon at the Invalides, were that of a slave or some anonymous individual.

Consequently, if one really wanted to do so, the Phoenician race, and all other related Negro races to whom humanity owes its access to civilization, could be much more precisely defined. We could even do this by anthropological means, although experience has shown that it is possible to sustain any theory one wishes in this field. Millions are spent on excavating clay mounds in Mesopotamia, in the hope of finding evidence to pinpoint with certainty and finality the birthplace of civilization in Western Asia.

Although those who undertake this have very slim hope of ever attaining their objective, they nonetheless continue, as if the routine had become a permanent habit. In contrast, the exact location of the Phoenician tombs is known. All that is needed is to go and open them for information on the race of the cadaver contained therein. But the chances are great that these will be so definitely Negro as to make denial impossible, so it is better not to touch them.

To discover the exact anthropological characteristics of the ancient Phoenicians, it would be necessary to examine the skeletons in the sepulchers of the great Phoenician epoch on the very shores where Tyre and Sidon developed their power as commercial centers. Unfortunately, these important documents have not yet been made available to ethnologists. They will certainly be made available someday, after systematic research leading to the conservation of archeological data and skeletons has been undertaken.[35]

That was written in 1924; since that date few excavations have been made in the region (excavations at Ras Shamra were interrupted in 1939). Many documents have been discovered by chance. The most ancient tombs found in Phoenicia, those at Byblos, which probably date back to the Eneolithic (Chalcolithic) epoch, were unearthed by Dunand. They reveal a human type that Dr. Vallois classifies in Sergi's brown Mediterranean race. Now, that so-called brown Mediterranean race is none other than the Negro race. Furthermore, some of the skulls present a deformity found today only among the Mangbetu Blacks of the Congo (cf. Contenau, *La Civilisation phénicienne,* p. 187).

Arabia

According to Lenormant,[36] a Kushite Empire originally existed throughout Arabia. This was the epoch personified by the Adites of

Ad, grandsons of Ham, the Biblical ancestor of the Blacks. Ched-dade, a son of Ad and builder of the legendary "Earthly Paradise" mentioned in the Koran, belongs to the epoch called that of the "First Adites." This empire was destroyed in the eighteenth century B.C. by an invasion of coarse, white Jectanide tribes, who apparently came to settle among the Blacks.

Before long, however, the Kushite element regained political and cultural control. The first White tribes were completely absorbed by the Kushites. This epoch was called that of the "Second Adites." (Cf. Lenormant, pp. 260–261.)

These facts, on which even Arab authors agree, prove, as will shortly become more evident, that the Arab race cannot be conceived as anything but a mixture of Blacks and Whites, a process continuing even today. These same facts also prove that traits common to Black culture and Semitic culture have been borrowed from the Blacks. The reverse is historically false. To attempt to explain the Negro Egyptian world by the so-called Semitic world should be impossible on the basis of no more than a few grammatical similarities, such as suffixal conjugations, pronoun suffixes, and *t* for the feminine. The Semitic world, as we conceive of it today, is too recent to explain Egypt. As we have seen, prior to the eighteenth century B.C., only Negroes (Kushites, in official terminology) were found in the region of Arabia. Infiltrations before the second millennium were relatively insignificant. Egypt conquered the country during the early centuries of the Second Adites, under the minority of Tuthmosis III. Lenormant believes that Arabia is the land of Punt and of the Queen of Sheba. We should remind the reader that the Bible places *Put,* one of the sons of Ham, in the same country.

In the eighth century B.C., the Jectanides, having become strong enough, seized power in the same manner—and during the same period—as the Assyrians won control over the Babylonians (also Kushites):

> Though they shared the same customs and the same language, the two elements that formed the population of southern Arabia remained quite distinct, with antagonistic interests, just as in the basin of the Euphrates, the Assyrians and Babylonians, the first of whom were likewise Semites, and the second, Kushites. . . .
> So long as the empire of the Second Adites lasted, the Jectanides

were under the Kushites. But a day came when they felt strong enough to become masters in their turn. Led by Iârob, they attacked the Adites and were able to overcome them. This revolution is usually dated at the beginning of the eighth century B.C.[37]

Lenormant reports that after the Jectanide victory, some of the Adites crossed the Red Sea at Bab el Mandeb to settle in Ethiopia, while the others remained in Arabia, taking refuge in the mountains of Hadramaut and elsewhere. This is the source of the Arab proverb: "As divided as the Sabaeans," and why southern Arabia and Ethiopia became inseparable linguistically and ethnographically. "Long before the discovery of the Hymyaritic language and inscriptions, it had been noted that *Ghez,* the Abyssinian language, is a living remnant of the ancient language of Yemen."[38]

Such were the relations between those two regions. But we are a long way from any notion of a migration by a civilizing white race during the prehistoric period, through Bab el Mandeb or any other place. We can see how inadmissible are the German linguistic theories which rest on such an assumption. Equally inadmissible are theories that take the same assumption (Capart) to explain the origin of Egyptian writing, whose essential symbols in reality represent the flora and fauna of the African interior, particularly Nubia, not Lower Egypt. Capart supposes that a hypothetical white Semitic race came from the African interior via Bab el Mandeb, stayed there a long time, and taught the natives to write. From what has been said above, it follows that no historical fact supports that theory.

The known migrations occurring in the region are much later than the dawn of Egyptian civilization and the invention of hieroglyphic writing. But since the objective is always the same, and it is always a question by whatever means of attributing the slightest phenomenon of civilization in Black Africa to some white race, even a mythical white race, a mathematical process is utilized: extrapolation. From the fact that a recent migration of Negro Adites (eighth century B.C.) took place in this area, one assumes that there must have been Semitic migrations there, even though we have no trace of any. The working hypothesis is transformed into a reality, and the riddle is solved. This is how it is possible to explain Egyptian civilization by pure abstractions which have nothing to do with historical facts; thus are the trusting but uninitiated deceived.

Institutions and Customs of the Sabaean Kingdom

According to the same author, the caste system, alien to the Semites, was the basis of social organization in Saba (the Biblical Sheba),
as in Babylon, Egypt, Africa, and the Malabar kingdom in India.[39]
"This regime is essentially Kushite and wherever we find it, it is easy
to detect that it originally came from that race. We saw that it flourished in Babylon. The Aryas of India, who adopted it, borrowed it
from the Kushite populations who had preceded them in the basins of
the Indus and the Ganges. "[40]

Circumcision was practiced. "Lokman, the mythical representative
of Adite wisdom, resembles Aesop, whose name seems to Mr.
Welcker to indicate an Ethiopian origin. In India also, the literature
of tales and fables appears to come from the Sudra [lowest-class
Hindus]. Perhaps this type of fiction, characterized by the role played
by animals, is a literary genre peculiar to the Kushites."[41]

It should be noted in passing that Lokman, who belongs to the second period of the Adites, is also the builder of the famous dam at
Mareb, whose waters "sufficed to irrigate and fertilize the plain over
a distance of seven days' walk from the city. . . . Still in existence
today are its ruins which several travelers have visited and studied."[42]

The Jectanides, "who, at the time of their arrival, were still little
more than barbarians," introduced nothing but a system of pastoral
tribes and military feudalism (cf. Lenormant, p. 385). The religion
was of Kushite origin and seemed to emanate directly from the Babylonian cult. It would remain the same until the advent of Islam. The
Sabaean gods were just about the same as the Babylonian gods and
all belonged to the same Kushite family of Egyptian and Phoenician
deities. . . . The only Triad revered was: Venus-Sun-Moon, as in
Babylon. The cult had a pronounced sidereal character, especially solar: they prayed to the sun at different phases of its course. There
was neither idolatry, nor images, nor priesthood.

They addressed a direct invocation to the seven planets. The 30-
day fasting period already existed, as in Egypt. They prayed seven
times each day, with their faces turned toward the north. These
prayers to the sun at different hours somewhat resemble Moslem
prayers which take place during the same phases, but which have
been reduced by the Prophet to five compulsory prayers "to relieve
humanity"; the other two prayers are optional.

There were also sacred springs and stones, as in Moslem times:

Zenzen, a sacred spring; *Kaaba,* a sacred stone. The pilgrimage to Mecca already existed. The *Kaaba* was reputed to have been constructed by Ishmael, son of Abraham and Hagar the Egyptian (a Negro woman), historical ancestor of Mohammed, according to all Arab historians. As in Egypt, belief in a future life was already prevalent. Dead ancestors were deified. Thus, all the elements necessary for the blossoming of Islam were in place more than 1,000 years before the birth of Mohammed. Islam would appear as a purification of Sabaeanism by the "Messenger of God."

So we have seen that the entire Arab people, including the Prophet, is mixed with Negro blood. All educated Arabs are conscious of that fact. The fabulous hero of Arabia, Antar, is himself a mixed-breed:

Despite the importance they attach to their genealogy and the pre-rogative of blood, the Arabs, especially the sedentary urban dwellers, do not keep their race pure of any mixture. . . .
But the infiltration of Negro blood, which spread to all parts of the peninsula and seems destined one day to change the race completely, began in very early Antiquity. It occurred first in Yemen, which geography and trade placed in continual contact with Africa. . . .
The same infiltration was slower and came later in Hejaz or in Nedjd. Yet, it too occurred earlier than one generally seems to think. Antar, the romantic hero of pre-Islamic Arabia, is a mulatto on his mother's side. Nevertheless, his thoroughly African face does not prevent his marriage to a princess of the tribes proudest of their nobility, so habitual had those black-skinned (Melanian) admixtures become. They had long been accepted in the mores, down through the centuries immediately preceding Mohammed.[43]

Contrary to Lenormant, we have made no distinction between "Kushite" and "Negro" for, outside of *a priori* statements, no one has ever been able to distinguish between the two.[44]

Consequently, it is important to change our notions about the Semite. Whether in Mesopotamia, Phoenicia, or Arabia, the Semite, insofar as he is discernible objectively, appears as the product of a Negro-White mixture. It is possible that the Whites who came to crossbreed with the Negroes in that area of Western Asia were distinguished by certain ethnic features, such as the Hittite nose.

The mixed character of Semitic languages could be explained in the same way. There are roots common to Arabic, Hebrew, Syriac, and Germanic tongues. This common vocabulary is more extensive than might be suggested by this very short list. No contact between Nordics and Arabs within the historical period of humanity explains it. It is an ethnic kinship, rather than a borrowing.

Arabic	*English*	*German*
ain	eye	auge
ard	earth	erde
asfar	fair	
beled	land	land
Qasr	castle	

In contrast, certain Arab words seem to be of Egyptian origin:

Arabic	*Egyptian*
Nabi: the Prophet	Nab: the master, master of knowledge
Nahâs: copper	Nahasi: copper (Sudanese tribes have known copper since early Antiquity.)
Rat: thunder	Ra: celestial, atmospheric god
El Baraka: divine blessing	Ba-Ra-Ka: blessing

It is even more absurd to explain the creation of the Empire of Ghana in the third century B.C. as a Semitic contribution from Yemen, for at that time Yemen was a Negro Ethiopian colony and remained so until the birth of Mohammed. In any event, if we remain in the realm of conclusive facts, it is impossible to prove that the civilization of any of those regions preceded that of Egypt; it is impossible to explain the latter by the former.

The new radioactive methods utilized in dating monuments and objects will make sense only if they succeed in dating man's work on matter, not the age of the matter employed. It would be easy to find anywhere on earth a plant fragment dating from earliest prehistory. We are referring here to the American method based on the decreasing period of radioactive carbon C^{14}.

CHAPTER VI

The Egyptian Race as Seen and Treated by Anthropologists

Since this problem is essentially anthropological, we might have expected the anthropologists to solve it once and for all, with positive, definitive truths. Far from it! The arbitrary nature of the criteria employed—to mention that fact alone—produces no generally acceptable conclusion and introduces so many "scholarly complications" that we sometimes wonder whether the solution might not have been easier had the anthropologists been bypassed altogether.

And yet, although the conclusions of the anthropological studies are unrealistic, they nevertheless testify overwhelmingly to the existence of a Black race from the most remote epochs of prehistory to the dynastic epoch. It is impossible to cite all those conclusions here; they have been summarized in Chapter X of Dr. Emile Massoulard's *Préhistoire et proto-histoire d'Egypte* (Paris: Institut d'Ethnologie, 1949). Here is a sample (pp. 402–403):

> Miss Fawcett believes that the Naqada crania are sufficiently homogeneous to justify speaking of a Naqada race. By the height of the skull, the auricular height, the height and width of the face, the height of the nose, the cephalic and facial indices, this race presents affinities with Negroes. By the nasal width, the height of the orbit, the length of the palate, and nasal index, it presents affinities with the Germans . . .
> In some features, predynastic Naqada probably resembled Negroes; in others, they probably resembled Whites.

The characteristics common to Negroes and the predynastic Egyptian race of the Naqada are basic in contrast to those they share with Germans. For that matter, if we were to judge by the "nasal index" of two Black races, the Ethiopians and the Dravidians, they too would present affinities with the Germans. Leaving us dangling between those two extremes, the Negro race and the German race, these measurements indicate the elasticity of the criteria utilized. Let us quote one of those criteria:

Thomson and Randall MacIver sought to analyze more carefully the importance of the Negroid factor in the series of skulls from El Amrah, Abydos, and Hou. They divided them into three groups: 1. Negroid skulls (those whose facial index is lower than 54 and nasal index above 50; that is, with low, broad face and wide nose); 2. non-Negroid skulls (those with facial index over 54 and nasal index below 50; high, thin face and narrow nose); 3. intermediate skulls (those belonging to one of the first two groups by their facial index and to the other group by their nasal index, as well as those on the borderline between the two groups). In the early predynastic epoch, the proportion of Negroids would be 24% among men and 19% among women; in the later predynastic epoch, 25% and 28% respectively.

Keith challenged the validity of the criterion used by Thomson and Randall MacIver to separate the Negroid from the non-Negroid crania. He estimated that if any series of present-day English crania were examined by the same criterion, one would find 30% Negroids.[1] Inversely, it could be said that, if the same criterion were applied to the 140 million Negroes in Black Africa today, a minimum of 100 million Blacks would come out "whitened" by that measurement. Moreover, the distinction between Negroids, non-Negroids, and intermediates is not clear. In actual fact, non-Negroid is not the equivalent of White, and "intermediate" even less so.

"Falkenburger continued the anthropological study of the Egyptian population in a recent work based on 1,787 male skulls dating from the early predynastic to the present. He distinguished four principal groups" (*ibid.*, p. 421).

The distribution of the predynastic skulls among those four groups was reported as follows:

Negroids 36%, Mediterraneans 33%, Cro-Magnoids 11%, and 20% individuals belonging to none of those three categories but related either to the Cro-Magnoids (type AC) or to Negroids (type BC). The proportion of Negroids is clearly higher than that of Thomson and Randall MacIver which Keith nonetheless found excessive.

Are Falkenburger's statistics realistic? It is not for us to decide. If they are accurate, the predynastic population, instead of representing a pure race, as Elliot Smith claimed, was composed of at least three different racial elements: more than one-third Negroid, one-third Mediterranean, one-tenth Cro-Magnoid, and one-fifth individuals more or less mixed (*ibid.*, p. 422).

Despite their differences, these conclusions attest to the Negro foundation of the Egyptian population in the predynastic epoch. They are incompatible with the notion that the Blacks did not filter into Egypt until later. On the contrary, the facts prove that the Black element was preponderant from the beginning to the end of Egyptian history, especially when we add that "Mediterranean" is not synonymous with "White." Instead, it probably refers to Elliot Smith's "brown or Mediterranean race": "Elliot Smith makes these early Egyptians a branch of what he calls the brown race, which is none other than Sergi's Mediterranean or ̣Eurafrican race" (*ibid.*, p. 418). The epithet "brown" here relates to skin color and is only a euphemism for Negro. Thus it is clear that the whole Egyptian race was Negro, with an infiltration of nomadic Whites during the Amratian period.

Petrie's study of the Egyptian race reveals an immense possibility of classification that will surely amaze the reader:

Petrie has published a study on the races of Egypt in the predynastic and protodynastic in which he takes only representations into account. In addition to the steatopygic, he distinguishes six different types: the aquiline type, characteristic of a white-skinned Libyan race; the type with plaited beard, belonging to a race of invaders perhaps from the shores of the Red Sea; the type with pointed nose, no doubt from the Arabian desert; the type with tilted nose, from Middle Egypt; the type with beard sticking straight out in front, from Lower Egypt; the type with straight nasal septum, from Upper Egypt. Judging from these representations, there were seven different racial types in Egypt during the epochs considered. In the following pages, we shall see that a study of the skeletons hardly authorizes such conclusions (*ibid.*, p. 391).

That classification shows how frivolous and unwarranted were the criteria applied to describe the Egyptian race. I had intended to examine microscopically the density of the pores in the epidermis of mummies, but the limited supply of specimens would not have produced any valid conclusion on a scale covering the entire Egyptian population.

In any case, we can see that anthropology has failed to establish the existence of any white Egyptian race; if anything, it would tend to establish the opposite. Nevertheless, in current textbooks, the problem is suppressed; most often they merely take it on themselves to assert categorically that the Egyptians were Whites. All honest laymen then get the impression that such an assertion must necessarily be based on solid studies previously conducted. But that, as we have seen, is simply not true. This is how the minds of so many generations have been warped.

> On the *south* of the Northwest Quadrant lay the teeming black world of Africa, separated from the Great White Race by an impassable desert barrier, the Sahara, which forms so large a part of the Southern Flatlands. Thus isolated and at the same time unfitted by ages of tropical life for any effective intrusion among the White Race, the negro and negroid peoples remained without any influence on the development of early civilization. We may then exclude both of these external races—the straight-haired, round-headed, yellow-skinned Mongoloids on the east, and the woolly-haired, long-headed, dark-skinned Negroids on the south—from any share in the origins or subsequent development of civilization.[2]

That is typical of current statements in textbooks today. The dictatorial nature of Breasted's assertion is equaled only by the absence of any foundation, for the author gets caught in his own contradiction by claiming, on the one hand, that the Sahara has always separated Negroes from the Nile and, on the other hand, that this valley was their only road to the north. A glance at the map of Africa shows that one can go from any point on the continent to the Nile Valley without crossing a desert.

Breasted's ideas stem from an erroneous conception of the peopling of the continent. Instead of there having always been Blacks all over Africa stagnating in little clusters while Egyptian civilization was developing, a mass of evidence inclines us to believe that the Blacks first swarmed over that valley before spreading out in all directions in successive migrations. This is also attested by the anthropological data already cited, indicating the presence of the Negro in the Nile Valley as early as prehistoric times. Furthermore, the Negro character of Egyptian civilization, as it is recognized today, rules out any possibility that this civilization was a monopoly of the white race. Numerous authors circumvent the difficulty by speaking of Whites with red skin or Whites with black skin. This does not seem incongruous to them for, as soon as a race has created a civilization, there can be no more possibility of its being Black.

"For the Greeks, Africa was Libya. This expression was already inaccurate since many other peoples lived there, along with the so-called Libyans, who figured among the Whites on the northern periphery, or the Mediterranean, if you prefer. As such, they were distinct from a great number of segments of Whites with brown or red skin (Egyptians) . . ."[3]

In a textbook for pupils in *cinquième* (eighth grade), we read: "A Black is distinguished less by the color of his skin (for there are Whites with black skin) than by his features: thick lips, flat nose, etc."[4] Only by similar definitions has one been able to whiten the Egyptian race, and this is the clearest proof of its blackness.

Breasted's stand on the problem of the Egyptian race is typically that of contemporary Egyptologists who, better informed than their predecessors, simply evade the topic by a few statements presented as if supported by previous scientific data. It is an intellectual swindle.

✳   ✳   ✳

Here ends the critical part of this volume. In the earlier chapters we have reviewed the various types of theses concerning the origin of the Egyptian race. Each of these theses belongs to one of the different types outlined above. I have selected them, not because they are presented by some authority or other, but because they have been advanced with the maximum number of details to enable us to expose the unsurmountable contradictions that all of them contain. This review is therefore quite complete indeed. The overall picture that emerges—the general failure of all those attempts to attain their objective—does not contain the slightest factor susceptible of convincing the reader.

We now move on to the constructive part of this book and to present the various facts that prove the Negro origin of the ancient Egyptians.

CHAPTER VII

Arguments Supporting a Negro Origin

Totemism

In his book, *From Tribe to Empire,* Moret had stressed the essentially totemic character of Egyptian society. His thesis was subsequently opposed, almost as if it were feared that grave consequences would inevitably result from it. As a matter of fact, Frazer was categorical on the origin of totemism; he insisted that it is found only in colored populations. There was no way to accept his thesis if one hoped to demonstrate the white origin of Egyptian civilization.

So one tried to deny Egyptian totemism while seeking traces of it in so-called white populations, such as the Berber and Tuareg. The zeal with which it was sought in those two groups proves that, if the search had been successful, there would no longer have been any doubt about Egyptian totemism. But the attempt failed: Arnold Van Gennep (1873–1957) could not detect any Berber totemism.

The debate finally drifted into philosophical abstraction: concrete ethnographic data were transformed into cogitation, into a problem of logic, into pure contemplation that no fact could henceforth disturb by implication. Without venturing into philosophy, it was impossible to deny that the "taboo" character of certain animals and plants in Egypt corresponds to totemism as it exists throughout Black Africa. By contrast, such "taboos" were alien to the Greeks and other Indo-European populations unaware of totemism. Thus the Greeks scoffed at the excessive veneration of the Egyptian for animals and even for certain plants.

After a certain stage of social development, which may be lower than the level of development and mixture that the Egyptian people had attained, endogamy and totemism are not mutually exclusive but coexist. Thus, today in Black Africa, some husbands and wives have the same totemic names: N'Diaye, Diop, Fall, and so on. Nowadays it never crosses their minds that such a practice could have been taboo. And yet, both husband and wife are clearly aware of being biologically parts of the very essence of the same totem. Both mates are quite conscious of sharing the same animal essence, the same biological essence; they are conscious of belonging originally to the same tribe, so much so that they often remind each other of that fact. Consequently, Van Gennep's notion that Egyptians, who often married their close relations, especially their sisters, could not be totemists, is definitely refuted here. Marriage with one's sister stems from another cultural trait equally pervasive in the Black world: matriarchy, which will be discussed shortly.

When exogamy was in force, a kind of relationship was finally established between clans that contracted marriage with one another (between two, or among three, four, or more clans). The memory of that relationship may explain today, for example, the *Kal*, a hypothetical clan relationship in Wolof society authorizing reciprocal ridicule.

Despite studies that attempt to expand the notion of totemism, we can say, with Frazer, that it is absent from white populations. Otherwise it would have been evident in the last white barbarian hordes who overran Europe in the fourth century. Those populations were at the ethnographic (clan, tribe) stage when totemism, if present, invests all acts of life and is evident at all levels of social organization.

Yet nothing, in the life of those hordes, reflected the idea of a biological relationship between man and beast, either in the individual or in the collective sense. In contrast, it cannot be denied that the Pharaoh participated in an animal essence (the falcon) just as we do today in Black Africa.

˙Circumcision

The Egyptians practiced circumcision as early as prehistoric times; they transmitted this practice to the Semitic world in general (Jews and Arabs), especially to those whom Herodotus called Syrians. To show that the Colchians were Egyptians, Herodotus cited these two indications:

> My own conjectures were founded, first, on the fact that they are black-skinned and have woolly hair, which certainly amounts to but little, since several other nations are so too; but further and more especially, on the circumstance that the Colchians, the Egyptians, and the Ethiopians, are the only nations who have practiced

circumcision from the earliest times. The Phoenicians and the Syrians of Palestine themselves confess that they learnt the custom of the Egyptians; and the Syrians who dwell about the rivers Thermodon and Parthenius, as well as their neighbors the Macronians, say that they have recently adopted it from the Colchians. Now these are the only nations who use circumcision, and it is plain that they all imitate herein the Egyptians.[1]

Anticipating the agreement of all logical minds, I call *Negro*[2] a human being whose skin is black; especially when he has frizzy hair. All who accept this definition will recognize that, according to Herodotus, who saw the Egyptians as plainly as the reader is now seeing this book, circumcision is of Egyptian and Ethiopian origin, and the Egyptians and Ethiopians were none other than Negroes inhabiting different regions.

Thus, we can understand why the Semites practice circumcision despite the fact that their traditions present no valid justification for it. The weakness of the arguments in Genesis is typical: God asks Abraham (and later Moses) to be circumcized, as a sign of a covenant with Him, without explaining how circumcision, considered from the standpoint of Jewish tradition, can lead to the notion of an alliance. This is all the more curious because Abraham was allegedly circumcized at the age of ninety. In Egypt he had married a Negro woman, Hagar, mother of Ishmael, the Biblical ancestor of the second Semitic branch, the Arabs. Ishmael was said to be the historical ancestor of Mohammed. Moses, too, wed a Madianite, and it was in connection with his marriage that the Eternal asked him to be circumcized. What should be noted in these legendary tales is the idea that circumcision was introduced among the Semites only as a result of contact with the Black world—which conforms to the testimony of Herodotus.

Only among Blacks does circumcision find an interpretation integrated in a general explanation of the universe, in other words, a cosmogony. Specifically, the Dogon* cosmogony that Marcel Griaule reports. In *Dieu d'eau,* he reminds us that, to make sense, circumcision must be accompanied by excision. These two operations remove something female from the male and something male from the female. To the archaic mentality, such an operation is intended to fortify the dominant character of a single sex in a given human being.

---

*The Dogon ethnic group in the Republic of Mali, formerly "French" Sudan.

According to Dogon cosmogony, a newborn baby is to a certain extent androgynous, like the first god:

> So long as it retains its foreskin and clitoris, indications of the sex opposite to the apparent sex, masculinity and femininity have equal strength. Thus it is not accurate to compare the uncircumcized to a woman; like a girl on whom excision has not been performed, he is both male and female. If this indecision about his sex were allowed to continue, he (or she) would have no interest in procreation. . . . These, then, are the various reasons for circumcision and excision: the need to rid the child of an evil force, the need for him (or her) to pay a debt of blood and to turn definitely toward one sex.[3]

For this explanation of circumcision to be valid, divine androgyny, the traditional cause of this practice in African society, must also have existed in Egyptian society. Only then can we be justified in identifying the ritual causes of circumcision among Egyptians and in the rest of Black Africa. As a matter of fact, Champollion the Younger writes in his letters to Champollion-Figeac about the divine androgyny of Amon, Supreme God of the Meroitic Sudan and Egypt: "Amon is the point of departure and the focal point of all divine essences. Amon-Ra, the Supreme, primordial Being, his own father and termed the husband of his mother, has his feminine portion enclosed in his own essence that is both male and female."

The Nile is also represented by an androgynous personage. Amon is likewise the god of all Black Africa. In passing it may be said that in the Meroitic Sudan, Black Africa, and Egypt, Amon is connected with the idea of humidity. His attribute in all these countries is the ram. Thus, in the significantly entitled volume, *Dieu d'eau* (God of Water), when Marcel Griaule writes of the Dogon god Amma, this deity appears in the form of the Ram-God, with a gourd between his horns. In Dogon ("French" Sudan) cosmogony, Amon descends from the sky on a rainbow, symbol of rain and humidity.

Although some Blacks have abandoned circumcision, through forgetfulness of their traditions or for various other reasons, although there is a growing trend in Black Africa to renounce excision, and although circumcision is a technically different operation for Egyptians and Semites, this does not alter the root of the problem. Yet, for the identification to be complete and the argument convincing, excision must also have existed in Egypt. Strabo tells us that this was the case:

"The Egyptians are especially careful in raising all their children and circumcize the boys and even the girls, a custom common to the Jews, a people originally from Egypt, as we observed when we discussed that subject" (Bk. 17, Chap. 1, par. 29).

Kingship

The concept of kingship is one of the most impressive indications of the similarity in thinking between Egypt and the rest of Black Africa. Leaving aside such general principles as the sacrosanct nature of kingship and stressing one typical trait because of its strangeness, we shall single out the ritual killing of the monarch. In Egypt, the king was not supposed to reign unless he was in good health. Originally, when his strength declined, he was really put to death. But royalty soon resorted to various expedients. The king was understandably eager to preserve the prerogatives of his position, while undergoing the least possible inconvenience. So he was able to transform the fatal judgment into a symbolic one: from then on, when he grew old, he was merely put to death ritualistically. After the symbolic test, known as the "Sed Festival," the monarch was supposedly rejuvenated in the opinion of his people and was once again deemed fit to assume his functions. Henceforth, the "Sed Festival" was the ceremony of the king's rejuvenation: ritualistic death and revivification of the ruler became synonymous and took place during the same ceremony. (Cf. Charles Seligman's *Egypt and Negro Africa; A Study in Divine Kingship*. London: Routledge, 1934.)

The monarch, the revered being par excellence, was also supposed to be the man with the greatest life force or energy. When the level of his life force fell below a certain minimum, it could only be a risk to his people if he continued to rule. This vitalistic conception is the foundation of all traditional African kingdoms, I mean, of all kingdoms not usurped.

Sometimes it operated differently; for example, in Senegal, the king could not rule if he had received wounds in battle; he had to be replaced until cured. It was during such a replacement that a paternal brother, who was the son of a woman of the people, seized the throne. As Lat-Soukabé, he initiated the Guedj dynasty, circa 1697.

The practice of replacing the king whenever his vital strength declines obviously stems from the same vitalistic tenets throughout the Black world. According to those beliefs, the fertility of the soil, the abundant harvests, the health of people and cattle, the normal flow of events and of all the phenomena of life, are intimately linked to the potential of the ruler's vital force.

In other regions of Black Africa, the events occur exactly as in Egypt with regard to the actual killing of the monarch. Certain peoples even set a time limit, after which he is assumed to be incapable of ruling and is then really put to death. Among the Mbum of Central Africa, this time limit is ten years and the ceremony takes place before the millet season.[4] The following peoples still practice the ritualistic death of the king: the Yoruba, Dagomba, Shamba, Igara, Songhay, the Hausa of Gobir, Katsena, and Daura, and the Shilluk. This practice also existed in ancient Meroë, i.e., Nubia, Uganda-Rwanda.

Cosmogony

Negro cosmogonies, African and Egyptian, resemble each other so closely that they are often complementary. To understand certain Egyptian concepts, one must refer to the Black world, as is attested by what we have said about kingship. In the latter case, it suffices to read Father Tempels's study, *Bantu Philosophy* (published in translation by Présence Africaine in 1959). It presents a systematized analysis of Negro vitalism which, according to Father Tempels, serves as the basis of the Bantu's daily acts.

This similarity of mores, customs, traditions, and thinking has already been sufficiently stressed by various authorities. Perhaps it would take more than a lifetime to report all the analogies between Egypt and the Black world, so true is it that they are one and the same. Paul Masson-Oursel emphasizes the Negro character of Egyptian philosophy:

> By accepting it [that philosophy] the intellectualism born of Socrates, Aristotle, Euclid, and Archimedes, conformed to the Negro mentality that the Egyptologist perceives as a backdrop for the refinements of a civilization at which he marvels. . . . Venturing to express what should be a cliché—the African aspect of the Egyptian mind—we can use it to account for more than one of its cultural traits.[5]

This identity of Egyptian and Negro culture, or rather, this identity of mental structure, as observed by Masson-Oursel, makes Negro mentality the basic trait of Egyptian philosophy; . . . [one that] should be obvious to anyone of good faith.

The oneness of Egyptian and Black culture could not be stated more clearly. Because of this essential identity of genius, culture, and race, today all Negroes can legitimately trace their culture to ancient Egypt and build a modern culture on that foundation. A dynamic, modern contact with Egyptian Antiquity would enable Blacks to discover increasingly each day the intimate relationship between all Blacks of the continent and the mother Nile Valley. By this dynamic contact, the Negro will be convinced that these temples, these forests of columns, these pyramids, these colossi, these bas-reliefs, mathematics, medicine, and all this science, are indeed the work of his ancestors and that he has a right and a duty to claim this heritage.

"From now on, in this type of research so invaluable for the investigation of thought, we are beginning to perceive that a great part of the Black continent, instead of being unpolished and savage as was previously supposed, has cast its influence in many directions across the immense isolation of desert or forest, an influence which came from the Nile and passed through Libya, Nubia, and Ethiopia."[6]

With respect to the incarnation process of the Dogon Octad and Ennead (eight or nine deified ancestors), and the Egyptian Octad and Ennead, it would almost be necessary to reproduce here entire pages of Griaule's *Dieu d'eau*. In both cases, four couples are engendered by the primitive god; they are the authors of creation and civilization. This suggests how the number eight has become the basis of the Dogon's numerical system; thus 80 is the equivalent of 100, and 800 the equivalent of 1,000.

This also helps us to understand how the ancestor cult has become the foundation of cosmogony in Black Africa as in Egypt. While the most distant ancestors are detached in some manner almost like a vapor to reach the heavens, the nearest ones, those who have just died and whose memory is not yet vague enough for them to be the forebears of an entire people, these closest ancestors are only family demi-gods. With the advent of the historical period, when diligence in recording events no longer permits vagueness, the deʹfication process becomes somewhat restricted. The cult of ancestors continues, but henceforth they remain more or less historical personages.

We could, for instance, insist on the similarity between the Dogon God-serpent and the God-serpent of the Egyptian Pantheon. Each of these dances in the dark. As a matter of fact, Amélineau writes that the God-serpent is called "the one who dances in the shadows." This refers to the serpent in an inscription on a sarcophagus at the Marseilles Museum, an inscription accompanying the representation of the tomb of Osiris (*Prolégomènes,* p. 41). In the Dogon Pantheon, the seventh ancestor, transformed into a serpent, has been killed by his men; his head has been buried beneath the blacksmith's cushion. From this sepulcher the Ancestor-serpent rises up to dance underground (i.e., in the darkness) and to move toward the tomb of the oldest man to devour him (cf. Griaule, *op.cit.,* p. 62).

We might emphasize this trait as a possible indication of a ritual man-eating, such as might also be found in Egypt at the beginning. This feature might also stem from the vitalistic principles which form the basis of Negro society. By assimilating the substance of others, one acquires their vital force; this increases one's invulnerability against the destructive forces of the universe.

By the same token, we might also compare the incestuous jackal-god of the Dogon Pantheon with the jackal-god of the Egyptians. He is the guardian of the pond where the dead are supposed to be cleansed. Currently, however, there is a tendency to assimilate the jackal-god with a dog-god. Finally, the importance attributed to the signs of the zodiac in Dogon cosmogony deserves attention. When one is also aware that the Dogon know the star Sothis (Sirius), one can only recall that the Egyptian calendar was based on the heliacal rising of that star.

Social Organization

The social stratification of African life is precisely that of Egypt. In Egypt the stratification was as follows:

peasants,
skilled workers,
priests, warriors, and government officials,
the king.

In the rest of Black Africa, we have:
peasants,
artisans or skilled workers,
warriors, priests,
the king.

Matriarchy

The matriarchal system is the base of the social organization in Egypt and throughout Black Africa. In contrast, there has never been any proof of the existence of a paleo-Mediterranean matriarchy, supposedly exclusively White. To support this statement, we need only cite the arguments of an author who devoted 437 pages to a vain attempt to whiten Black Africa:

> Succession to the throne is regulated in Kano [Nigeria] by matriarchy, a paleo-Mediterranean legacy, until the epoch of Fulani domination. We are told that the Queen of Daura had a saddle-ox. This reminds us of the customs of the ancient [Libyan] Garamantes; so we again encounter ancient White Africa with its matriarchal system. Closely related are the peoples of Kordofan [Sudan] and Nubia, including Teda and Tuareg, as well as the sovereigns of the Sudan. (Baumann, *op. cit.*, p. 313.)

It will be noted that these statements whose seriousness is equaled only by their vagueness, follow from a single unimportant fact: the Queen of Daura rode a saddle-ox. In passing, Baumann has even whitened the sovereigns of Western Sudan, in line with a well-known Nazi procedure that consists of explaining any African civilization by the activity of a white race or its offspring, even if we have to decree that white "Blacks" or "dark red" Whites exist, all of whom are grouped under the convenient term "Hamites."

If the matriarchal system, inherited from some white paleo-Mediterranean, were anything but a mental fantasy, it would have lasted throughout the Persian, Greek, Roman, and Christian periods, just as it has continued until today in Black Africa. But this obviously is not the case. Cyrus arranged his succession in advance by designating his eldest son, Cambyses, who killed his younger brother to avoid competition. In Greece, succession was simply patrilineal, as in Rome.

In reality, there never was a monarchical tradition in Greece. Except for the ephemeral reign of Alexander, the country was never unified. The kings of the heroic epoch of whom Homer speaks, were only rulers of cities, village chiefs, such as Ulysses. Hostilities between those villages even seemed childish: stones were thrown at inhabitants of a neighboring town as they passed through another community. In the best periods, such Greek cities as Athens were governed by adventurous, ambitious merchants who gained control by intrigue. Alexander was a foreigner from Macedonia. The absence of queens in Greek, Roman, or Persian history can be noted; the Byzantine Empire must be considered as a separate complex. In contrast, during those remote epochs, queens were frequent in Black Africa. When the Indo-European world acquired enough military strength to conquer the old countries that had civilized it, they encountered the fierce, unyielding resistance of a queen whose determined struggle symbolized the national pride of a people who, until then, had commanded others. This was Queen Candace, of the Meroitic Sudan.[7] She impressed all Antiquity by her stand at the head of her troops against the Roman armies of Augustus Caesar. The loss of an eye in battle only redoubled her courage; her fearlessness and scorn of death even forced the admiration of a chauvinist like Strabo: "This queen had courage above her sex." At the beginning of Western civilization, the Frankish kings gradually acquired the habit of arranging their succession in advance, excluding any notion of matriarchy. Thus, in the West, political rights are transmitted by the father—this does not mean that a daughter is not allowed to receive them.

On the other hand, Negro matriarchy is as alive today as it was during Antiquity. In regions where the matriarchal system has not been altered by external influences (Islam, etc.), it is the woman who transmits political rights. This derives from the general idea that heredity is effective only matrilineally.

Another typical aspect of African matriarchy, an aspect often misunderstood, is the dowry paid by the man, a custom reversed in European countries. Misconstrued in Europe, this custom has made people think that woman is bought in Black Africa, just as an African might say that a woman buys a husband in Europe. In Africa, since woman holds a privileged position, thanks to matriarchy, it is she who receives a guarantee in the form of a dowry in the alliance called marriage. What proves that she is not bought like a slave, is that she is not riveted to the conjugal home by the dowry; if the husband is really at fault, the marriage can be broken within a few hours to his disadvantage. Contrary to the legend, the least onerous tasks are reserved for women.

What is the origin of Negro matriarchy? We do not know for certain at the present time; however, current opinion holds that the matriarchal system is related to farming. If agriculture was discovered by women, as is sometimes thought, if it be true that they were the first to think of selecting nourishing herbs, by the very fact that they remained at home while the men engaged in more dangerous activities (hunting, warfare, etc.), this, along with matriarchy, would explain an important but almost unnoticed aspect of African life: woman is the mistress of the home in the economic sense of the word. She is in charge of all the food, which no one, not even the husband, can touch without her consent. Frequently a husband, within reach of food prepared by his own wife, dares not touch it without her authorization. It is degrading for a man to enter a kitchen in Black Africa. Accordingly, woman exercises a kind of economic ascendancy over African society, the more marked because it is so generally applied. The hypothesis (that woman discovered agriculture) would also enable us to understand why women still habitually cultivate a small garden around the hut. This is their own domain, where they grow their condiments.

It might be assumed that agriculture appeared everywhere during the same period, circa the eighth millennium B.C. Yet, scarcely anywhere except in the Sahara, do we find vestiges of farm life that can positively be traced back to that epoch. That farming was done by a "Negroid," "steatopygic" (Black) race, as Théodore Monod suggests. Agriculture must have spread quite early over the whole intertropical zone, from the Sahara to India, perhaps as far as Lake Baikal, while the Eurasian plains, absolutely unfavorable to farming and sedentary life, seem to have always been the cradle of nomadism. This was why the Indo-Europeans, molded by their geographical surroundings, were to have views diametrically opposed to those of Blacks.

The end of the Aegean epoch was marked by the rejection of Negro matriarchy, though the Indo-Europeans had been influenced by it to some extent. Since matriarchy is a basic trait of Negro agricultural civilization, it would be absurd to expect it to regulate succession in a government created by Whites. And so, despite the *Tarikh el Fettach*, it is difficult to accept that hypothesis. Moreover, Kâti begins Chapter V of his chronicle as follows: "It is time now to return to our subject: the biography of the Askia.* In fact, little could be obtained because almost all the tales that precede are mendacious."[8]

Many African Moslems alter their genealogical tree, adding branches back to Mohammed, thus claiming Moroccan ancestry.

---

*Title of several emperors of Songhay, the most famous of whom was Mohammed Touré, Askia the Great, who reigned from 1493 to 1529.

Such must have been the tendency of the Sara princes in ancient Ghana when they became Sarakolé, that is, when an infiltration of Arab blood, accompanied by Islamization, marked the Ghanaian dynasty. Thanks to Arab chroniclers of the Middle Ages, it is known that the Black rulers of Ghana reigned over the Berber-Tuareg of Aoudaghost, who paid them tribute. "Aoudaghost" sounds curiously like a Germanic root; it recalls such names as Visigoths and Ostrogoths. This notion fits in with the hypothesis of a Vandal—Germanic—origin of the Berbers.

Ibn Battuta, who visited Sudan in the Middle Ages, was impressed by the Negro matriarchal system. He claimed to have encountered a similar phenomenon only in the Indies among other Black populations: "They take the name of their maternal uncle, not that of their father. It is not the sons who inherit from their father, but rather the nephews, sons of the father's sister. I have never found this custom anywhere else, except among the infidels of Malabar in India."[9]

Matriarchy must not be confused with the reign of the African Amazons or that of the Gorgons. Those legendary regimes in which woman allegedly dominated man were characterized by a technique intended to debase the male: in his education, they avoided assigning him tasks that might develop his courage or revive his dignity. He served as a nurse in place of women who defended the society and had their breasts removed to improve their archery. However little we can trust the legend, we are compelled to assume an early ferocious domination of men over women, perhaps an epoch of a "patriarchal" regime, followed by the emancipation of women and a period of revenge, that of the Amazons. This revolt and victory of women over men must have been merely partial, for there were allegedly but two nations of Amazons and Gorgons in early Antiquity. The fact that the Amazons were intrepid horsewomen inclines us to think that they came from the Eurasian plains, if that region is indeed the original habitat of the horse, as is claimed.

The matriarchal system proper is characterized by the collaboration and harmonious flowering of both sexes, and by a certain preeminence of woman in society, due originally to economic conditions, but accepted and even defended by man.

Kinship of the Meroitic Sudan and Egypt

If we consider that present-day Ethiopia[10] is not the Ethiopia of the

Ancients, which designated essentially the Sudanese civilization of Sennar, we must react against a misleading modern terminology that unconsciously transfers ancient Ethiopia toward the east, to Addis Ababa. The kings who drove the Libyan usurpers from the throne of Egypt, under the Twenty-fifth Dynasty circa 750 B.C., were in reality Sudanese monarchs.[11]

In 712 Shabaka ascended the throne of Egypt, after routing Bocchoris, the usurper. The enthusiastic welcome accorded him by the Egyptian people, who saw him as the regenerator of the ancestral tradition, attests once again in favor of that original kinship between Egyptians and Negro Ethiopians. Ethiopia and the African interior have always been considered by Egyptians as the holy land from which their forebears had come. This passage from Chérubini indicates the reaction of the Egyptians to the advent of the Black Dynasty from the land of Kush (the Sudan):

> In any event, it is remarkable that the authority of the king of Ethiopia seemed recognized by Egypt, less as that of an enemy imposing his rule by force, than as a guardianship invited by the prayers of a long-suffering country, afflicted with anarchy within its borders and weakened abroad. In this monarch, Egypt found a representative of its ideas and beliefs, a zealous regenerator of its institutions, a powerful protector of its independence. The reign of Shabaka was in fact viewed as one of the happiest in Egyptian memory. His dynasty, adopted over the land of the Pharaohs, ranks twenty-fifth in the order of succession of national families who have occupied the throne.[12]

This kinship of Egypt and Nubia, of Mesraim and Kush, both sons of Ham, is revealed by many events in Egypto-Nubian history. After Chérubini, it is Budge's turn to note it: "Observing at Semma that the temple of Ti-Raka was dedicated by this king to the spirit of Osorta-Sen III, addressed as a divine father, Budge expressed the opinion that the local Ethiopian kings considered the Egyptian conquerors as their ancestors. . . . Nevertheless, Budge takes into account the Egyptian's conviction that he was united by close bonds to the people of Punt, that is, to the Ethiopia of today. . . . He notes finally that the inhabitants of Punt had been described as wearing, in that very remote epoch, the time of Queen Hatshepsut, the peculiar plaited beard that adorns the face of the gods on all Egyptian representations."[13]

That quotation hardly needs comment. The last factor mentioned, the plaited beard, is still seen in Black Africa. The Egyptians were convinced, not only of the close ties between two peoples, but also of an original biological kinship, that of having the same ancestor as the Blacks who then inhabited the land of Punt. This was the common ancestor that Egyptians and Nubians both adored as the god Amon who, as we have seen, is the god of all Black Africa today.

Until the close of the Egyptian Empire, the kings of Nubia (Sudan) were to bear the same title as the Egyptian Pharaoh, that of the Hawk of Nubia. Amon and Osiris were represented as coal-black; Isis was a black goddess. Only a citizen, a national, in other words, a Black could have the privilege of serving the cult of the god Min. The priestess of Amon at Thebes, the Egyptian holy site par excellence, could not be other than a Meroitic Sudanese. These facts are basic, indestructible. In vain has the scholars' imagination sought to find for them an explanation compatible with the notion of a White Egyptian race.

"The god Kush had altars in Memphis, Thebes, Meroë under the name of Khons, god of the sky to the Ethiopians, Hercules to the Egyptians" (Pédrals, p. 29). In Wolof, Khon means "rainbow"; it means "to die" in Serer. "Khon being understood to mean: dead in the other world, but not yet having attained to the divine condition." There is also a land named Khons on the Upper Nile.

Accordingly, Nubia appears to be closely akin to Egypt and the rest of Black Africa. It seems to be the starting point of both civilizations. So we are not astonished today to find many civilizing features common to Nubia, whose kingdom lasted until the British Occupation, and the remainder of Black Africa. Right after the end of Egypto-Nubian Antiquity, the Empire of Ghana soared like a meteor from the mouth of the Niger to the Senegal River, circa the third century A.D. Viewed in this perspective, African history proceeded without interruption. The first Nubian dynasties were prolonged by the Egyptian dynasties until the occupation of Egypt by the Indo-Europeans, starting in the fifth century B.C. Nubia remained the sole source of culture and civilization until about the sixth century A.D., and then Ghana seized the torch from the sixth century until 1240, when its capital was destroyed by Sundiata Keita. This heralded the launching of the Mandingo Empire (capital: Mali) of which Delafosse would write: "Nevertheless, this little village of the Upper Niger was for several years the principal capital of the largest empire ever known in

Black Africa, and one of the most important ever to exist in the universe."[14] Next came the Empire of Gao, the Empire of Yatenga (or Mossi, still in existence), the kingdoms of Djoloff and Cayor (in Senegal), destroyed by Faidherbe* under Napoleon III. In listing this chronology, we have simply wanted to show that there was no interruption in African history. It is evident that, if starting from Nubia and Egypt, we had followed a continental geographical direction, such as Nubia–Gulf of Benin, Nubia–Congo, Nubia–Mozambique, the course of African history would still have appeared to be uninterrupted.

This is the perspective in which the African past should be viewed. So long as it is avoided, the most learned speculations will be headed for lamentable failure, for there are no fruitful speculations outside of reality. Inversely, Egyptology will stand on solid ground only when it unequivocally officially recognizes its Negro-African foundation. On the strength of the above facts and those which are to follow, we can affirm with assurance that so long as Egyptology avoids that Negro foundation, so long as it is content merely to flirt with it, as if to prove its own honesty, so long will the stability of its foundations be comparable to that of a pyramid resting on its summit; at the end of those scholarly speculations, it will still be headed down a blind alley.

What could be more normal than to find the entire Egypto-Nubian Pantheon almost intact in Africa? Pédrals quotes Morié, who relates a Coptic tradition about two kings; one is unidentified, the second is King Shango, Iakouta, or Khevioso (depending on the dialect). This ruler, worshiped all over the Slave Coast (Guinea) under these different names, as the god of thunder and destruction, was, according to stories related by the Blacks, a king of Kush, whence his surname Obbato-Kouso, Shango. He passionately loved war and the hunt, and his conquests took him as far as Dahomey. The kings Biri (god of the darkness) and Aido-Khouedo (god of the rainbow) were his slaves.

As Morié puts it, this Obba-Kouso was born at Ife, a locality with which our author is completely unacquainted. Adorned with the title, "first-born of the Supreme God," he resulted from the incestuous love of Orougan, god of the south, and Yemadja, mother of Orougan, herself a sister of Agandjou, god of Space. Chango-Obba-Kouso's brothers are Dada, god of nature, and Ogoun, god of hunters and blacksmiths. He has three wives: Oya, Osoun, and

*General Louis Faidherbe (1818–1889), France's most famous governor of Senegal.

Oba. It is quite evident that Orougan and Yemadja resemble the incestuous couple Amon (Kham) and Mout. Their son, moreover, has the surname "King of Kush." It is also evident that Osoun resembles Asoun, wife of Toubboum-Set-Typhon, later wed by Hor, son of Mesraim-Osiris, and that Dada resembles Dedan, son of Kush in one version, and of Reama in another version, with an uncertainty that the Bible aggravates even more. Finally, the Ethiopians claim that Kush also had married three women, his sisters.

Morié's testimony . . . summarizes an essential bit of the tradition common to countries coasting on the Gulf of Benin (Togo, Dahoney, Nigeria), to the Ewe, Guin, Fon, and Yoruba. The latter call their holy city Ife. (Pédrals, pp. 30–31.)

This testimony Morié had taken, as Pédrals discovered, from a booklet translated from the Arabic and published in Paris in 1666*. The tradition it reveals was noted by the Copts themselves, a fact all the more important because this tradition blends with that found today in West Africa, among the populations of Dahomey, Togo, Nigeria, etc. Shango and Orougan are gods of Nigeria and the whole Gulf of Benin in general. Ife, the city whose name Morié takes from the Coptic texts without knowing that it is Nigeria's holy city, shows the close connection between Egyptian history and that of Black Africa. Orougan, god of the south, suggests the etymology of Ouragan (hurricane), a West Indian word, thus probably of African origin, introduced into the Antilles by voodoo. Yakouta, god of destruction, suggests the Wolof Iakou, also meaning destruction. Note that the Mossi king is currently called "Naba," which was also the name of a monarch who reigned over a part of Nubia (cf. Pédrals, p. 36).

During the reign of Psammetichus, when the Egyptian army was mistreated, some 200,000 of them, led by their officers, went from the Isthmus of Suez to the Nubian Sudan to place themselves at the service of the King of Nubia. Herodotus reported that the Nubian ruler settled the entire army on lands that it farmed, and its elements were finally assimilated by the Nubian people. That happened at a time when Nubian civilization was already several millennia old. Consequently, we are amazed when historians try to use this fact to explain Nubian civilization. On the contrary, all the earliest scholars who studied Nubia, even those to whom we owe the discovery of

---

L'Egypte de Mourtadi, fils du Gaphiphe.

Nubian archeology (such as Cailliaud) conclude that Nubia had priority.

Their studies indicate that Egyptian civilization descended from that of Nubia, in other words, Sudan. As Pédrals observes, Cailliaud bases this argument on the fact that in Egypt all the objects of worship (thus, the essence of sacred tradition) are Nubian.[15] Cailliaud assumes then that the roots of Egyptian civilization were in Nubia (the Sudan) and that it gradually descended the valley of the Nile. In this, he was merely rediscovering or confirming to some extent the unanimous opinion of the Ancients, philosophers and writers, who judged the anteriority of Nubia to be obvious.

Diodorus of Sicily reports that each year the statue of Amon, King of Thebes, was transported in the direction of Nubia for several days and then brought back as if to indicate that the god was returning from Nubia. Diodorus also claims that Egyptian civilization came from Nubia, the center of which was Meroë. In fact, by following data provided by Diodorus and Herodotus on the site of that Sudanese capital,[16] Cailliaud (circa 1820) discovered the ruins of Meroë: 80 pyramids, several temples consecrated to Amon, Ra, and so on. In addition, quoting Egyptian priests, Herodotus stated that of the 300 Egyptian Pharaohs, from Menes to the Seventeenth Dynasty, 18 rather than merely the three who correspond to the Ethiopian "dynasty" were of Sudanese origin.

Egyptians themselves—who should surely be better qualified than anyone to speak of their origin—recognize without ambiguity that their ancestors came from Nubia and the heart of Africa. The land of the Amam, or land of the ancestors (*man*=ancestor in Wolof), the whole territory of Kush south of Egypt, was called land of the gods by the Egyptians. Other facts, such as the tornadoes and torrential rains mentioned on the pyramid of Unas, make one think of the tropics, i.e., the heart of Africa, as Amélineau observes. . . .

Significantly, excavations in the area of ancient Ethiopia reveal documents worthy of the name only in Nubia proper, not in modern Ethiopia. In reality, it is in Nubia that we find pyramids similar to those in Egypt, underground temples, and Meroitic writing, not yet deciphered, but closely related to Egyptian writing. Strangely enough, though this point is not emphasized, Nubian writing is more evolved than Egyptian. While Egyptian writing, even in its hieratic and demotic phases, has never completely eliminated its hieroglyphic essence, Nubian writing is alphabetical.

Of course, one could confidently expect that efforts would be made to rejuvenate Nubian civilization and explain it by that of Egypt. This is what the American Egyptologist George Andrew Reisner (1867–1942) thought he had accomplished in a study covering little more than the period of Nubian history from the Assyrian epoch, or the first millennium. He claimed that Nubia was previously governed by a Libyan dynasty, which the Black dynasties merely prolonged. Once again, the mythical White created civilization and then withdrew miraculously, leaving the place to the Blacks. All the Negro civilizations of Black Africa—from Egypt, Nubia, Ghana, Songhay, to the kingdom of Benin, passing through Rwanda-Urundi, to name only these—have been victims of these general frustrating attempts which finally become as monotonous as an uninteresting face that no longer provokes even a smile.

Reisner could not have failed to know that Nubian civilization dates back to 1500 B.C., that is to say, prior to the appearance of the white Japhetic Libyan in Africa. Consequently, the problem is not to seek Libyans in recent Nubian history, but to find some at the start of that civilization about 5000 B.C. This task Reisner was careful not to attempt.

When Mohammed was born, Arabia was a Negro colony with Mecca as its capital. The Koran refers to the army of 40,000 men sent by the King of Ethiopia to crush the Arab revolt. One corps of that army consisted of warriors mounted on elephants. Delafosse, himself, is obliged to record that suzerainty of Ethiopia over Arabia:

> If one thinks of the part that this empire has played in the destinies of ancient Egypt; if it is remembered that at the birth of Mohammed (570) it exercised suzerainty of the other side of the Red Sea, over the Yemen, and that it sent an army of almost 40,000 men against Mecca; if one considers the extraordinary renown that the power of the famous Prester John enjoyed in Europe during the Middle Ages . . . one is obliged to suppose that a like force could not have failed to spread among the people with whom it came in contact.[17]

Cradles of Civilization Located in the Heart of Negro Lands

No less paradoxical is the fact that the Indo-Europeans never created a civilization in their own native lands: the Eurasian plains.

The civilizations attributed to them are inevitably located in the heart of Negro countries in the southern part of the Northern hemisphere: Egypt, Arabia, Phoenicia, Mesopotamia, Elam, India.

In all those lands, there were already Negro civilizations when the Indo-Europeans arrived as rough nomads during the second millennium. The standard procedure consists of demonstrating that these savage populations brought all the elements of civilization with them wherever they went. The question which then comes to mind is: Why did so many creative aptitudes appear only when there was contact with Blacks, never in the original cradle of the Eurasian steppes? Why did those populations not create civilizations at home before migrating? If the modern world disappeared, one could easily detect, thanks to the many traces of civilization in Europe, that this was the focal point from which modern civilization had spread over the earth. Nothing similar can be found in the Eurasian plains. If we refer to the most remote Antiquity, the evidence forces us to start from the Black countries to explain all the phenomena of civilization.

It would be incorrect to say that civilization was born of racial mixture, for there is proof that it existed in Black lands well before any historical contact with Europeans. Ethnically homogeneous, the Negro peoples created all the elements of civilization by adapting to the favorable geographical conditions of their early homelands. From then on, their countries became magnets attracting the inhabitants of the ill-favored backward lands nearby, who tried to move there to improve their existence. Crossbreeding, resulting from this contact, was thus a consequence of the civilization already created by Blacks, rather than its cause. For the same reason, Europe in general—and Paris or London in particular—are gravitational poles where all the races in the world meet and mix every day. But, 2,000 years hence, it will be inaccurate to explain European civilization of 1954 by the fact that the continent was then saturated by colonials each of whom contributed his share of genius. On the contrary, we can see that all the foreign elements, outdistanced, require a certain length of time to catch up, and for a long time can make no appreciable contribution to technical progress. It was the same in Antiquity; all the elements of Egyptian civilization were in existence from the beginning. They remained as they were and at most simply disintegrated on contact with the foreigner. We are well aware of the various White invasions of Egypt during the historical period: Hyksos (Scythians), Libyans, Assyrians, Persians. None of these brought any new development in mathematics, astronomy, physics, chemistry, medicine, philosophy, the arts, or political organization.

The foregoing likewise enables us to reject *a posteriori* explanations which, reasoning from the situation in the modern world, decree that the temperate zone is preeminently favorable to the flowering of civilizations, all of which were born in that zone. Historical documents prove the contrary: that at the time when the earth's climate was already fixed, all the earliest civilizations existed outside of that zone.[18]

Languages

It is as easy to prove the profound unity of Egyptian and Negro languages as it is difficult to support—much less to prove—the kinship of Egyptian, Indo-European, and Semitic tongues. "A young scholar, N. Reich, decided to compare certain Egyptian roots with certain others still used by the Negro populations of Central Africa and Nubia. He showed without difficulty that they were absolutely identical." (Amélineau, *Prolégomènes*, p. 216.)

After Reich, Miss Homburger [Professor of African languages in Paris] supports the relationship between Egyptian and Negro-African languages in Chapter XII of her *Les Langues négro-africaines* (Paris: Ed. Payot, 1941). But her thesis merely implies an Egyptian influence on a Negro substratum which originally could have been ethnically and linguistically different from the Egyptian substratum. Granting Miss Homburger's studies the importance refused them until now, I find her difficult to follow on this last point. The quasi-identity of Egypt and Black Africa, in all aspects, ethnic and otherwise, does not justify her conclusion.

The linguistic comparison between Egyptian and Wolof which, although limited, will be more convincing because of its precision, will refute the notion of two different linguistic backgrounds. *A priori* one might think such a comparison impossible by contending that in 2,000 years Latin was so completely transformed into other languages: French, Spanish, Italian, etc., that we would be unable to relate those tongues to it if we did not have previously written testimony.

For two reasons, that observation has not deterred me:

First, the evolution of languages, instead of moving everywhere at the same rate of speed, seems linked to other factors: such as, the stability of social organizations, or the opposite, social upheavals. Understandably, in relatively stable societies, man's language has changed less with the passage of time. This is not simply hypothesis: the twenty Berber sentences available, dating back to the twelfth century, reveal a language identical with modern Berber, whereas a comparison between the French of the first Capetians [1,000 years ago] and modern French discloses profound differences.

In Black Africa proper, the scanty evidence we have of those earlier tongues, other than the Meroitic as yet undeciphered, given the present state of our knowledge, consists of a few disparate words in the texts of Arab authors from the tenth to the fifteenth centuries. Thus, we read in Ibn Battuta's *Voyage au Soudan* (p. 15): "The guerti is a fruit similar to the plum with a very sweet taste; but it is unhealthy for Whites. Its kernel is crushed to extract the oil." The word *guerté* must have been applied to the peanut at the time of its recent introduction into Black Africa. If we consider the Wolof form of the word which must have been borrowed from Sarakolé, and if we accept Ibn Battuta's spelling as accurate, the current word (*guerté*) differs from the fourteenth-century term (*guerti*) only in the change of the final vowel.

"Whites who profess the Sunnite doctrine and observe the Malekite ritual, are called 'Touri' here," says Ibn Battuta (p. 17). Touré is a Sudanese name. Thus, the Touré were probably mixed-breeds, partly descended from the Arab minority living in the Sudan during the fourteenth century. Similarly, he refers to Farba Hosein of Valata. Hosein, an Arab term, was correctly written by the author. In the transcription, Valata became Valaten, which seems to reflect a Berber ending. With that exception, the structure and pronunciation of the word have remained the same. Farba designates an administrative function in Serer and has been incorporated verbatim into Wolof. "The King of Ghana was called Maga," a word probably as old as the third century B.C., like the Sarakolé language if we can assume that it was spoken at the beginning of that empire. As already noted, *Mag*=great, a great person, in Wolof, whereas *Ganâr* denotes present-day Mauritania, that is, the northwest of the ancient Ghanaian empire. *Killa*=calabash (in the fourteenth century); currently, in Wolof, it means wooden utensil. Those few examples show the relative stability of African languages.

Secondly, the comparison of the African languages to Egyptian leads not to vague relationships that can at best be considered as possibilities, but to an identity of grammatical facts too numerous to be attributed to coincidence. Consequently, we have here a phenomenon similar to that which a few years ago confronted the physico-chemical world in the incandescent lamp. Refusal to examine these concrete facts and to seek an explanation for them is unscientific. Instead, this attitude is entirely analogous to that of the learned philosophers who, seeing the filament of that lamp become intermittently incandescent, nonetheless concluded that the phenomenon was an impossibility, because it was contrary to the principles accepted up to that time, contrary to their previously held convictions.

Can we simply disregard such similarities as the following? Egyptian expresses the past tense by the same morpheme, *n*, as Wolof; it has a suffixal conjugation which reappears verbatim in Wolof; most pronouns are identical with those in Wolof. We find the two Egyptian pronoun suffixes, *ef* and *es,* with the same meaning in Wolof; demonstratives are the same in both languages; the passive voice is expressed by the same morpheme, *u* or *w* in both languages . . . It is enough to replace *n* in Egyptian by *l* in Wolof to transform an Egyptian word into a Wolof word with the same meaning:

Egyptian	*Wolof*
Nad: to ask	Lad: to ask
Nah: to protect, hide	Lah: to protect, hide
Nebt: braid, to braid	Let: braid, to braid
Ben-ben: source, spring	Bel-bel: to spring
Funa: sure, regular, authentic	Fula: worthy, regular conduct

Without listing all the vocabulary common to both, there are too many similarities to be ascribed to mere chance.

CHAPTER VIII

Arguments Opposing a Negro Origin

If Blacks created Egyptian civilization, how can we explain their present decline? That question makes no sense, for we could say as much about the Fellahs and Copts, who are supposed to be the direct descendants of the Egyptians and who, today, are at the same backward stage as other Blacks, if not more so. Nevertheless, this does not excuse us from explaining how the technical, scientific, and religious civilization of Egypt was transformed as it adjusted to new conditions in the rest of Africa.

Around the mother valley, States developed very early, though we cannot fix the exact date of their appearance. By successive migrations as time passed, Blacks slowly penetrated into the heart of the continent, spreading out in all directions and dislodging the Pygmies. They founded States which developed and maintained relations with the mother valley until it was stifled by the foreigner. From south to north, these were Nubia and Egypt; from north to south, Nubia and Zimbabwe; from east to west, Nubia, Ghana, Ife; from east to southwest, Nubia, Chad, the Congo; from west to east, Nubia and Ethiopia.

In Ethiopia and Nubia—completely Negro territory—we still find a profusion of stone monuments, such as obelisks, temples, pyramids. Temples and pyramids are found exclusively in the Meroitic Sudan. We have already stressed the dominant role played by that country in spreading civilization to Black Africa; we need not return to that subject.

To modern minds, the term "Ethiopia" conjures up Addis Ababa. Here again, we must insist on the fact that in this region, except for one obelisk and two pedestals of statues, nothing is found. The civilization of Axum, former capital of Ethiopia, is more a word than a reality attested by historical monuments.

It is in the Meroitic Sudan, Sennar, that temples and pyramids (84) abound. Thus, place names have been falsified to provide a more or less Oriental and discreetly Asiatic origin by way of the Bab el Mandeb for Negro-Egyptian civilization. In reality, we must react against a whole terminology: *Chamites* or *Hamites, Oriental* and *Ethiopian,* and even *African* are, in modern historical writing, euphemisms enabling one to speak of Negro-Sudanese-Egyptian civilization without once using the term "Negro" or "Black."

In Zimbabwe—which may well be an extension of the land of the Macrobian Ethiopians mentioned by Herodotus—we find ruins of monuments and cities built of stone, with the falcon represented, "over a radius of 100 to 200 miles around Victoria," writes D.P. de Pédrals (p. 116). In other words, those ruins extend over a diameter almost as great as that of France.

In the region of Ghana, Pédrals (p. 61) also speaks "of the city of Kukia, which the Tarikh es Sudan claims already existed at the time of the Pharaoh." Louis Desplagnes, who excavated in that area, reported vestiges of it. The same author also mentioned the site of Kumbi*, excavated by a French district officer, Bonnel de Mézières, who discovered tombs of great dimensions, "sarcophagi of schist, metallurgical workshops, ruins of towers and of various buildings."

We can still distinguish clearly the outline of an avenue, bordered by houses with walls more than one meter or one and a half meters above ground. The roofs have collapsed. Farther on, a strip of flat ground for a public square, with walls which seem to have once supported upper floors. Sometimes the buildings are so well preserved that little would be needed to make them livable again. The building lines are still visible because of the presence of hewn stone. All around, remains of a low enclosure; outside the tombs, bits of pottery everywhere, pearls, red copper débris. Some distance away, on a laterite plateau, traces of a metallurgical workshop. . . .

The other constructions are complicated. One consists of five rooms four meters deep, with communicating halls. The masonry is perfect. The walls are thirty centimeters thick. (Pédrals, p. 62.)

In the Lake Debo region (in Mali, on the Niger), pyramids are also found, and these were dubbed "mounds," as might be expected. This is the usual procedure in the attempt to disparage African values. In contrast, there is the reverse procedure consisting of de-

---

*Capital of the ancient Empire of Ghana.

scribing a clay tumulus—a real mound—in Mesopotamia, as the
most perfect temple that the human mind can imagine. It goes without saying that such reconstructions are generally mere wishful
thinking.

On the other hand, here is what Pédrals has to say about the pyramids of the Sudan:

> These are massive clusters of clay and stone, in the form of trun-
> cated pyramids, with a terra cotta summit of red brick. All of them
> date from the same chronological period and were built for the
> same purpose. . . . They rise from 15 to 18 meters high on a base
> of 200 square meters. Desplagnes excavated one of these mounds
> on the site of El Waleji, at the confluence of the Issa Ber and Bara
> Issa. In the central part, he discovered a mortuary chamber ori-
> ented east-west, 6 meters at its longest part and 2½ meters at its
> widest. . . . In the chamber, on a sandy bed around a large jar,
> Desplagnes found numerous pieces of pottery, two human skele-
> tons, jewels, weapons, swords, knives, arrowheads and spear-
> heads, beads, pearls, earthenware figurines representing animals,
> and, finally, awls and bone needles. The pearls were made of a
> glassy blue paste, covered either by whitish spiral bands or by
> enameled incrustations resembling Egyptian glass of the Middle
> Empire (Tell Amarna). The pottery indicates a ceramics industry
> much more advanced than that of the present inhabitants of the
> area. . . . The metal work is likewise excellent, judging from the
> jewels of precious metal, sometimes in filigree. (*Ibid.,* pp. 59–60.)

It is impossible to describe here all the riches of the civilization of
Ife. They are such that Frobenius, following the usual pattern, vainly
sought an external White origin for them.[1]

In the Nile Valley, civilization resulted from man's adaptation to
that particular milieu. As declared by the Ancients and by the Egyptians themselves, it originated in Nubia. This is confirmed by our
knowledge that the basic elements of Egyptian civilization are neither
in Lower Egypt, nor in Asia, nor in Europe, but in Nubia and the
heart of Africa; moreover, that is where we find the animals and
plants represented in hieroglyphic writing. . . .

The Egyptians usually measured the height of the flood waters with
a "Nilometer," and from it they deduced the annual yield of the harvests by mathematical calculation. The calendar and astronomy also

resulted from that sedentary farm life. Adaptation to the physical surroundings gave birth to certain hygienic measures: mummification
(to avoid epidemics of the plague from the Delta), fasting, diets, and
so on, which gradually led to medicine coming into existence. The development of social life and exchanges required the invention and use
of writing.

Sedentary life led to the institution of private property and a whole
ethic (summarized in the questions asked the deceased at the Tribunal of Osiris). This code of ethics was the opposite of the warlike,
predatory habits of the Eurasian nomads.[2]

When, as a consequence of the overpopulation of the valley and of
social upheavals, the Negroes of the Nile penetrated more deeply into
the interior of the continent, they were to encounter new physical and
geographical conditions. A given practice, instrument, technique, or
science, formerly indispensable on the banks of the Nile, was no
longer vitally needed on the Atlantic coast, on the banks of the
Congo and the Zambezi. Thus it is understandable that certain factors
of Negro culture in the Nile Valley may have disappeared in the interior, while other factors, not the least fundamental ones, have lasted
until our day.

The absence of papyrus in some areas contributed to the scarcity
of writing in the heart of the continent but, despite solemn statements
to the contrary, it was never entirely absent from Black Africa. At
Diourbel, chief town of Baol, in Senegal, in the Ndounka quarter
near the railway, not far from Daru Mousti Road, there is a baobab
tree covered with hieroglyphics, from its trunk to its branches. As I
recall, these consisted of signs of hands, of animal paws—no longer
the same as the camel hoofs of Egypt—signs of feet, and other objects. It would have been useful to take prints of these and study
them. But, at the time, I was neither old enough nor sufficiently
trained to be interested. One might get an idea of the period—ancient
or recent—during which those symbols had been engraved on the
bark by analyzing the thickness of the bark, the nature of the symbols, the objects represented, and the displacement of those signs
along the trunk and branches as the tree grew. It must be added that
such trees are considered sacred and one rarely removes the bark to
make rope. It must also be added that they are not rare in the country.

In short, since the subsoil of Black Africa is practically intact, we
can expect later diggings to produce unsuspected written documents,
despite the climate and its torrential rains, which are unfavorable to

the conservation of such pieces. An authentic hieroglyphic writing, called Njoya, exists in the Cameroon. It would be interesting to learn whether it is as ancient as is claimed. It is exactly the same type of writing as Egyptian hieroglyphics. Finally, in Sierra Leone, there is a type of writing different from that of Bamun (Cameroon); this is Vai, which is syllabic. According to Dr. Jeffreys, the writing of the Bassa is cursive. That of the Nsibidi is alphabetical. (Cf. Baumann & Westermann, *op. cit.*, p. 444.)

Thus it can be said that, until the fifteenth century, Black Africa never lost its civilization. Frobenius reports:

Not that the first European navigators at the end of the Middle Ages failed to make some very remarkable observations. When they reached the Bay of Guinea and alighted at Vaida, the captains were astonished to find well-planned streets bordered for several leagues by two rows of trees; for days they traversed a countryside covered by magnificent fields, inhabited by men in colorful attire that they had woven themselves! More to the south, in the Kingdom of the Congo, a teeming crowd clad in silk and velvet, large States, well ordered down to the smallest detail, powerful rulers, prosperous industries. Civilized to the marrow of their bones! Entirely similar was the condition of the lands on the east coast, Mozambique, for example.

The revelations of the navigators from the fifteenth to the eighteenth centuries provide positive proof that Black Africa, which extended south of the desert zone of the Sahara, was still in full bloom, in all the splendor of harmonious, well-organized civilizations. This flowering the European conquistadors destroyed as they advanced. For the new land of America needed slaves which Africa offered: hundreds, thousands, whole shiploads of slaves! Nevertheless, the black slave trade was never a safe business; it required justification; so they made the Negro half-animal, a piece of merchandise. Thus was invented the notion of the fetish, as a symbol of African religion. Made in Europe! As for me, I have never anywhere in Africa seen natives adoring fetishes.

The idea of the "barbaric Negro" is a European invention that boomeranged and dominated Europe until the start of this century.[3]

The texts of the Portuguese travelers, quoted by Frobenius, agree with those of Arab authors of the tenth to fifteenth centuries. The social organization of Negro States in the fourteenth and fifteenth centuries, to which Frobenius refers, the royal pomp displayed there, are described by an Arab writer who visited the Empire of Mali at the time. This is a passage in which Ibn Battuta reports audiences granted by the Mandingo King, Suleyman Mansa. The author visited the Sudan in 1352–1353, at the time of the Hundred Years' War. . . .

On certain days the sultan holds audiences in the palace yard, where there is a platform under a tree, with three steps; this they call the *pempi*. It is carpeted with silk and has cushions placed on it. Over it is raised the umbrella, which is a sort of pavilion made of silk, surmounted by a bird in gold, about the size of a falcon. The sultan comes out of a door in a corner of the palace, carrying a bow in his hand and a quiver on his back. On his head he has a golden skullcap, bound with a gold band which has narrow ends shaped like knives, more than a span in length. His usual dress is a velvety red tunic, made of the European fabrics called *mutanfas*. The sultan is preceded by his musicians, who carry gold and silver two-stringed guitars, and behind him come 300 armed slaves. He walks in a leisurely fashion, affecting a very slow movement, and even stops from time to time. On reaching the *pempi* he stops and looks around the assembly, then ascends it in the sedate manner of a preacher ascending a mosque-pulpit. As he takes his seat the drums, trumpets, and bugles are sounded. Three slaves go out at a run to summon the sovereign's deputy and military commanders, who enter and sit down. Two saddled and bridled horses are brought, along with two goats, which they hold to serve as a protection against the evil eye. Dugha stands at the gate and the rest of the people remain in the street, under the trees. . . .
The Negroes are of all people the most submissive to their king and the most abject in their behavior before him. They swear by his name.[4]

Ibn Battuta next tells us that Kankan Musa, predecessor of Suleyman Mansa, had given Es Saheli, who had built a mosque for him at Gao,* about 180 kilograms (approximately 400 pounds) of gold. This gives us an idea of the country's wealth in the precolonialist period.

---

*Gao, old trading city on the Middle Niger, capital of the Empire of Songhay.

Another passage by Ibn Battuta demolishes the legend that insecurity reigned in Black Africa before European colonization and that this colonization brought with it peace, liberty, security, and so on.

Among the admirable qualities of these people, the following are to be noted:

1. The small number of acts of injustice that one finds here; for the Negroes are of all peoples those who most abhor injustice. The sultan pardons no one who is guilty of it.[5]
2. The complete and general safety one enjoys throughout the land. The traveler has no more reason to fear brigands, thieves, or ravishers than the man who stays at home.
3. The Blacks do not confiscate the goods of the white man [i.e., of North Africans] who die in their country, not even when these consist of big treasures. They deposit them, on the contrary, with a man of confidence among the Whites until those who have a right to the goods present themselves and take possession.[6]

In that period, how did Blacks conduct themselves in the presence of Whites, or of races deemed white? Ibn Battuta answers this question in a text describing the reception of his caravan at Walata where the Farba Hosein represented the King of Mali:

Our merchants stood in his presence and he addressed them through a third person, though they were standing close to him. That showed how little consideration he had for them and I was so displeased that I bitterly resented having come to a country whose inhabitants show themselves to be so impolite and evince such scorn for white men.[7]

Delafosse, whose comment on the importance of the Mali Empire was quoted earlier, observed: "Gao, however, had recovered its independence between the death of Kankan Musa and the advent of Suleyman Mansa and, about a century later, the Mandingo Empire began to decline under attack by the Songhay, though retaining enough power and prestige for its sovereign to negotiate as an equal with the King of Portugal, who was then at the height of his glory."[8]

Accordingly, the emperors of Black Africa, far from being mere kinglets, negotiated on an equal footing with their most powerful Western counterparts. On the strength of documents in our possession, we can go further and emphasize the fact that the neo-Sudanese empires preceded by several centuries the existence of comparable empires in Europe. The Empire of Ghana was probably founded about the third century A.D. and lasted until 1240. As we know, Charlemagne, founder of the first Western Empire, was crowned in 800.

Ghana's magnificence was in every respect similar or superior to Mali's. Such, then, were the African States at the time they were about to enter into contact with the modern Western world. At that time there were only absolute monarchies in the West, whereas in Black Africa monarchies were already constitutional. The king was assisted by a People's Council, whose members were chosen from the various social strata. This type of organization existed in Ghana, Mali, Gao, Yatenga, Cayor, and so on. This could not have been the beginning, but rather the result of a long evolution, the start of which we can discover only by going back to Nubia and Egypt. In no other way can we reestablish the continuity of that chain. From whichever side the history of Africa is considered, one constantly falls back on the Meroitic Sudan and Egypt.

When contact was made a second time between Europe and Black Africa, via the Atlantic, it was above all else the far-ranging navies and the firearms available in Europe, thanks to the continued technical progress in the Northern Mediterranean, that gave Europe its superiority. They enabled it to dominate the continent and to falsify the Negro's personality. That is how things still stand, and that is what has caused the subsequent alteration of history concerning the origin of Egyptian civilization.

Along with political unity, cultural unity was already asserting itself within the different empires. Certain languages, having become official because they were spoken by the emperor, served as administrative languages and were beginning to dominate the others, which tended to become regional dialects, just as Breton, Basque, and Provençal in France have become patois. . . .

By destroying these and other cultural ties, colonization brought the dialects back to the surface and favored the development of a linguistic mosaic. Similar results might have occurred in France after a few centuries of German Occupation, had it encouraged the rise of the aforementioned patois to the detriment of French, already attained to the status of a national tongue.

Consequently, it is evident that there has indeed been a decline in

Black Africa, especially at the level of the masses, but this is due to colonization. That can surely be charged with the retrogression of certain tribes which have gradually been hybridized and pushed back into the forest. It would therefore be doubly inaccurate today to take the condition of those populations which have become more or less primitive as evidence that Black Africa never had a civilization or a past; that the Black has a primitive, non-Cartesian mentality, hostile to civilization, and so on. This regression alone can explain how, in a relatively backward State, these populations still retain intact a tradition that reveals a stage of social organization and a conception of the world that no longer correspond to their cultural level.

An analogous fact in Europe can be cited: the retrogression of the white populations residing today in Swiss valleys isolated by snow, such as the valley of Lötschenthal. These Whites are savages today, in the Bushman or Hottentot sense of the word; they make masks, grimacing and tormented, indicating a cosmic terror equaled only by the Eskimo. The Geneva Museum possesses a fine collection of these masks. In contrast, one can observe that the serenity of Negro art reflects the clemency of the physical setting, but also a taming, at least spiritual, of universal forces. Instead of being inexplicable phenomena that terrify the imagination, these forces were already integrated in a general system to explain the world. Considering its period, that system was equivalent to a philosophy. The Negro had dominated nature, partly by technique, but mostly by his spirit: Nature no longer frightened him. By the same token, Negro expressionist art (in the Ivory Coast and the Congo) was not to reflect torment but would appear as a kind of plastic sport.

Problems Caused by Straight Hair and So-called Regular Features

At this point we must say that neither straight hair nor regular features are a monopoly of the White race. There are two well-defined Black races: one has a black skin and woolly hair; the other also has black skin, often exceptionally black, with straight hair, aquiline nose, thin lips, an acute cheekbone angle. We find a prototype of this race in India: the Dravidian. It is also known that certain Nubians likewise belong to the same Negro type, as this sentence by the Arab author, Edrissi, indicates: "The Nubians are the most handsome of Blacks; their women have thin lips and straight hair."[9]

Thus, it is inexact, anti-scientific, to do anthropological research, encounter a Dravidian type, and then conclude that the Negro type is absent. This is what Dr. Massoulard does on reporting Miss Stoessiger's work on Badarian crania. The contradiction is all the more flagrant because these crania are prognathous and prognathism is found only in Negroes or Negroids—by Negroid, I mean any element born of the Negro:

> Badarian skulls differ very little from other less ancient predynastic skulls; they are just a bit more prognathous. Next to these, they most resemble primitive Indian skulls: Dravidians and Veddas. They also present a few affinities with Negroes, due no doubt to a very ancient admixture of Negro blood. (Massoulard, *op. cit.,* p. 394.)

By this kind of fictitious opposition, it has been possible to whiten the Egyptian race which, even in the prehistoric epoch, as this text shows, was still Negro, despite allegations without scientific foundation which contend that the Egyptians were originally Whites, "bastardized," let us say "mixed," subsequently with Negroes.

It is customary to mention the straight hair of certain carefully chosen mummies, the only ones found in museums, to affirm that they represent a prototype of the White race, notwithstanding their prognathism. These mummies are displayed conspicuously in an attempt to prove the whiteness of the Egyptians. The very coarseness of their hair precludes acceptance of that contention. When such hair exists on the head of a mummy, it merely indicates the Dravidian type, in reality, whereas the prognathism and black skin—pigmented, not blackened by tar or any other product—excludes any idea of a white race. The meticulous selection process to which they have been subjected rules out any possibility of their being a prototype. In fact, Herodotus told us, after seeing them, that the Egyptians had woolly hair. As we have already observed, one may well wonder why mummies with such characteristics are not exhibited. Those that should be the most numerous are currently the least discoverable, and when we are lucky enough to stumble upon one, we are assured that it represents a foreign type.

One observation that could prove Herodotus' statement about the Egyptian's woolly hair is the artificial coiffure still worn by Black African women. Why would a white woman with naturally beautiful hair hide it under the coarse, artificial hair-do of the Egyptian? We should rather view this as a manifestation of the black woman's constant anxiety over the hair problem.

In any case, it is obvious that we cannot rely on the quality of the hair to guarantee the whiteness of a race. . . .

An Enslaved Black Race

Certain books attempt to spread the notion of an enslaved black race living throughout Antiquity alongside a white race and slowly transforming the characteristics of the Whites. Contacts between these two races as far back as prehistory can be taken as an authentic fact, without any determination on our part as to the importance of those contacts in the different regions where they took place. But objective examination of the documents available from those distant epochs compels us to reverse the relations it has been attempted *a priori* to establish between those two races, from Elam to Egypt. Dieulafoy's excavations reveal that the first Elamite dynasties belonged to the Black race. The series of Amratian statuettes show us a white race captive in Egypt beside an unfettered black race. The White race did not liberate itself completely until the close of the Aegean epoch which marked the arrival of the northern Mediterranean on the scene.

Reddish-brown Color of the Egyptians?

It seems quite probable that the infiltration, from prehistoric times, of that conquered captive race depicted on those statuettes may have helped to whiten the Egyptian's complexion. In other words, it seems likely that a white minority appeared later to graft itself onto an early Negro substratum, because of the valley's attraction for the coarse Aryan and Semitic shepherds. But what is certain is the preeminence of the Negro element from the beginning to the end of Egyptian history. Even the intensive crossbreeding of the low period did not succeed in eliminating the Negro characteristics of the Egyptian race. This mixture of the Egyptian Negro and the proto-Semite or Aryan followed a fanlike development in the course of Egyptian history as a result of commercial trends. During the Aegean epoch it is reflected in the kidnapping of Io by the Phoenicians. In fact, the Phoenicians, a Negroid people, more or less cousins of the Egyptians, served as their mariners throughout that period. Among other commercial exchanges between a civilized Egypt and a then barbaric Europe, they engaged in the white slave trade. Io, as we have noted, kidnapped from Greece and sold to the Pharaoh for a high price, because her white skin was a rarity, merely symbolized that trade. It would be extremely difficult to deny or minimize the extent of such trading.

This could explain the so-called "reddish-brown" complexion of the Egyptians, though they continued to have "thick lips, even everted," a "mouth a bit too wide," and "a fleshy nose," to quote Maspero. Obviously, the Egyptians never ceased being Negroes. The special color attributed to them can be seen today among millions of Negroes in all parts of Black Africa.

It is common to mention the mastaba or Egyptian tomb paintings as a place to distinguish the *Nahasi* from the *Rametou,* that is, the Blacks from the so-called Egyptians. That is tantamount to distinguishing Wolof from Bambara, Mossi from Toucouleur, and mistaking the latter for Whites, or for a race distinct from the black race represented by the Wolof. For an African, this is an accurate evaluation of the distinctions usually made on the basis of Egyptian paintings. Or it would be if it were possible to date those paintings with some degree of certainty. Moreover, all those mastaba paintings were known before Champollion; those color shades had been seen before. It had nonetheless been affirmed that the types depicted were Negroes, because up to that time Egypt had always been recognized as a Negro country. Egyptian art itself was considered Negro art, and therefore uninteresting.

This opinion did not change until the day it was recognized with amazement that Egypt was the Mother of all civilization. Then eyesight suddenly improved and it was possible to distinguish, on the frescoes where everyone had previously recognized Negroes, evidences of a "white race with red skin," a "white race with dark red skin," a "white race with black skin." But they never distinguished, as Egyptians, a white race with white skin.

The Inscription on the Stela of Philae

Because of this inscription which marked off the border between the Meroitic Sudan and Egypt after the troubles of the Twelfth Dynasty, it is often concluded that this separated two distinct races, that this stela barred Blacks from entering Egypt. Such a conclusion is a grievous error, for the term "Black" was never used by the Egyptians to distinguish the Meroitic Sudanese from themselves. Egyptians and Meroitic Sudanese belonged to the same race. They designated each other by tribal and regional names, never by epithets related to color, as in cases involving contact between a black race and a white race.

If modern civilization should disappear today, but leave libraries untouched, survivors could open almost any book and perceive immediately that persons living south of the Sahara are called "Blacks." The term "Black Africa" would suffice to indicate the habitat of the Black race. Nothing similar is found in Egyptian texts. Whenever the Egyptians use the word "Black" (*khem*), it is to designate themselves or their country: *Kemit,* land of the Blacks.

Not one of the many modern texts is authentic that mentions the term "Blacks" as if it had ever been used by the Egyptians to distinguish themselves from Negroes. Whenever these texts relate some fact reported by the Egyptians about "Blacks," it is a distortion. They translate *Nahasi* by "Blacks" in order to serve the cause. Strangely enough, the word *Kushite* becomes incompatible with the idea of "Blacks" as soon as it refers to the first inhabitants who civilized Arabia before Mohammed; the land of Canaan, prior to the Jews (Phoenicia); Mesopotamia, prior to the Assyrians (Chaldean epoch); Elam; India, before the Aryans. This is one of the many contradictions that betray the specialists' fear of revealing facts they must have detected. Their reasoning process can perhaps be described as follows: Given the ideas I have been taught about the Negro, even if the evidence proves objectively that civilization was created by the said Negroes (Kushites, Canaanites, Egyptians, etc.), it must be wrong. By searching diligently, we must be able to find the opposite. Thus, the sure, indispensable method to discover the truth contained in these documents, despite appearances, rests in the interpretation of such terms as Kushite, Canaanite, etc. Though these words in the documents mean "Blacks," this is an obvious mistake. Let us therefore say that any race is involved except the Black race, or perhaps a black race that is not Black: the brown race for example.

A similar falsification occurs when ancient authors such as Herodotus, Diodorus, or the first Carthaginian travelers, are quoted. We are given to believe that those authors distinguished between Egyptians and Blacks. This is true of Delafosse (by no means the only one), when he writes in *Les Noirs de l'Afrique* (pp. 20–21):

A passage in Herodotus' *History* is very instructive in this regard.

In Book II (paragraphs 29–30), the Greek author has more or less fixed for us the northern limits reached in his day in the Nile Valley by the Blacks, whom he calls "Ethiopians." These limits are almost identical with those attained in our day. Blacks were already found, he tells us, "above the Elephantine" (Aswan), that is to say, upriver from the first cataract, some of them sedentary, others nomadic, living side by side with the Egyptians.

Checking this against the original, we can perceive the distortion; it leads us to believe that, according to Herodotus, Blacks and Egyptians were different. Book II of Herodotus, which Delafosse quotes, informs us that the Egyptians had black skin and woolly hair. This is the process by which ancient authors are made to say the contrary of what they had written. At other times, their embarrassing testimony is merely passed over in silence. Occasionally one insults them or tries to mask one's anger by casting doubt on their evidence, thus attempting to discredit them. These altered, falsified quotations are quite serious to the extent that they give the layman the illusion of authenticity.

As early as 4000 B.C. Egyptian documents indicate that the Meroitic Sudan was a prosperous country which maintained commercial ties with Egypt. Gold was plentiful. About that time the Meroitic Sudan probably transmitted to Egypt the twelve hieroglyphs that were the first embryonic alphabet.

After several attempts at conquest, Sudanese and Egyptians became allies and joined forces in expeditions to the Red Sea, led by Pepi I (Sixth Dynasty). Nubia was then governed by a king named Una who, under the successor of Pepi I, became governor of Upper Egypt. That alliance lasted at least until the Twelfth Egyptian Dynasty. Sesostris I then successfully set up a trusteeship over Nubia:

> But the yoke is rejected under Sesostris II, in circumstances that make Egypt itself fear invasion. Ramparts and fortresses are erected between the first and second cataracts to stop the Nubians. Egypt is so uneasy that it appeals to Bedouin tribes led by a certain Abshal, from Syria. In four campaigns, Sesostris III puts an end to the threat. The border is restored upriver, where new fortresses are built, at the same time that a new stela is erected barring the passage of Blacks. (Pédrals, p. 45.)

Except for the incorrect use of the term "Blacks" which ends the quotation and for which the author, known to be a man of good will, is not entirely responsible, that passage reveals the nature of the facts that prompted the Stela of Philae. They show that, at a given moment, the Sudanese ally nearly conquered Egypt which, for that reason, organized its defense, whence the Stela of Philae. Thus, it could not possibly mean what others would like to see it mean.

From the Battle of Danki (fifteenth century) to that of Guilé (nineteenth century), Cayor and Djoloff experienced the same periodic antagonism as Egypt and Nubia. Did that make Cayorians and Djoloff-Djoloff any less Negro?

34.   The Tower of Babel. (Example of the restoration
of monuments.) The tower is in the background, with the
Hanging Gardens of Babylon in front of it.

35.   Zimbabwe: The falcon and crocodile are echoes of Egypt. (Photo by Summers.)

36. Zimbabwe: Cyclopean Architecture. The stones are placed one on the other without cement to hold them together.

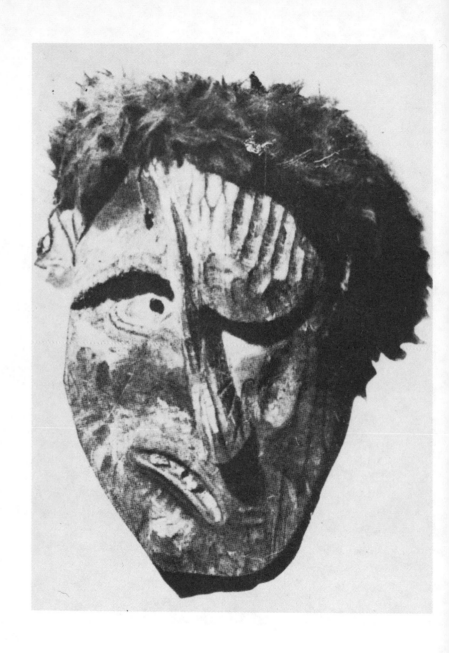

37. Grimacing Swiss Mask.

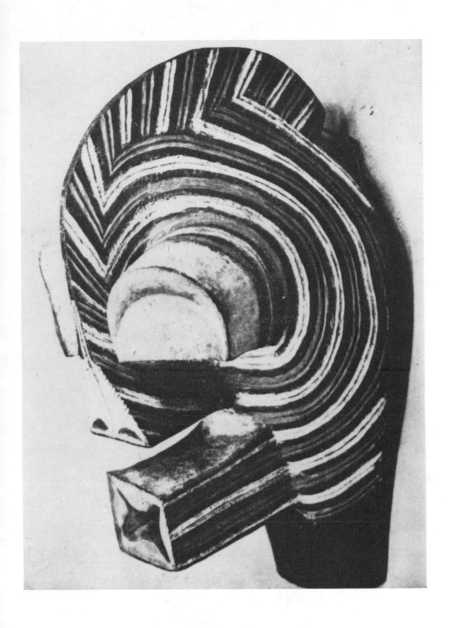

38. Congolese Cubist Mask. Compare with preceding figure. (A.P.A.M. photo.)

39.   Ife (Nigeria) Head. Compare the coiffure with the
Uraeus of the Egyptian Pharaoh. (Lagos Museum.)

40. Benin Bronze Head: "Court Dignitary" (British Museum cast, Nigeria). (Courtesy of the American Museum of Natural History.)

41. Tower of the Gao Mosque. Resembling a step pyramid, this is the tomb of the Askias.

CHAPTER IX

Peopling of Africa from the Nile Valley

The arguments advanced to defend the theory that Black Africa was settled from Oceania by way of the Indian Ocean are without foundation. No fact, archeological or otherwise, authorizes us at present to seek the Negro's original habitat outside of Africa. West African legends report that Blacks migrated from the east, from the region of the Great Water. Without any additional proof, Delafosse, perhaps as a working hypothesis, identified the "Great Water" with the Indian Ocean. Moreover, the cradle of humanity was then assumed to be in Asia, because of the discovery of Pithecanthropus (in Java) and Sinanthropus (in China), and because of the Bible (Adam and Eve). Opinion hardened around that identification; for a long time it was forgotten that this was merely an *a priori* affirmation, and the hypothesis was accepted as a demonstrated theorem.

From what we know about the archeology of South Africa, where humanity seems to have been born; from what we know about Nubian civilization, probably the oldest of all; from what we know about the prehistory of the Nile Valley, we can legitimately assume that the "Great Water" is none other than the Nile. No matter where we collect legends on the genesis of a Black African people, those who still remember their origins say they came from the east and that their forebears found Pygmies in the country.[1] Dogon and Yoruba legends report that they came from the east, while those of the Fang, who as recently as the nineteenth century had not yet reached the Atlantic coast, indicate the northeast. Bakuba legends list the north as their provenance. For peoples living south of the Nile, traditions suggest that they came from the north; this is true of the Batutsi of Rwanda-Urundi. When the first sailors to reach South Africa disembarked at the Cape several centuries ago, the Zulu, after a north-south migration, had not yet reached the tip of the Cape.

This hypothesis squares with the fact that the traditions of Blacks in the Nile Valley mention only a local origin. Throughout Antiquity, Nubians and Ethiopians never claimed any other, unless it were one farther south. This summarizes the ancient legends as reported by d'Avezac with an irony that does not diminish their importance:

> Others, erudite dreamers or ingenious physiologists, instead of seeking the early history of Africans in traditions now almost lost, have preferred to seek it in risky hypotheses, and their conjectural narrations present the Negro as the oldest man created, son of the soil and of chance, born in the snowy Mountains of the Moon (Central Africa) which later cradled the man who went down to Sennar and engendered the Egyptian and the Arab and the people of Atlantis. The Black race, long the most numerous, first overpowered and dominated the Whites; but the latter, having gradually multiplied, shook off the yoke of their masters. The ex-slave, becoming master in his turn, condemned the Blacks to bear the chains that he had just broken. Centuries have passed, but his anger is not yet appeased.[2]

That legend compresses the history of humanity into a few lines.[3] What is noteworthy here is the southern origin of the inhabitants of the Nile Valley, which Nubians and Egyptians have always asserted. What also stands out is the early arrival of the Negro on the road to civilization and the current reversal of the situation. He is the man who comes down to Sennar which, no doubt, is the plain located between the White Nile and the Blue Nile, point of departure for the Meroitic Sudanese civilization. Sennar is also the name of the Mesopotamian plain, likewise between two rivers: the Tigris and the Euphrates. Which of these appellations is correct and authentic? The second seems a replica of the first. Rectification of this error would again reverse the direction of history. It would then become natural for Egypt to be peopled from the plain of Sennar and the legend would agree with history.

Along with current legends of African peoples, almost all of which mention the Nile basin and the Pygmies who inhabited the interior before the dispersion of the Blacks, let us cite two passages from Herodotus which confirm them. The first concerns two Nasamonians who left Syrtis (Cyrenaica), followed the Mediterranean coast westward, then headed toward the interior across the Sahara, and arrived on the banks of a river where only black Pygmies lived:

> The young men therefore despatched on this errand by their comrades with a plentiful supply of water and provisions, travelled at

first through the inhabited region, passing which they came to the wild beast tract, whence they finally entered upon the desert, which they proceeded to cross in a direction from east to west. After journeying for many days over a wide extent of sand, they came at last to a plain where they observed trees growing; approaching them, and seeing fruit on them, they proceeded to gather it. While they were thus engaged, there came upon them some dwarfish men, under the middle height, who seized them and carried them off. The Nasamonians could not understand a word of their language, nor had they any acquaintance with the language of the Nasamonians. They were led across extensive marshes, and finally came to a town, where all the men were of the height of their conductors, and black-complexioned. A great river flowed by the town running from east to west, and containing crocodiles (p. 92).

It would seem therefore, that at a certain time the interior was inhabited exclusively by Pygmies. The river in question might well have been the Niger, since we know now, contrary to what Herodotus believed, that beyond Ethiopia the Nile does not bend around to flow from south to north after crossing Africa from the northwest to the southeast.

The second passage refers to the voyage of Sataspes, son of Teaspes. Ordered by Xerxes to be impaled, Sataspes was conditionally pardoned, thanks to an appeal by his mother, who happened to be the sister of Darius. He crossed the Strait of Gibraltar and sailed southward. Though he did not complete the trip, he was able to make the following observations on the Atlantic coast of Africa:

> . . . He reported to Xerxes that at the farthest point to which he had reached, the coast was occupied by a dwarfish race, who wore a dress made from a palm-tree. These people, whenever he landed, left their towns and fled to the mountains; his men, however, did them no wrong, only entering their cities and taking some of their cattle (p. 217).

In short, there is agreement between Negro legends now current and these facts reported by Herodotus 2,500 years ago.[4]

So the Pygmies were probably the first to occupy the interior of the continent, at least at a certain period. They settled there prior to the arrival of larger Blacks. It can be assumed that the latter formed a kind of cluster around the Nile Valley. In the course of time they spread out in all directions, as a result of the population growth and the upheavals that occur during the history of a people.

This is neither a mere mental conception nor a simple working hypothesis. Our knowledge of African ethnography enables us to distinguish between a hypothesis and a confirmed historical fact. To be sure, a cultural foundation common to all African Blacks, particularly a common linguistic base, seems to justify the idea in the main. But, above all, there are the totemic clan names borne by all Africans, either collectively or individually, according to the extent of their dispersion; the analysis of these names combined with a proper linguistic examination enables us to progress from the realm of probability to the level of certainty.

Egypt proper and Senegal have the following names in common:

Egypt	Senegal
Atoum	Atu
Sek-met	Sek
Kéti	Kéti
Kaba	Kaba, keba, kébé
Antef	Anta
Fari: the Pharaoh	Fari: title of emperor
Meri, Méri	Meri, Méri
Saba (Kush)	Sébé
Kara, Karé	Karé
Ba-Ra	Bara, Bari (Peul)
Ramses, Reama	Rama
Bakari	Bakari

In Chapter X of his *Archéologie de l'Afrique Noire,* Pédrals mentions the Burum, found in the Upper Nile and the Benue region of Nigeria; the Ga-Gan-Gang, in the area of the Great Lakes and Ghana, Upper Volta, and Ivory Coast; the Goula-Goulé-Goulaye, on both the Nile and the Shari. We should add that Gilaye is a Senegalese name of Sara origin.

Kara-karé

According to Pédrals, the Kara form a nucleus living on the border of the "Anglo-Egyptian" Sudan and Upper Ubangi. The Karé live near the Logone River; the Karékaré, in the northeast of Nigeria.

Karékaré is only the redoubling of Karé, a word combining Ka+Ra, or Ka+Ré. The Kipsigi-Kapsigi are found in the area of the Great Lakes and in Northern Cameroon; the Kissi, northeast of Lake Nyasa and in the forest areas of Upper Guinea. . . .

This list could be prolonged indefinitely and thus localize in the Nile Valley the early habitat of all the Negro peoples scattered today over the different parts of the continent. This identity of names could suggest a recent migration. It is therefore preferable to probe more deeply into the origin of a few peoples, such as the Yoruba, Serer, Toucouleur, Peul, and Laobé, and show that their point of departure was indeed the valley of the Nile.

Before doing so, we shall comment on the legendary people called Ba-Fur, sometimes referred to as Red, sometimes as Black. *Ba* is the collective prefix preceding all names of peoples in Africa. It can be compared with *Wa* in Egyptian, Coptic, and Wolof, meaning: those of, them, etc. This plural ending in languages where it appears as a suffix, could explain the origin of the Egyptian plural in *w:*

Bak-w: servants (Egyptian)
Sumba-wa: the Sumbs
Zimbab-we.

Ba-Fur has the same formation as Ba-Pende: the Pende; Ba-Luba: the Luba. Without venturing to draw a conclusion, I must point out that in Wolof *Pour*=yellow. Ba-Fur could designate not a tribe of Red men or Blacks, ancestors of the Serer, but a tribe of the Yellow race. This would explain the Mongoloid features found in West Africa and also perhaps the cultural relations between Africa and America, attested by the resemblance of such words as:

Loto: canoe, in Wolof, and in North American Indian languages (as in Sara and Baguirmian).
Tul: name of a city in Senegal.
Tulé: name of an Eskimo land; German song.
Tula: name of a city in Mexico.
Inuit: men, in Eskimo (cf. Gessain, *Les Esquimaux du Groenland à l'Alaska,* p. 5).
Init, Ai-nit: men, in Wolof.

In the nineteenth century Bory de Saint Vincent described the Eskimos, some of whom were almost as black as the blackest of Africans, despite the latitude:

> Whatever the reason, both sexes, more tanned than people in Europe and Central Asia, darker than any other Americans, are even blacker the farther north one goes; an additional proof that it is not, as generally believed, the heat of the sun that causes black skin-color in certain intertropical regions. It is not rare to find Eskimos, Greenlanders, and Samoyeds at 70 degrees latitude who, darker than Hottentots at the opposite extreme of the old continent, are almost as black as Wolof or Kaffirs on the Equator.[5]

Egyptian Origin of the Yoruba

In his volume, *The Religion of the Yorubas* (Lagos: C.M.S. Bookshop, 1948), J. Olumide Lucas traces the Egyptian origin of this people as follows:

> CONNECTION WITH ANCIENT EGYPT. Whilst it is doubtful whether the view of an Asiatic origin is correct, there can be no doubt that the Yorubas were in Africa at a very early date. A chain of evidence leads to the conclusion that they must have settled for many years in that part of the continent known as Ancient Egypt. The facts leading to this conclusion may be grouped under the following heads:
> A. Similarity or identity of language;
> B. Similarity or identity of religious beliefs;
> C. Similarity or identity of religious ideas and practices;
> D. Survival of customs and names of persons, places, objects, etc.
> (Introduction, p. 18).

The author then cites many words common to Egyptian and Yoruba:

ran: name
bu: place name
Amon: concealed
miri: water
Ha: large house
Hor: to be high
Fahaka: silvery fish
naprit: grain (or seed).

On the identity of religious beliefs, Lucas cites impressive facts:

> Abundant proof of intimate connection between the ancient Egyptians and the Yoruba may be produced under this head. Most of the principal gods were well known, at one time, to the Yoruba. Among these gods are Osiris, Isis, Horus, Shu, Sut, Thoth, Khepera, Amon, Anu, Khonsu, Khnum, Khopri, Hathor, Sokaris, Ra, Seb, the four elemental deities, and others. Most of the gods survive in name or in attributes or in both (p. 21).

Ra survives among the Yoruba with his Egyptian name: Rara. Lucas cites the word *I-Ra-Wo,* which designates the star that accompanies the rising sun. This word starts with a vowel prefix, typical of Yoruba, an essentially phonetic language according to the author (we would say: like all African languages). Its other components are: *Ra,* the Egyptian word, and *Wo:* to rise. Lucas suggests that *Rara,* meaning: not at all, in Yoruba, indicates that they formerly swore by this god.

Similarly, the name of the lunar god, Khonsu, is found among the Yoruba as Osu (the moon). Lucas reminds us that the occlusive *kh* does not exist in Yoruba, and that if a foreign word contains *kh,* it must follow this procedure: if *kh* is followed by another consonant, a vowel is added and forms a syllable according to the consonant-vowel rule in Yoruba. If *kh* is followed by a vowel in a word of more than one syllable, it is simply dropped. This is the case with the word *Osu.*

Amon exists in Yoruba with the same meaning it has in ancient Egyptian: hidden. The god Amon is one of the first deities known by the Yoruba and the words *Mon* and *Mimon* (holy, sacred) are probably derived from the name of that god, according to Lucas. *Thoth* · would become *To* in Yoruba.

Next the author offers an interesting etymological analysis of the word *Yoruba.* He points out that the West African term meaning "to exist" becomes *ye* by changing one vowel. When doubled into *yeye* it means: she who makes me exist, whence *yeye mi*: my mother, she who gives me life. Incidentally, *yaye* means "mother" in Wolof, Sara, Baguirmian, etc. *Yeye* is often contracted into *ye* or *iya; yemi:* my creator, in Yoruba, is applied to the Supreme Deity.

Furthermore, the Egyptian term *Rpa* is the name of the hereditary prince of the gods, by which Seb was known in ancient Egypt during the feudal period (the author says). *Rpa* probably evolved into *ruba,* in accordance with Yoruba linguistic rules: introduction of a vowel between two consonants and changing *p* to *b*. If we consider *yo* as merely a variant of *ye,* we get *Ye+Rpa*=Yoruba, which would probably mean "the living *Rpa* or the creator of *Rpa.*"[6]

Lucas presents an equally interesting analysis of the name applied to sheep by the Yoruba. He starts from the fact that the Greek word *aiguptos* is usually derived from the Egyptian: *Khi-khu-ptah,* which means the temple of the soul of Ptah. The walls of that temple were covered by pictures of sheep, along with other animals. Consequently, the name of the temple could be applied by the people to the animals depicted. In Yoruba, *a-gu-to*=sheep, and is to be compared with *ai-gup-tos* of the Greeks. This example would seem to indicate that the emigration of the Yoruba came later than the contact between Egypt and the Greeks. . . .

Finally, with regard to identical religious beliefs, the author cites the idea of a future life and that of a judgment after death:

the deification of the king;
the importance attached to names;
the strong faith in a future life.

Here Lucas recalls that all the ontological notions of the ancient Egyptians, such as Ka, Akhu, Khu, Sahu, and Ba, are found in Yoruba. These words exist verbatim in Wolof and Peul, as will be seen below. The belief in the existence of a guardian spirit is but one aspect of *Ka.* Lucas expands, for 414 pages, on the study of these beliefs and discusses in detail their identification with Egyptian beliefs. He concludes by noting the existence of Yoruba hieroglyphics and cites several examples. The identity of the Egyptian and Yoruba Pantheon alone would suffice to prove early contact.

What we know of the Yoruba people—even its legends—shows that it probably settled in its present location relatively recently, after a migration from east to west. With Lucas, we can thus consider as an historical fact the joint possession of the same primitive habitat by the Yoruba and the Egyptians. The Latinized form of Horus, from which the Yoruba Orisha seems to derive, would lead us to think that their migration was not only later than the contact with the Greeks, but also later than contact with the Romans.

To conclude, let us note that Pédrals mentions, on page 107, the

Kuso Hill near Ife and the existence of a Kuso Hill in Nubia, near ancient Meroë, west of the Nile "in the heart of the land of Kush."

Origin of the Laobé

Where do they come from? In my opinion they are a fragment of the survivors of the legendary Sao people. As a matter of fact, what do we learn about the Sao from the Bornu manuscripts and the excavations of Messrs. Griaule and Lebeuf?

1. Their name was *Sao* or *So;* 2. they were giants; 3. they danced all night long; 4. they left innumerable terra cotta figurines; and 5. these statuettes reveal an ethnic type with pear-shaped head.

All five of those traits are found in the Laobé.

Like the Sao, the Laobé bear as their sole totemic name that of So or Sow, which has been mistaken for a Peul name. The only sacred object still left them, the instrument with which they carve, is called a *Sao-ta*. They are all giants, both men and women, easily attaining a height of six feet or more, when they are relatively unmixed. In addition, they have extraordinarily handsome limbs and are always built like athletes. Their skulls are pear-shaped, identical with those of the ethnic type seen on Sao statuettes.

The Laobé's only occupation is to carve wooden kitchen utensils made from tree-trunks for all the other castes in African society, not only for the Peul. This fact, in addition to their height, helps us to place their original habitat in the vicinity of a mountainous wooded area. A basic preoccupation of the Laobé woman, who spends much of her time dancing, is to make figurines, baked or not, for the children of other castes.

The Laobé were wrongly considered to be a caste of Peul and Toucouleur sculptors. This error was partly caused by the fact that they speak Peul and Toucouleur, which led people to believe that this was their mother tongue. That was not true. It was overlooked that the Laobé are always bilingual, at least in Senegal. They speak Wolof as fluently as Peul, and their accent in Wolof is not that of a Peul or Toucouleur. They seem to be a people that has lost its culture and whose scattered remnants adapt haphazardly to circumstances by learning the languages of the regions in which they reside. We have already noted that their basic totemic name is *Sow*. The other totemic names borne by the Laobé reflect their mixture with the Peul, Toucouleur, and other ethnic groups. The reverse is also true; thus, one can explain how the Peul can be named *Sow* as well as *Ba* and *Ka* which, in my view, are the only appropriate names for them. (Ba+ Ra = Bari.)*

The dissolute nature of the Laobé's morals confirms the idea of a people that has lost its culture and is no longer attached to any tradition. An equally essential preoccupation of the Laobé is to steal donkeys to make up a herd to serve as a dowry at the time of the numerous ephemeral marriages they contract. The real ownership of the donkeys handed over to the bride's family matters little. Besides, the family is under no illusion and its strategy is to get rid of the animals within 48 hours, either by selling them or trying, not always successfully, to make the unsold animals unrecognizable by dyeing them a different color. Despite all these "legitimate" precautions, if the victims are able to identify and seize their beasts—not without encountering strong verbal resistance from the Laobé—the marriage remains no less solid than any other Laobé union, for the bridegroom has fulfilled his duty and is free from all reproach.

Furthermore, a Laobé woman knows that sculpture is merely a pretext and that the principal source of wealth is the herd of donkeys. She is economically secure only when she weds a talented thief. If her mate does not excel in this field, the wife will constantly throw this up to him and the marriage will last even less time than usual. For all these reasons, the usual distinction between two categories of Laobé, sculptors and non-sculptors, is no longer very important.

The Laobé are bellicose but seldom come to blows. The classic scene is that of two adversaries advancing one toward the other at a pace slow enough to allow the crowd time to intervene. Swearing and hurling insults with all his might, each antagonist drags behind him a long stick weighing several pounds. As soon as the onlookers have separated them, both opponents feel that they have done their duty; the scuffle is ended but the insults continue.

The Laobé are the noisiest and the most socially undisciplined of all the Africans I know. A Laobé woman spends her time quarreling and deceiving her husband. . . .

The Laobé live scattered over different villages in Senegal and elsewhere. They have no fixed dwellings; it is inaccurate to say that they inhabit the Futa Toro (in Senegal) or the Futa Jallon (in

---

*See "Origin of the Peul," below.

Guinea), territories of the Toucouleur and Peul. They form sporadic groupings within larger ethnic groups. The Laobé of Senegal can no longer pinpoint their original habitat; their social organization has completely dissolved; they no longer have traditional chiefs. The most respected member of the group rides a mule, while donkeys are reserved for the others. . . .

They seem to have borrowed circumcision from other Senegalese populations. They swear by the Sao-ta, the instrument they use to hollow out the tree-trunks after these have been felled by the axe; they use the same instrument for circumcision. A Laobé often excessively resorts to the expression: "May God make me flee from the sao-ta if ever I do such a thing!" He then breaks his oath almost immediately. . . .

In other words, the Laobé are a branch of the Sao, scattered after the destruction of their culture. Other branches probably went elsewhere. At Wadi-Halfa, in Nubia, Champollion discovered a stela depicting Mandu,[7] a Nubian god, offering to Osorta-Sen, a Pharaoh of the Sixteenth Dynasty, the peoples of Nubia, which included two tribes called Osaou and Schoat. These names are strangely reminiscent of the legendary people called the Sao, who were known to have settled around Lake Chad. There are still Schoat on the banks of the Logone. (Cf. Baumann; Delafosse, however, identifies these Schoat as Arabs.)

Origin of the Peul

At first sight, one might believe that the Peul originally came from that part of West Africa where Semitic Moors and Blacks long remained in contact (Delafosse, *The Negroes of Africa*). Though the hypothesis of this crossbreeding must be accepted, the initial site where it took place must be sought elsewhere, despite appearances.

Like other West African populations, the Peul probably came from Egypt. This theory can be supported by perhaps the most important fact to date: the identity of the only two typical totemic proper names of the Peul with two equally typical notions of Egyptian metaphysical beliefs, the *Ka* and the *Ba*. What was the role of the *Ka* and the *Ba* in ancient Egypt? Moret answers this question in *Le Nil et la civilisation égyptienne* (p. 212):

The *Ka,* which united with the *Zet,* is a divine being that lives in the sky and does not appear until after death. We were wrong to define it, with Maspero, as the double of the human body, living with it, but leaving it at the moment of death, and being restored to the mummy by the Osirian rites. The formula for the spiritualization of the king shows that while Horus purifies the *Zet,* dematerializing it in the Basin of the Jackal, he purifies the *Ka* in another basin, that of the Dog. . . . *Ka* and *Zet* were thus separated . . . and had never lived together on earth. . . . In the texts of the Old Kingdom, the expression "to pass to one's *Ka*" means "to die." Other texts specify that an essential *Ka* exists in the heavens. This *Ka* presides over one's intellectual and moral forces; at the same time, it purifies the flesh, embellishes the name, and gives physical and spiritual life. . . .

Once the two elements are united, *Ka* and *Zet* form the complete being who attains perfection. This being possesses new properties which make of him an inhabitant of the heavens, called *Ba* (soul?) and *Akh* (spirit?). The soul (Ba), represented by the bird Ba, with a human head, lived in the heavens. . . . As soon as the king is joined by his *Ka,* he becomes *Ba.* . . .

It matters little whether Moret's interpretation of the Egyptian *Ka* and *Ba* is entirely accurate or not. What is essential is that these two notions unquestionably play a role in Egyptian ontology. *Ka* and *Ba* are the only typical totemic names of the Peul. According to what has just been said about the Laobé, we believe that the Peul borrowed from them the name Sow that we hesitate to identify with the third Egyptian term: *Zet. Bari,* another totemic Peul name, is merely a combination of Ba + Ra.

The fourth term in Moret's text, *Akh,* does not correspond to a totemic name, so far as I know, but it has an obvious ontological meaning, in Wolof, even today. In Wolof, *Akh*=that which one is forced to render to others at the time of judgment after death, before attaining eternal bliss. It refers to the fraction of the personality alienated from someone else, directly or indirectly, by inroads made on that person's possessions.

Zet, in Egyptian: the corpse purified and rigid.
Sed, in Egyptian: symbolic death of the aged king and his ritual rejuvenation.
Set, in Wolof: cold, condition of the cadaver; as a verb: to die.

Ka, in Egyptian: can be summarized as meaning the essence of a being who lives in the heavens. Accordingly, it is depicted by two arms raised toward the sky. It has the following meanings: high, above, large, standard, height. In Egyptian, *Ka* would be pronounced *Kao,* which means: high, above, elevated, etc., in Wolof.

Ba, in Egyptian: is represented by a bird with a human head, who lives in the sky. But *Ba,* in Egyptian, also designated an earthbound bird with a long neck. In Wolof, *Ba=*ostrich.

Thus, it is evident that these Egyptian metaphysical notions met with different fates, depending on the peoples who transmitted them. While, in Wolof, the Egyptian meaning is preserved, in Peul, some of them, notably *Ka* and *Ba,* have become totemic and, as it were, ethnic names.

We would have to assume that the Peul are one of the numerous tribes which produced Pharaohs in the course of history. This is also true of such Serer tribes as the Sar, the Sen, and others. Until the Sixth Dynasty (period of the proletarian revolution), only the Pharaoh had a right to the Osirian death and, consequently, fully enjoyed his *Ka* and his *Ba.* Several Pharaohs bore that name, among others, King Ka, of the protodynastic epoch; his tomb was discovered at Abydos by Amélineau. This would be in line with a Peul branch called Kara.

The other Peul names, such as Diallo, are proper names acquired later in other milieus. As for the Peul language, it is naturally related to all other Senegalese languages, in particular, and to Black African languages in general. The relationship among Peul, Wolof, and Serer emphasizes their basic unity.

Originally the Peul were Blacks who later mixed with a foreign white element from the exterior. The birth of the Peul branch would have to be dated in the period between the Eighteenth Dynasty and Lower Egypt, a period of considerable crossbreeding with the foreigner.

Origin of the Toucouleur

Like the other populations that constitute the Negro people, the Toucouleur came from the Nile basin, the region called the "Anglo-Egyptian" Sudan. This is proved by the fact that today in that region, among the Nuer, we find the typical totemic names of the Toucouleur who live on the banks of the Senegal River, thousands of kilometers away.

"Anglo-Egyptian" Sudan	Senegal (Futa-Toro)
Kan	Kann
Wan	Wann
Ci	Sy
Lith	Ly
Kao	Ka (Peul)

In the same region, in the Nuba Mountains (Hills of Nubia), we find the Nyoro and Toro tribes. In Uganda-Rwanda, we also find the Kara tribe. At the present time in Abyssinia, there is a tribe called Tekruri, which leads us to think, in the event that the Senegalese Toucouleur (Tukulor) are a fraction of that tribe, that the region of Tekrur, instead of giving its name to the Toucouleur, acquired it from them when they settled there. In addition, there is a Nyoro tribe in the "French" Sudan, where the Toucouleur also sojourned before reaching the area to be called the Tekrur, north of the Senegal. From there, they slowly went down toward that river, whose banks were immediately named Futa-Toro.

A skeptical reader might nonetheless deem these parallels insufficient, so we add still another. We know for a fact that, during the second half of the nineteenth century, the Toucouleur, already Islamized, had left the banks of the Senegal River to penetrate the interior, settle in Sine-Salum and convert the Serer of that region. The great Toucouleur marabout (religious teacher) who tried to accomplish this, a contemporary of Lat Dior,* was named Ma Ba Diakhou. The area won over to Islam by the Toucouleur was baptized Nyoro by the ancestors of Ma Ba: Nyoro du Rip. According to their own traditions, the Toucouleur now living on the banks of the Senegal had probably once resided in the area called Nyoro of the Sudan. . . .

Origin of the Serer

The Serer probably came to Senegal from the Nile basin; their route was said to be marked by the upright stones found at the same latitude, from almost as far away as Ethiopia to Sine-Salum. This hypothesis can be supported by a series of facts taken from the analysis

---

*Lat Dior, Senegalese patriot, Damel (King) of Cayor. Converted to Islam by Ma Ba, he led the resistance to the French, died in 1886.

of an article by Dr. Joseph Maes on the upright stones in the "French" Sudan village known as Tundi-Daro.[8]

Dr. Maes attributes the origin of those stones to Carthaginians or Egyptians, whom he supposes to be Whites. He explains the name of the village as follows: *Tundi,* he reports, derives from a Songhay word meaning stone. *Daro* probably comes from the Arab *Dar,* meaning house: the final *o* is dropped so that what remains may be identical with the Arab word. Thus, Tundi-Daro would mean: house of stone.

That analysis could be acceptable if only those stones represented a house, or if one could somehow find that they look like a house. But Dr. Maes knows that this is impossible and his text reports a group of facts ruling out any idea of human habitation:

> They are monoliths cut in the shape of a phallus, usually with the head (glans) well delineated, the grooves follow the lines of the glans, and the pouch is depicted by rounded bulges whose longitudinal folds resemble those of the scrotum. Other smaller stones are not phallus-shaped. Deprived of rounded protuberances, with the triangle outlined in the form of a pubis, by the union of the lower two-thirds with the upper third they seem instead an attempt to represent the female organ.

How does he then interpret them? "It can be accepted as plausible that these monoliths mark the site of a cemetery, each stone marking the grave of a male or female corpse." This idea would be interesting and arguable if one could find even a semblance of bones under those stones. But Dr. Maes adds: "The fact that we have found only a few bone fragments has very little weight against this hypothesis. It is possible that the bodies were cremated and only the ashes and a few bones spared by the flames were buried."

That line of reasoning is unacceptable from start to finish. These cannot be considered graves because there are no skeletons. The few bones that Dr. Maes was ready to identify prove that, if there had originally been skeletons there, they would not yet have been destroyed.

What do the stones really represent? They correspond to an agrarian cult; they symbolize the ritual union of Sky and Earth (by depicting the two sexual organs) to give birth to vegetation (female), vegetation that nourishes mankind; in other words, to make the seed grow.

As a matter of fact, according to archaic beliefs, the rain corresponds to the fecundation of the Earth (Mother Goddess) and the Sky (Father God), heavenly deity who becomes atmospheric with the discovery of agriculture (a concept borrowed from Mircea Eliade). Vegetation growing after that union was considered a divine product. Whence the idea of a cosmic Trinity that evolved through a process of successive incarnations until the Trinity of the Father, the Son, and the Virgin Mother, later replaced by the Holy Spirit, passing through the Triad: Osiris, Isis, Horus.

Since like begets like, they cut the two sexual organs into the stone to invite the deities to unite so that the lifegiving vegetation might grow. In short, it was his eagerness to assure his material existence that incited man to this practice. The vital instinct, archaic materialism, could accept only this transposed, disguised form of metaphysics that would evolve uninterruptedly toward idealism.

There, then, in our opinion, is the sense of those representations. Incidentally, such phallic stones are not tied to a solar cult except insofar as the sun is related to the rain; it is inaccurate to make it into sun worship, allegedly pastoral—and thereby Hamitic (including the nonsense usually associated with that word). Such sun worship, supposedly due to shepherds and warriors, stems from the imagination, not from any verifiable fact.

On the contrary, a people who practiced such a cult had to be essentially agricultural; this automatically eliminates the Eurasian steppes and Nordic regions, cradles of nomadic shepherds. Needless to say, there are no phallic stones in those areas. These are found only in lands inhabited by Negroes or Negroids, or in places that they have frequented, the area that Speiser calls "the great megalithic civilization," which extends from Africa to India, Australia, South America, Spain, and Brittany. It is known that the menhirs and dolmens of Brittany date back to an epoch of an agricultural and copper civilization. Moreover, Spain and Brittany were stopovers for the Phoenicians, a Negroid group, en route to pick up tin from the British mines. That megalithic civilization in Brittany belongs to the second millennium, the period when the Phoenicians frequented those regions. This combination of facts should leave no doubt on the southern and Negro origin of the megaliths in Brittany.

Having proved the agricultural character of the societies to which we owe those megaliths, let us call attention to another contradiction in Dr. Maes's article. He assumes that the dead were cremated. But cremation is practiced by nomads who, by virtue of their vagabond-age, cannot worship at fixed tombs. They retain this custom every-where, even when they become sedentary (Romans, Arya of India). Corpses are burned so they may be carried along, not buried. The ag-ricultural people to whom the Tundi-Daro megaliths must be attrib-uted could not have burned their dead. It must be possible to find their bones by following indications that we shall provide presently.

But Dr. Maes goes into detail about the people responsible for those stones: "Anyone familiar with Black psychology can state al-most categorically that these works which require a considerable amount of effort, without any immediate apparent usefulness, without any relationship to the natural functions of eating and copulating which alone interest the black man, have not been executed by the black race."

Because of its contradictions, that is perhaps his most interesting passage. In fact, it is inconceivable, according to the logic supposedly characteristic of the mature, cultured, modern Western mind, that the same pen which described the "well-delineated glans" and the stones shaped like a woman's sex could have written a few lines later: "without any relationship to the natural functions of eating and copu-lating which alone interest the black man."

Nor could one expect the same writer who has just interpreted "Tundi-Daro" as "house of stone" to call these stones "works which require a considerable amount of effort without any immediate appar-ent usefulness." And why does the author get bogged down in his own contradictions? Simply to be able to say, at the end, that a Car-thaginian or Egyptian origin must be sought for the stones. In other words, to bring everything back to a source that he believes or wants to believe white.

This attitude, typical of the Western world when we are concerned, shows how absolutely necessary it is for us to dig out our own past, a task that no one people can do for another, because of passions, na-tional pride, and racial prejudice resulting from an education dis-torted from the ground up. If pebbles were found in Africa, one would seek an outside origin for them with the preconceived idea, ex-pressed or tacit, that "anyone familiar with the Blacks can assert cat-egorically" that this pile of pebbles cannot be attributed to them.

Who, then, is responsible for those upright stones? Not the current residents of the Tundi-Daro region. On that point the author is firm: "No oral tradition has survived among the present inhabitants of

Tundi-Daro. When questioned, the oldest and most learned residents reply that those stones were always known to their fathers and grandfathers, but that the latter knew nothing about the men who had worked them." That statement by the author is not an interpretation, but a fact, so we can use it.

But, who, then, is really responsible for those stones? In all probability, the African people still located in the same area, at a relatively short distance from Tundi-Daro, a people which still practices the cult of upright stones. This ethnic group is the Serer. We suggest them for the following reasons:

The Serer still practice the cult of upright stones in Sine-Salum. For them it has several meanings, including the one listed above. The Serer are still the only rainmakers in northern Senegal. They are essentially farmers and it is solely for agricultural reasons that they invoke the rain by traditional rites. . . . To support this hypothesis, we can suggest a deeper and more cogent reason resulting from an analysis of the name Tundi-Daro: *Tund*=hill, in Wolof and Serer. *Daro*= union, in the sexual sense of the term. Note, however, that *Daro* is a most respectful term, not to be confused with the vulgar expression, but nonetheless referring to sexual relations. Thus, it could easily be a question here of a ritual union.

The final *i* indicates the plural. Tundi-Daro: the hills of union, in Wolof. In Wolof today, it would not be possible to find a more perfect or more grammatically correct expression to translate this idea: the hills of union. Besides, this expression is exclusive, the only adequate one. It translates the notion of a ritual union which takes place on the hills. Why on the hills? Precisely because these rites of union took place on high ground, mountains, hills, considered sacred because they represent the point where sky and earth seem to touch: the idea of the "center of the world," Jerusalem, the Kaaba of Mecca, the sacred mountain of the Mongolian *Shaman* (sorcerer-priest).[9]

But, in this particular instance, if our theory is correct, if our analysis of the name Tundi-Daro is more than an attractive coincidence, it is at least indispensable that hills exist in Tundi-Daro. This condition is fulfilled; there are indeed hills in Tundi-Daro. "Tundi-Daro is backed against reddish sandstone hills, partly covered by sand," writes Dr. Maes in the same article. Hence, we are dealing here with an identity: the name of the village results from two palpable realities that surround it: the hills and the phallic stones in their ritual meaning. . . .

Until the contrary is proved, we must maintain that the Serer passed through Tundi-Daro and spent some time there. If that is true, it must be possible to produce further proof by a systematic search for graves in the surrounding mounds. The Serer bury their dead as the Egyptians did; except that mummification had to be abandoned because of the scarcity of cloth and the improvement of hygienic conditions which had caused it in Egypt. Above the tomb, instead of a pyramid, the Serer place a cone-shaped roof that covers the soil. On this plain, where stone is scarce, brick construction is replaced by straw. The roof finally crumbles and may cave in, but there generally remains a small mound of earth on the site of the ancient grave.

The corpse's attire depends on the financial status of his relatives; he is placed in the grave with all his household utensils and the familiar objects used during his lifetime for, like the Egyptians, the Serer believe that life continues after death just as it unfolded on earth.[10] Once again we can see the importance of analyzing ethnological facts in African history and the relative certainty that linguistic considerations can provide. We also see the advantage to be derived from ethnographical research judiciously carried out.

The magnitude of the doctor's errors, his state of mind which makes him distort problems before attacking them—a characteristic over which he has no monopoly—indicates how necessary it is for us to interpret our own culture, instead of persisting in seeing it only through Western eyes. We must retain from these works all the facts that are carefully and objectively reported, but the interpretations, that is, the efforts to understand those facts, to explain them, and to establish ties of cause and effect between them, should not simply be taken for granted.[11]

Our reasoning, however, although persuasive, is marred by a contradiction which could have passed unnoticed had we not called attention to it. But, since we seek nothing but the truth, our zeal for objectivity forces us, whenever the occasion arises, to emphasize the factual and remove any possible doubt. The Serer indeed still practice the cult discovered at Tundi-Daro. But their language, though very close to Wolof, is not the source of the term Tundi-Daro. This expression is basically Wolof, not Serer. This fact deserved mention. Unless we are faced here with a chance phenomenon, the cradle of the

Wolof language would have to be extended toward the east, toward the bend of the Niger, to the ancient site of Ghana. Or else, the area of Wolof expansion would cover a much broader area than it currently does: banks of the Senegal, bend of the Niger, Chad, and perhaps even beyond. Other facts support the Nilotic origin of the Serer. The holy city that they created on arriving at Sine-Salum is named Kaôn. This is also the name of an Egyptian city where hieroglyphics have been found.

The Serer's celestial god, whose voice is the thunder, is named Rôg, to which one often adds *sen,* an adjective indicating nationality. While Rôg is to be compared with the Egyptian god Ra or Ré, also a celestial deity, *Sen* recalls certain Nubian kings, certain Egyptian Pharaohs, such as Osorta-Sen, Perib-Sen. This observation is the more striking because the Nubian monarch, Taharqa, claimed Osorta-Sen as his ancestor. Furthermore, Perib-Sen restored the coat-of-arms of Upper Egypt when he came to power. Thus, the Sen Pharaohs were essentially from the south. Finally, the plain of Sen-aar or Sin-aar, recalls the plain of Sin in Senegal, inhabited by the Serer. Currently, in Central Africa, there is a people called Séré, whom we cannot automatically identify with the Serer. It would be more helpful here to try to sift out the common stem of all these names:

Séré: man, in Séré-hulé, altered form: Sarakollé, Sarakole.
Sara: peoples of Chad.
Séré: tribe in Central Africa.
Sérère: Serer, a people of Senegal.

We may assume that the root common to all these names would be the generic term for man, as is the case with the Bantu. In fact, *Ba-Ntu*=the men. The stem *Ntu* of Bantu occurs in Wolof: *Nit*=man; and in Egyptian: *Nti*=man, someone; in Peul: *Neddo*=man. This designation of a people by a generic term meaning man has been general throughout Black Africa, starting with Egypt.

South of the Nuer and the Dinka, we find the Luoluo, a name resembling that of the Lolo in Senegal, a tribe of the Séré, and Falli are found to the south of the Chad, south of the Kotoko and Choa. This last name resembles that of the Nubian Schoat tribe (Baumann, pp. 319–320). Fall, incidentally, is a typical Serer name.

To quote Pierret, Serer means: he who fixes the limits of the temples, in Egyptian. This meaning would be consistent with the religious fervor of the Serer, one of the rare ethnic groups in Senegal not yet converted to a modern foreign religion.

Champollion the Younger reported the existence in Egypt of a caste of priests called *Sen.* Nobility and clergy had the same rank; there were often priestly kings. Several Pharaohs of the earliest dynasties were Serer, judging from their names: Pharaoh Sar and Pharaoh Sar-Teta, both of the Third Dynasty (cf. Pierret, *Dictionnaire archéologique*); Pharaoh Perib-Sen, fifth Pharaoh of the First Dynasty, and Osorta-Sen, of the Sixteenth Dynasty.

At the time of those early dynasties (excluding, of course, the last Pharaoh listed), the Negro Egyptian race was still practically free of any racial admixture, as proved by the monuments from those periods depicting a distinctly Black type. Yet, all the civilizing elements were already present, including writing and sciences. From that epoch to the end, Egyptian civilization simply lived on the knowledge acquired during those first dynasties and the earlier period. Much later the Scythian, Greek, Persian, Roman, Arab, and Turkish invasions altered the Egyptian type, but it never ceased to retain its basic Negro features (modern Fellahs, several Peul tribes).

Origin of the Agni

The Agni (Añi) also seem to be of Egyptian origin if we consider the first name that always accompanies that of the king: Amon, an Egyptian deity. There was, for example, Amon Azenia, an Añi king who lived in the sixteenth century, and Amon Tiffou, an Añi ruler of the seventeenth century,[12] and Amon Aguirc, an Añi monarch of the nineteenth century, who signed a treaty of alliance with Louis-Philippe (cf. *Encyclopédie mensuelle d'outre-mer,* April 1952).

We could compare: Añi, Oni (name of the Nigerian king of Ife), Oni (name of Osiris), Anu (name of a predynastic Black race of Egypt). In *The Book of the Dead,* there are several passages where the name of Osiris is followed by the ethnic term Ani: Hymn of Introduction to *The Book of the Dead;* the Judgment, etc.; Hymn to Ra at Sunrise. In Chapter XV we find the Hymn to Osiris, taken from the Ani papyrus, and in the same chapter we read: "Osiris Ani, the royal scribe in truth . . . " (*The Book of the Dead,* translated by Wallis Budge. London, 1898).

Origin of the Fang and Bamum

In an article published in the *Encyclopédie de la France d'outre-mer* (December 1951, pp. 347–348), Pédrals reports that Father Trilles, after making a series of studies, is convinced that the Fang had "some contact with Christian Ethiopia during their ancient migration." This is a people who, as we noted earlier, still had not reached the coast during the nineteenth century in its northeast-southwest trek.

Similar studies by M. D. W. Jeffreys point to a connection between the Bamum and the Egyptians; Pédrals writes:

> Having noted in several books on Egypt the vulture-pharaoh and serpent-pharaoh relationships, and especially the fact pointed out by Diodorus: that the Ethiopian and Egyptian priests kept an asp curled up in their hats; having also noted various examples of zoomorphic two-headed representations, particularly in *The Book of the Dead (Ani papyrus)*, folio 7, M. D. W. Jeffreys declared himself convinced that "the Bamum cult of the king derives from a similar Egyptian cult."

This observation by M. D. W. Jeffreys can be linked to the legend that a Damel of Cayor had a vulture which was fed exclusively on the human flesh of slaves. The legend probably exaggerates by reporting that whenever the vulture uttered cries of hunger, a slave was killed so that the vulture might feast on his entrails. This vulture belonging to the king of Cayor (Senegal) was named Geb. In Egyptian, Geb signifies the Earth, the reclining god.

Origin of the Moors

The Moors are Arabs, recent arrivals from Yemen, having come during the Islamic invasions (seventh century). As already indicated, their numerous manuscripts, that carefully reproduce their genealogy and the date of their departure from Yemen, fully prove this. The Moors produce these manuscripts on any occasion. They are certainly not ignorant of their origin which they know down to the smallest detail. Their testimony must be taken seriously.

It is useless to disregard those manuscripts and try to find origins and an antiquity on the African continent, which the Moors do not have—merely to make them a part of the hypothetical white race that supposedly settled Egypt early, only to disappear gradually after a long period of crossbreeding.

LADIES KNEELING ON MATS HAVE THEIR EAR-RINGS ARRANGED BY A LITTLE SERVING—MAID.

FROM A WALL-PAINTING IN THE TOMB OF NAKHT AT THEBES   DYN. XVIII (ABOUT 1425 B.C.)

GUESTS SEATED IN CHAIRS ARE BEING SERVED WITH FOOD AND DRINK AND ADORNED WITH ORNAMENTS. BOTH MEN AND WOMEN WEAR COLLARS AND BRACELETS AND HAVE CONES OF FRAGRANT OINTMENT ON THEIR HEADS. THE WOMEN ALSO WEAR EAR-RINGS AND FIL-LETS WITH LOTUS FLOWERS DROOPING OVER THE FOREHEAD.

FROM A WALL-PAINTING FROM A THEBAN TOMB, NOW IN THE BRITISH MUSEUM   DYN. XVIII (ABOUT 1500 B.C.)

GUESTS AT FEASTS WITH ATTENDANTS

42.   The Peul Type. Note the beads worn about the waist, a practice linked with Negro African sensuality.

43. The Peul Type. Ramses II, as a boy (reproduced by Pirenne in Vol. II of his work). Note the typical braid of prepubescent noble children, and compare with Black Africa. (Musée du Louvre.)

CHAPTER X

Political and Social Evolution of Ancient Egypt

A. First Cycle: The Old Kingdom

The political unification of the Nile Valley was effected for the first time from the south, from the kingdom of Nekhen in Upper Egypt. Narmer's Tablet, discovered by Quibbell in Hierakonpolis, retraced its various episodes. Capart rightly identified, it seems, King Narmer with the legendary King Menes depicted on Plate 5.

The capital of the united kingdom was transferred to Thinis near Abydos. This was the period of the first two Thinite dynasties (3000–2778). By the Third Dynasty (2778–2723), centralization of the monarchy was complete. All the technological and cultural elements of Egyptian civilization were already in place and had only to be perpetuated. For the first time in Egypt, Pharaoh Zoser introduced architecture in hewn stone.[1] His strong Negro face with characteristic features dominated that period (pl. 6). In reality, the other Pharaohs of the dynasty were no less Negroid; Petrie affirmed that this dynasty, the first to give Egyptian civilization its almost definitive form and expression, was of Sudanese Nubian origin.[2] It was easier to recognize the Negro origin of the Egyptians when the initial display of their civilization coincided with an unquestionably Negro dynasty. The equally Negro features of the protodynastic face of Tera Neter and those of the first king to unify the valley, also prove that this is the only valid hypothesis (pl. 4). Similarly, the Negro features of the Fourth Dynasty Pharaohs, the builders of the great pyramids, confirm this (pl. 7–10).

Examining the figures in chronological order, we see a homogeneous, ethnological picture, able to enlighten us on the true origin of the ancient Egyptians. This is because, under the Old Kingdom, prior to the widespread contacts with white-skinned races of the Mediterranean, the Negro Egyptian race was practically untouched by cross-breeding. . . .

"With administrative centralization in the Third Dynasty," writes Jacques Pirenne, "there was no longer any noble or privileged class."[3] However, the clergy, guardian of the faith that established the king's authority, was a corps apart, well organized and relatively independent. Until then it had exercised its spiritual guardianship at the coronation of the king in the temple at Heliopolis. But, to make his power absolute, the king clashed with the clergy. From then on he renounced the Heliopolis coronation and had himself crowned in his own palace at Memphis. He proclaimed the principle of his omnipotence by divine right, added "Great God" to his titles, and was free from any human control. The advent of the Fourth Dynasty, with the Giza pyramids, showed that the monarchy had reached its zenith.

Thereafter the regime again evolved toward feudalism. The courtiers constituted a special corps of dignitaries which would make itself hereditary by usage, and soon by right. The cycle just described was twice more to be repeated almost identically and the history of ancient Egypt was to end without ever developing into a republic nor creating true secular thought. The feudal system that had just triumphed with the Fifth Dynasty reached its peak with the Sixth. It then engendered general stagnation in the economy and the administration of the State in urban as well as rural areas. And the Sixth Dynasty was to end with the first popular uprising in Egyptian history.

Obviously, division of labor on the basis of craftsmanship already existed. The cities doubtless were active centers of trade with the eastern Mediterranean. Their idle poverty-stricken masses would take an active part in the revolt. The mores of the nobility created a special class of men: servants contracted for varying tenure. The text describing these events[4] shows that the country had plunged into anarchy; insecurity reigned, especially in the Delta with the raids by "Asiatics." The latter monopolized the jobs intended for Egyptians in the various workshops and urban building yards.

The wretched of Memphis, capital and sanctuary of royalty, pillaged the city, robbing the rich and driving them into the streets. The movement soon spread to other cities. Saïs was temporarily governed by a group of ten notables. The situation throughout the city was poignantly described in that text:

Thieves become proprietors and the former rich are robbed. Those

dressed in fine garments are beaten. Ladies who had never set foot outside now go out. The children of nobles are dashed against the walls. Towns are abandoned. Doors, walls, columns are set aflame. The offspring of the great are thrown into the street. Nobles are hungry and in distress. Servants now are served. Noble ladies flee . . . [their children] cringe in fear of death. The country is full of malcontents. Peasants wear shields into the fields. Man slays his own brother. The roads are traps. People lie in ambush until [the farmer] returns in the evening; then they steal whatever he is carrying. Beaten with cudgels, he is shamefully killed. Cattle roam at will; no one attends them. . . .
Each man leads away any animals he has branded. . . . Everywhere crops are rotting; clothing, spices, oil are lacking. Filth covers the earth. The government stores are looted and their guards struck down. People eat grass and drink water. So great is their hunger that they eat the food intended for the swine. The dead are thrown into the river; the Nile is a sepulcher. Public records are no longer secret.

It would seem that an attempt was made at the same time to desecrate the sacred texts, but this is difficult to verify. . . .

Apparently, the poor, at least for a time, retained the position thus acquired, for economic life and trade regained their normal course; wealth reappeared, though no longer in the same hands: "Luxury is widespread but it is the poor who now are affluent. He who had nothing, possesses treasures, and the great flatter him . . . "

So the first cycle of Egyptian history ended with the collapse of the Old Kingdom. It had begun with the feudalism that preceded the first political unification; it closed in anarchy and feudalism. Monarchy sank into feudalism without being directly attacked. In fact, the principle of monarchy could not have been gravely threatened. Perhaps there were a few timid attempts at self-government in the Delta cities, as at Saïs. But this was probably a temporary solution dictated by the suddenness of the crisis and the lack of public authority that followed the invasion of the Delta by the Asiatics. Cities on the invasion route were abruptly compelled to assure their own safety as they faced the common enemy. Confronted by this situation, the former provincial governors in Upper and Middle Egypt set themselves up as independent feudal lords, freed henceforth from any royal overlordship, though they did not ever question the principle of monarchy itself. On the contrary, each in his own way was trying to be king; they called themselves kings of their own regions. Apparently, the bureaucratic apparatus, which weighed so heavily on the poor, along with royal absolutism, was the main target. . . . After that revolution, all Egyptians had a right to the "Osirian death," the privilege of survival in the hereafter, previously reserved for the Pharaoh as the only one with a *Ka,* a soul, in the sky.

Two facts, however, must be noted. The discontent was strong enough completely to disrupt Egyptian society throughout the entire country. But it lacked direction and coordination, the strength of modern movements. That would have required a level of popular education incompatible with the possibilities and forms of education at the time. Above all, it was the size of the territory that overcame the insurgents. The country was already unified and royalty could take temporary refuge in the surrounding provinces, if only in the guise of an embryonic feudalism. The sack of Memphis shows that the monarchy could have been definitely conquered and swept away if the Egyptian kingdom were reduced to the size of a single city comparable to the Greek city-state.

Throughout history, until technical progress and education paved the way for better coordination of insurrectional activity (1789), peoples have always been conquered by the size of the kingdoms whose social regimes they wished to transform. A study of the Asiatic mode of production really boils down to an analysis of the historico-economic factors that led to early unification in Egypt and opposed it in Greece. A comparison of the two societies reveals a residual factor, linked to the prior stage of nomadic life among the Greeks. To be sure, it is reasonable to assume that all peoples, including the Egyptians, experienced a period of nomadism before becoming sedentary. But nowhere did nomadic life have so profound or so prolonged an effect as among the Indo-Aryans of the Eurasian plains. Their civilization has remained marked by it even in our day and many practices of civilized nations in Europe today are related ethnologically to that period, for example, cremation of the dead, the patriarchal family, and so on.

When we consider the failure of a revolution during Antiquity, it is evident that the non-revolutionary character of the social structure is less important than the size factor. In reality, whatever may have been the "virtues" of Egypt's social organization, it finally created, like Greece, intolerable abuses and uprisings as virulent as the Greco-Latin revolts. These revolts in Egypt would surely have triumphed if the territorial dimensions had been the same. Only the size of the kingdom condemned the insurrections in advance. During the period of anarchy, most of the Egyptian cities temporarily had autonomous governments, which disappeared with the revival of the kingdom.

B. Second Cycle: The Middle Kingdom

The second cycle of Egyptian history covers the period from the Sixth to the Twentieth Dynasty. In the course of the Sixth Dynasty, Memphis, the capital, was sacked by the rebels. After that Dynasty, royalty gradually took refuge in its less-accessible southern homeland. . . . This happened repeatedly in Egyptian annals. Whenever the nation was threatened by an invasion of Whites from Asia or Europe via the Mediterranean, whenever such incursions disrupted national life, the political power migrated to the south, toward its ancestral habitat. Inevitably, salvation, in other words, the reconquest of political power, reunification, and national rebirth were achieved through the efforts of the legitimate Black dynasties indigenous to the south. In the Delta, were concentrated all the branded White slaves, the fruits of the victories of Merneptah and Ramses II over the Indo-European hordes. Their freed descendants, from the time of Psammetichus on, were to seal Egypt's doom, as we shall see.

The city of Heracleopolis, in Middle Egypt, temporarily played the role of capital during the Ninth and Tenth Dynasties. There were parallel reigns throughout that period of anarchy. In Upper Egypt, the city of Thebes never failed to act as the guardian of tradition and legitimacy. Its princes founded the Eleventh Dynasty, which immediately undertook national reconstruction. However, it required no less than two centuries of struggle and effort to reunify Egypt in 2065 B.C. This was the second reunification for which southern kings were responsible.

The Eleventh Dynasty revived the administrative centralization of the Third Dynasty, with all of its corollary effects. To weaken the great lords, the throne depended on the little people, the merchants. According to Pirenne, administrative centralization brought about abolition of the inalienability of landed property which might be shared by the various descendants of the owner. This disrupted family solidarity a second time. The Twelfth Dynasty fully established the triumph of administrative centralization.

Suddenly Egypt was invaded by new Asiatic hordes: the Hyksos (1730–1580). . . . They presumably introduced war chariots and the horse into the country. In reality, they occupied only the eastern region of the Delta, with Avaris as their capital. Their barbarism was indescribable. The Theban kings continued to reign in Upper Egypt, where royalty again found asylum.

During the reign of the Hyksos ruler, Apophis, hostilities erupted between the "Semitic-Aryan" invaders and the Black dynasty of Upper Egypt, which represented the Egyptian people's determination to liberate the nation. Mobilizing the country under its authority, it expelled the Hyksos in 1580 B.C. and reunified Egypt for the third time with the founding of the glorious Eighteenth Dynasty under Queen Hatshepsut. In the eyes of the Egyptian nation, she personified monarchical legitimacy.

On the death of Queen Hatshepsut, the great reign of the Eighteenth Dynasty began under Tuthmosis III, that other outstanding southern monarch, whose mother was a Sudanese Nubian. He overpowered all the States of Western Asia and the islands of the Eastern Mediterranean, reducing them to the status of vassals compelled to pay annual tribute. This was the case with Mitanni (an Indo-European state on the Upper Euphrates), Babylonia, Cilicia, the Hittite State, Cyprus, Crete, etc. Syria and Palestine were simply integrated into the Egyptian kingdom. It was at this time that, according to Herodotus,[5] the garrison which would become the Colchians, was stationed on the shores of the Black Sea; but this seems questionable.

In any case, Egypt was then the foremost technical, military, and imperial power in the world. Foreign vassal rulers vied with each other in submissiveness; each tried to use the most obsequious formulas in addressing the Pharaoh: "I am your footstool. I lick the dust from your sandals. You are my sun," a Syrian vassal wrote to Amenophis IV. After the Eighteenth Dynasty, the Egyptians acquired the habit of holding as hostages the sons of vassal rulers of Asia and the Mediterranean, training them in the Pharaoh's court in the hope that they might later govern their countries as good vassals. This was one of several causes of the extensive, profound, and almost exclusively Egyptian influence on Western Asia and the Mediterranean.

Like the Third Dynasty, the Eighteenth promoted administrative centralization. Administrative posts again ceased to be hereditary.

According to Pirenne, even in the priestly domain, property again became alienable; the family was dislocated anew by the disappearance of the right of the eldest son, the power of the husband, and paternal authority. The regimen of written contracts sanctioned by royal registry, income tax, and written and scholarly red tape returned (cf. Pirenne, I, 20). Naturally, we could expect Egyptologists to criticize Pirenne; his book is the most important postwar synthesis of the "mysterious" history of Egypt. By no stretch of the imagination could such a work on so delicate and difficult a subject fail to be criticizable. Nevertheless, his volume brings rationality to a subject too often treated in a way to defy human reason. With Pirenne, the first elements of rational explanation of the political, economic, and social history of Egypt make their appearance.

In reality, the basic contradictions in the Asiatic economic system were sufficiently developed in Egypt for the germs of dissolution to be visible. Though the land might be the property of the Pharaoh, the people had enough free access to it to continue their economic activity. It had become alienable. An individual could bequeath or sell it. Thus, the collective aspect of land ownership had become extremely theoretical. On the other hand, the State collected taxes, shrewdly assessed, but everyone worked for himself. Except for the conquered Indo-Europeans, systematically enslaved and branded to prevent their escape, Egypt, unlike Greco-Roman and feudal societies, had no servile labor force.

The labor force was therefore free and contractual in urban or rural communities, comparable in that respect to workers in capitalist regimes today. In this second form, capitalism could appear and, as a matter of fact, there was a marginal capitalism with the appearance of a business class who rented land in the countryside and hired hands to cultivate it. Like the farmers of capitalist Europe, their sole aim was to amass huge profits. The same business practices were carried on in the cities: interest-bearing loans, renting or subletting personal property or real estate for the purpose of financial speculation. Apparently, the only safeguard to prevent these practices from developing into a strong capitalism was the practically inalienable liberty of the Egyptian citizen. This was a special basic feature of the juridical organization and the Egyptian ethical code.

In Greco-Latin Antiquity, capitalist production depended on a slave market, 99.99 percent of which consisted exclusively of White slaves from the North and Northwest of Europe. Etymologically, "slave" derives from "Slav." In the Middle Ages, the master had power of life and death over the slave. During the European capitalist period, it has been shown, especially in England,[6] how the State favored the subjugation of the people by the industrial middle class. To the great satisfaction of nascent capitalism, peasants whose lands were confiscated and who no longer had anything but their labor to sell in the cities, as well as all the unemployed whose numbers both delighted and disturbed the bosses of bourgeois business, were reduced to the level of convicts or of branded slaves. The imperialist State somehow took it upon itself to find a cheap, servile, docile labor force for the budding industry of the economically dominant middle class.

The alienation of the worker in the Egyptian countryside never had more than minor importance. The State was responsible for organizing production and achieving the optimum yield from the soil. So the division of labor on the administrative level was extremely sophisticated. It is hard to imagine today the technical efficiency that the Egyptian state organization had attained. Facing the threat of the Asiatic hordes and Indo-European barbarians, for a long time Egypt was saved by the headstart it had made in the field of organization. This enabled it to recover with surprising speed after an invasion or a period of anarchy.

After the period of administrative centralization under the Eighteenth Dynasty, the monarchy again took the path of absolutism . . . This phase was inaugurated by Amenophis IV (Akhnaton), who first sponsored official monotheism, to make it the universal religion of an Empire that had itself become "universal." Though his religious reform failed, his absolutist policy survived and was consolidated under the Nineteenth Dynasty with the deification of Ramses II.

Meanwhile, at the end of the reign of Amenophis and under Horemheb, Egypt was faced with social conflicts of great scope. These were created by the excesses of bureaucratic agents, the crushing weight of taxation, and the poverty of the people. Horemheb decided to espouse social justice and enacted a series of laws intended to protect the weak and improve their living conditions. These laws were designed to punish government employees, soldiers, and judges guilty of theft or fraud against the little people. But the reforms had only a temporary effect. With the deification of Ramses II, feudal privilege and royal absolutism reappeared. The clergy recovered its former prerogatives, as at the time of the Sixth Dynasty. The temples again profited from immense holdings, endowed with immunity which empowered them to dispense justice to their tenants (cf. Pirenne, I, 21). At the same time they received tens of thousands of Aryan slaves branded with a hot iron. These were the only cases of a slave labor force in Egypt for large-scale production.

Ramses II and his father, Seti I, founder of the Nineteenth Dynasty, did not belong to the original Egyptian nobility. They owed their accession to the throne to the arbitrary choice by Horemheb, himself a ranking Egyptian army officer before becoming Pharaoh, of an officer in the "foreign" war chariot corps as his successor: Ramses I.[7] The latter's grandson, Ramses II, distributed plots of land to the professional army that he had created; it became a privileged corps.

The end of the reign of Ramses II and that of Merneptah witnessed great migrations of peoples that upset the ethnic balance around the Mediterranean and in Western Asia. Circa 1230 B.C., Merneptah conquered the first large coalition of Indo-Europeans led by Merirey, as we have seen. . . . Another group, probably the Etruscans, under Aeneas, settled in Italy; these were the same ones who had joined the Libyan coalition defeated by Merneptah. On the Egyptian inscriptions they were designated by the name Tursha. After the defeat, the survivors followed the coasts of Cyrenaica as far as Queen Dido's Carthage, or traveled there by the open sea. In any event, according to the ancient tradition related by Virgil, it was probably after that detour that Aeneas and his men, the Etruscans, reached Italy. Herodotus ascribes the same Asian origin to the Etruscans, who were perhaps the survivors of the destruction of Troy by the Achaeans. Only a few decades separate the fall of Troy (1290?) and the great Dorian drive. So the Tursha could certainly have left Asia Minor either during the siege of Troy or a few years later with the Dorians.

But Carthage was not founded until the ninth century B.C. If the visit of the Etruscans to that port were proved, three or four centuries elapsed between their departure from Asia Minor and their arrival in Italy. What could they have been doing en route? Should we then assume that they spent considerable time in Libya, where their stay is in fact mentioned in Egyptian documents? Perhaps they remained there after the coalition was defeated by Merneptah. During that sojourn they doubtless acquired various elements of Egyptian culture (sarcophagus, agrarian life, the divining art, architectural skills) which they definitely lacked at the outset. The 9,000 or so captives taken in battle Merneptah gave as slaves to the various temples to express his gratitude to the gods. . . .

So it was as a prisoner of war, transformed into a slave, chained and branded, that the white man first entered Egyptian civilization. Careful study of the documents could lead to no other conclusion. One may pretend to be ignorant of these facts, but they are indestructible. The white man contributed nothing to Egyptian civilization, any more than Black Africa today contributes anything to modern technical civilization. . . . This is why it is inaccurate to speak of components of separate Egyptian civilization—for it was Negro, devoid of any outside European or Semitic contribution, as shown by Egypt's deep affinities with Negro psychology. Its civilization may have disappeared precisely because it was unable to borrow from later cultures and became a victim of its own homogeneity. Accordingly, there is good reason to attack that new form of deception which lists separate components in Egyptian civilization (as history textbooks did in French-speaking Africa as recently as 1965). What then would we not have to say about Greek, Roman, Spanish, or French civilizations or "races"? Here again we detect that tendency to dissolve Black African historical consciousness in the fragmentation of minute details.

From then on Egypt continually had to defend its borders against the immense thrust of white-skinned peoples from the north, from the sea, and the east. After his victory over the Libyans west of the Delta, Merneptah set out on an expedition to pacify Palestine, where the first migratory wave of "sea peoples" had arrived. A passage inscribed on the "Stela of Israel," quoted by Pirenne, described those events. . . . Incidentally, this was the first mention of the name Israel in history (1222 B.C.). Palestine owes its name to the Palestiou. This was what the Egyptians called the Philistines, Indo-Europeans, probably Achaean fugitives, who settled in the region during that epoch.

Pharaoh Merneptah speaks of all those peoples as rebellious vassals. The text specifically states that the land of the Hittites is pacified. This confirms the notion that, after the conquests of Tuthmosis III (1580 B.C.), the Hittite land never ceased being a vassal of Egypt. . . . Merneptah sent them wheat to avoid a famine, just as a colonial power today might do for one of its dependencies.[8] The end of his reign saw an expansion of feudalism (cf. Pirenne, II, 464). The White slaves given to the temples were employed by the priests either in farming or in the local militia. With the collapse of the central power, local militias increasingly assumed local security func-

tions. Taking advantage of the anarchy, Syrian, Palestinian, and Libyan slaves had rebelled under the leadership of foremen and military officers of their race who supervised their labor. Pirenne quotes
a passage from Diodorus relating that Aramaean slaves captured by
Ramses II took advantage of the turmoil to revolt and create near
Memphis a village that they controlled and called Babylon, in memory of their country. Similarly, Phrygians founded a shortlived village
called Troion, in memory of Troy.

Efforts to quell the disorders came once again from the south.
Seti, viceroy of the Nubian Sudan, marched on Thebes to reestablish order in Egypt. He obtained the support of Amon's clergy,
wed Tausert, Queen of Upper and Lower Egypt, widow of Minep-
tah-Siptah, who seemed in the eyes of the people to symbolize monarchical legitimacy. As Seti II, he reigned from 1210 to 1205 and
succeeded temporarily in restoring law and order.

Shortly thereafter, Egypt again sank into anarchy and insecurity,
under the great feudal lords. This lasted until Setnekht created the
Twentieth Dynasty (1200). After he had reigned for two years, his
son, Ramses III, succeeded him under extremely difficult conditions.
He had to face a new invasion of "sea peoples," by land and sea,
especially by the Palestinian Philistines. He reinforced the Egyptian
fleet assigned to defend the mouths of the Nile. The most formidable
coalition ever witnessed during Antiquity was formed against the
Egyptians. It comprised the whole group of white-skinned peoples
who had been unstable since the first migrations in the thirteenth century; . . . they set up their immigration camp north of Syria. . . .

Thanks to superior organization, the Egyptian armed forces scored
a dual victory, on land and sea, over that second alliance. The fleet of
the "Peoples of the North" was entirely destroyed and the invasion
route through the Delta was cut. At the same time a third coalition of
the same white-skinned Indo-Aryans was being assembled, again in
Libya, against the Black Egyptian nation. Yet, this was not a racial
conflict in the modern sense. To be sure, the two hostile groups were
fully conscious of their ethnic and racial differences, but it was much
more a question of the great movement of disinherited peoples of the
north toward richer and more advanced countries.

Ramses III demolished that third coalition as he had destroyed the
first two. . . . As a result of this third victory over the Indo-Aryans,
he took an exceptional number of prisoners. This enabled him to increase appreciably the slave labor force on royal construction sites

and in the army. Such was invariably the procedure for acclimating white-skinned persons in Egypt, a process that became especially widespread during the low period. By bearing this in mind, we may avoid attributing a purely imaginary role to people who contributed absolutely nothing to Egyptian civilization.

Ramses III then carried his defense to Phoenicia (*Djahi,* in Ancient Egyptian[9]), on the northern frontier of the Egyptian Empire. He took personal command of the fleet and, near the Palestinian coast, he annihilated the fourth coalition in 1191 B.C. This disaster was unprecedented; the enemy fleet was totally destroyed to prevent its escape. A new slave labor force was now available. But he could not import an entire people into Egypt. So he settled them on the very land where they had been defeated. This was the origin of the Philistines. The "sea peoples" were definitely demoralized after that setback. Yet, we can understand, after all those upheavals, to what extent the ancient ethnic groups must have been disrupted all around the Mediterranean, except for Egypt which alone had been able to repulse the Indo-Aryan invasion.

Meanwhile, the Libyans in the western part of the Delta, were organizing still another coalition, the fifth directed against the Black Egyptian nation by the Indo-Europeans. Ramses III defeated them at Memphis in 1188 B.C. After that date the White Libyans never again revolted against Egypt, but they tried by every possible means to infiltrate peacefully and to settle there as serfs or semi-serfs, working at various kinds of manual labor, as farmers or artisans, especially in the Delta. They were also employed in the army as an auxiliary foreign corps called *Kehek.*[10]

The situation was identical in the Nubian Sudan where Libyans were also used as semi-serfs in the army. But the Libyans settled in the Delta, because of its proximity. These people, whose alien slave origin was obvious, would gradually be freed by Egyptian law. Later, some would become notables as a reward for "loyal" services to the Egyptian ruler. Yet, their slave origin would never be forgotten by the true Egyptian national, even when they took advantage of troubled periods to exercise control of a given district in the Delta where military command had been entrusted to them by the Pharaoh. We shall see how these foreign elements, who felt no real sentimental attachment to Egyptian soil, were to undermine political mores beginning with Psammetichus.

To protect the country against invasion, Ramses III had to resort to conscription, drafting one Egyptian national out of ten (cf. Pirenne, II, 476). Because of their immunity, we do not know whether this measure was applicable to the temple properties. Since Ramses II, Libyans and other White foreigners who were recruited into the auxiliary armed services had farmed land belonging to the royal domain, of which the well-informed Egyptian administration kept a strict accounting. To prevent their flight in troubled periods, Ramses III had them all branded with the seal of the local administration. This old Egyptian practice leaves no doubt about their slave status, whether they were farmers in peacetime or enrolled in the auxiliary forces in time of war. Authors often misuse the term "mercenaries" to designate those who were, in fact, slaves bearing the indelible mark of their royal master. . . .

The Egyptian army was losing its nationality. It was rapidly becoming a force of free mercenaries or semi-slaves commanded by national officers; only the high command and a few detachments of archers remained Egyptian (cf. Pirenne, II, 477). This procedure reached its climax under the Libyan usurpers of the Twenty-sixth Dynasty, more precisely, under Psammetichus. . . .

The political and social situation under Ramses III and immediately after his death is described in detail by the Harris Papyrus, an exceptionally long document of some 115 pages. A review of the land registry shows that the temple properties constituted one-seventh of the arable lands which, according to modern authors, covered about 5 million acres. Lands allocated to the Theban temples, enjoying general immunity, amounted to approximately 585,000 acres, with 86,436 slaves to farm them. For Heliopolis, there were 113,000 acres and 12,364 slaves; for Memphis, 6,800 acres and 3,079 slaves.

Donations to the temples by Ramses III during the 31 years of his reign were of comparable modesty:

3,648 deben (328 kg.) or 722 lbs. of gold;
6,027 deben (525 kg.) or 1155 lbs. of silver;
18,854 deben (1696 kg.) or 3730 lbs. of copper and bronze;
28 deben (2.3 kg.) or 5 lbs. of precious stones;
155,381 jars of wine, or 5,012 per year; and
2,418 head of cattle, or 78 per year.

Pirenne, who reports those statistics, observes that the donations were hardly enough to provide for the celebration of the cult of the king. All the figures cited seem ridiculously low, compared with the size and density of the population at the time. Quoting several ancient writers, Marcel Reinhard and André Armengaud[11] adopt an average of seven to eight millions for the population of Egypt, corresponding to a density on the order of 200 per square kilometer (some 520 per square mile).

Though the White slaves were rather numerous, the Egyptian population could easily absorb them. The 30,000 slaves acquired during the Asian expedition of Ramses III represented a small minority when we consider the density of the indigenous national population. We can easily understand how that indigenous population was able to remain ethnically Black throughout Antiquity, despite the influx of Whites. This was why, strictly speaking, Egypt never adopted an economy dependent on slaves; that always remained marginal.

On the other hand, it is clear that demographic pressure alone is not a determining revolutionary factor for, if that were true, the most violent revolutions in history would have taken place in Egypt, not in Greece. The Egyptian fortress resisted the tempest provoked by the great migrations of the twelfth century. After those, Ramses III succeeded more or less in stabilizing the situation on the administrative, economic, and financial levels. Egypt enjoyed a century of domestic tranquility with an uneventful succession of rulers from Ramses III to Ramses XI.

Nevertheless, the germs of feudalization had reappeared and were again undermining Egyptian society. Reinforcement of the clergy's administrative autonomy and the intensification of its immunity finally created a veritable clerical state within the Egyptian State. Like the king, the high priest of Amon centralized enormous powers in his hands; clerical justice was often rendered by oracle. This defective system, which would even be utilized to select the king and other officials and to make governmental decisions, passed over into Greece where it long continued, alongside the secular institutions.

The end of the Twentieth Dynasty was characterized by vigorous social conflicts, the most important of which were strikes by workers at the Theban necropolis. The form of their grievances indicates that they were absolutely free but disciplined workers; their demands for food could hardly endanger the monarchical principle. They broke through the barricades set up by the guards who supervised their labor. Then they marched on Thebes, the capital. The vizier (*djit*)[12] of Upper Egypt received the written complaints of their delegates and, with the assistance of the high priest of Amon, gave them 50 sacks of wheat. The strikers went back to work, which shows how mild their demands were (cf. Pirenne, II, 501). Beyond the bounds of legality, there were acts of banditry and desecration of sepulchers.

While Upper Egypt was becoming feudalistic, Libyans in Middle Egypt fomented a revolt that quickly spread to the Delta. This involved White slaves who had been in Lower Egypt since Ramses II and III and who were settled on plots of rigorously inventoried land. During the low period, they tried to seize every opportunity to become free and even to establish a kind of military feudalism. Facing this definite threat to national unity, the country was saved for the fifth time by the South, the Nubian Sudan. Ramses XI appealed to the viceroy of Nubia, who destroyed the city of Hardai, center of the insurrection (cf. Pirenne, II, 506). . . .

The social decomposition of the regime reached a climax and experienced a phase similar to that of the Sixth Dynasty. Thus, Egyptian history again described a cycle that ended in feudalism without a frontal attack on the monarchical system. Nevertheless, Egypt's prestige abroad was so intact that the "King" of Tyre declared: "All industries came from Egypt and all sciences first shone forth there" (cf. Pirenne, II, 505).

C. Third Cycle: Later Evolution

For the third time Egypt sank into feudalistic anarchy that lasted about three centuries: 1090 to 720 B.C. It did not end until a Sudanese Nubian intervention ignited a rebirth of national consciousness. With the entire Egyptian people behind them, the Pharaohs whose reigns formed the Twenty-fifth Dynasty then stimulated a veritable national renaissance. . . . [13]

The whole history of that dynasty was a supreme effort to form a united front against the foreign invader. Under the Twenty-second and Twenty-third Dynasties, feudalism had attained its zenith. All the Libyan and Achaean "freedmen" who occupied posts of any importance in the army set themselves up as chiefs or "princes" in their localities. Political power was thus usurped and fragmented by the Whites of the Delta, more commonly designated by the generic term

"Libyan." Not one of them, however, was able to impose his authority over the country; anarchy and decadence became general.

When the Libyan usurper, Osorkon, tried to force his son on Thebes as an Amon priest, the Theban clergy fled to the Nubian Sudan. The King of Sudan, Piankhi, moved immediately to reforge Egyptian unity by subduing one after another all the foreign rebels of Lower Egypt. These aliens had formed a new northern coalition under Tefnakht. Only two of the alien feudal lords in the north had refused to join that alliance. . . .

So the country was divided into two camps: in the north, the coalition of White rebels, former slaves; in the south, the authentic Egyptian nation solidly behind the Sudanese king. In the eyes of the clergy, the guardian of tradition, this full-blooded Black from the land of the ancestors was monarchical legitimacy incarnate.

The battle began at Heracleopolis. Tefnakht was defeated; Nimrod of Hermopolis surrendered. The siege of that city was led by Piankhi in person. He had trenches dug around the town and wooden towers constructed from which catapults hurled projectiles on the besieged city. As a sign of submission, Nimrod sent Piankhi "his diadem and a tribute in gold" (Pirenne, p. 67). Then it was the turn of Memphis, which Tefnakht vainly tried to defend with an army of "8,000 infantrymen and marines." Piankhi attacked from the river, through the port, penetrated the city, and sacked it. He then entered Heliopolis where he was solemnly and ritually crowned Pharaoh of Upper and Lower Egypt.

At Athribis Piankhi accepted the surrender of the last northern rebels, among them Osorkon IV and Tefnakht himself, whose oath of fidelity has been preserved. The colorful description of the Sudanese Pharaoh's extraordinary epic would be inappropriate here. We must call attention, however, to the unity of the authentic Black Egyptian nation fighting under his command against the maneuvers of Libyan feudalism in the Delta. Once again, on the initiative of its prestigious priestly corps, Egypt had sought and found salvation in the south, birthplace of the race's forebears.

In 706 B.C. Shabaka succeeded his brother Piankhi on the throne of Napata and Egypt. Bocchoris had replaced his father, Tefnakht, at the head of the rebels in the Delta. On putting him to death after taking Saïs, Shabaka felt that he was burning a heretic. . . .

The Sudanese dynasty sparked a powerful movement of cultural revival and national resurgence. Shabaka proceeded to restore the great Egyptian monuments. Under his reign, Thebes was governed by another Sudanese prince, who was at the same time fourth prophet of Amon. The King of Napata, the Sudanese Pharaoh, also served as first priest of Amon, so he was both king and priest. Thus, under the Twenty-fifth Dynasty, the Sudan revived theocratic monarchy and extended it over the whole country.

Shabaka transferred his administrative capital to Memphis, then to Tanis, indicating his determination to stamp out any moves toward independence by the feudal lords of the Delta. After the execution of Bocchoris, his son Necho had succeeded him, but as a vassal of Shabaka. After Shabaka died in 701, his nephew Shabataka became Pharaoh.

War with Assyria erupted over Palestine. Commanded by Taharqa,* youngest son of Piankhi, the Egyptian army invaded Asia and marched against the forces of Sennacherib. At first the Egyptians were repulsed. Shabataka was betrayed by the alien vassals of the Delta who refused to aid him against the foreign enemy. But once again the people rallied to his cause and saved Egypt. Artisans and shopkeepers from the Delta cities volunteered to form a militia which routed the Assyrians. Peace was restored and lasted for 25 years. After having Shabataka assassinated, Taharqa ascended the throne in 689 B.C. He proclaimed himself the son of Mout (Queen of the Sudan) and erected a temple in her honor. He continued the same policy of centralization by imposing royal authority even more severely "on the twenty feudal lords who shared the Delta." "To overcome their resistance, he did not hesitate to deport the wives of the princes of Lower Egypt to Nubia, in 680 B.C." (cf. Pirenne, p. 100). The economic, cultural, and especially the architectural renaissance was strengthened by the construction of such monuments as the Column of Taharqa in Karnak, the statues of Mentuemhat and Amenardis. Taharqa intervened in Asia in an effort to regain Egypt's international prestige.

He was betrayed a second time by the alien chiefs of the Delta. This was flagrant in the case of Necho, son of Bocchoris. As soon as the Assyrian army entered Egypt, he selected Assyrian names for Saïs and for his own son, Psammetichus. Saïs became Kar-Bel-Matati and Psammetichus was now called Nabu-Shezib Anni. Necho became the vassal of the Assyrian king, who entrusted him with the principal-

---

*The Biblical Tirhakah.

ity of Athribis (cf. Pirenne, II, 105). With the treason of the Libyan feudal lords, Lower Egypt became an Assyrian province.

Taking refuge at Thebes, Pharaoh Taharqa enjoyed the complete support of the clergy, which refused to legitimize the sovereignty of the Assyrian. Mentuemhat, governor of Thebes, remained loyal to Taharqa, as did the "divine spouse of Amon." Exceptionally energetic, Taharqa returned to the offensive in 669 B.C., recaptured Memphis, and remained there until 666. Again betrayed by the alien feudal lords of the Delta, he escaped to Napata, where he died two years later. His sister was adopted by Amenardis, whom she succeeded as "divine spouse of Amon. . . . "

Shabataka's son, Tanutamon, inherited the throne of Napata. He recruited an army in the Sudan, was acclaimed at Thebes as the legitimate heir of the Pharaohs by the clergy and the divine spouse of Amon. He then attacked Memphis and waged war against a new coalition of all the northern feudal lords. This alliance was defeated and Necho of Saïs was killed in the battle. All the leaders of foreign military feudalism surrendered as humbly as they had previously sworn allegiance to the Assyrian conqueror. Tanutamon proved his magnanimity by restoring them to their former posts. Only Psammetichus, son of Necho, remained loyal to Assyria and fled to the court at Nineveh.

In 661 B.C. Ashurbanipal attacked Egypt and pillaged the city of Thebes. Tanutamon escaped to Napata. The fall of the most venerable city of all Antiquity aroused deep emotion in the world of that time and marked the end of the Nubian Sudanese or Twenty-fifth Ethiopian Dynasty. That date also marked the decline of Black political supremacy in Antiquity and in history. Egypt gradually fell under foreign domination, without ever having known a republican form of government, or secular philosphy, throughout three millennia of cyclical evolution.

Such authors as Malet and Isaac, in their standard French textbook for *sixième* (seventh grade), used to train the younger generation since 1924, have systematically ignored the extraordinary epic of the Twenty-fifth Dynasty, and have tried to play up the reign of "Psammetichus–Nabu-Shezib Anni," the unworthy Libyan usurper who disguised his name to please the alien invader. It would be difficult to imagine a history of France written according to those criteria. The reign of Psammetichus served only to pave the way for foreign rule. . . .

Between Egypt and Greece the ties became progressively closer. Egypt's military and economic alliance with the King of Lydia opened the coasts of Asia Minor and the Sardian kingdom to Egyptian cultural and intellectual influence. This explains why Ionia experienced a cultural awakening earlier than continental Greece. Miletus flourished while Athens and Sparta were still scarcely emerging from barbarism. The Lydians invented or popularized the use of money, which the new economic relations had rendered indispensable.

Psammetichus inaugurated the Twenty-sixth Dynasty (663–525 B.C.), but its most characteristic reign was perhaps that of Amasis (568–526). Under the latter, Egypt definitely lost its independence with the Persian conquest of 525 B.C. . . . Amasis was brought to power by his troops and the mob during the troubles under the reign of Apries (588–569). His popular origins probably explain his secular and democratic conception of government. His legal reforms were extremely important in both the public and private sectors, but Egypt was no longer a power. At the head of the Persian army, Cambyses conquered the country and put Amasis to death.

From a comparison between Greco-Roman society on the one hand, and Egyptian society on the other, it is apparent that, despite its long history, Egypt did not practice slave, feudal (in the Western sense), or capitalist systems of production. Those three economic systems existed there only marginally. In politics, Egypt remained a monarchy, a principle that seems not to have been questioned even during acute crises. Habeas corpus was fully recognized. There was no national slavery (an Egyptian could not be enslaved), all were citizens in the full sense of the word. An individual enjoyed all the liberty consistent with a public law conceived to serve all. The monarchy had succeeded in embodying this idea of the public good; on three separate occasions, the failure of feudalism to supplant it, while preserving its principles and ethics, only made its return inevitable.

There was no solid support for republican ideas; they were not even contemplated. Like the rest of Black Africa, Egypt was unaware of them. The role played by the special characteristics of the social structure can be detected in the nonviolence and moderation of social protest which, except during the crises that terminated the Old Kingdom, never presented the turbulent aspect of revolutions in Greek cities. Yet, assuming that no social organization is perfect and that, despite the virtues of their own set-up, the Egyptians of certain epochs would willingly have shaken off the political regime responsible for social injustice, we can ascribe the failure of such movements in the territorial kingdom to only one factor: size. . . .

In the final analysis, the moving force of history lies in the determination of the oppressed classes to free themselves from their condition. If that condition is intolerable and humanly inadmissible, the rebellious conscience becomes revolutionary. Until now, man has invented nothing worse than slavery to degrade and exploit his fellow man. Hence, the truly revolutionary regimes are the slave regimes, whether the brutal slavery of ancient Greece or the barely disguised but no less virulent slavery of the Western Middle Ages. That is why, with the development of ancient or modern capitalist production, both those societies led to revolution.

But revolution can occur only if the dissatisfied slave element, alienated without compensation, becomes numerically preponderant. This was the case in all the industrial Greek cities of Antiquity, where the citizens (the free men) constituted scarcely one-tenth of the total population.

In Black African kingdoms, where relative detribalization, wars, and the division of labor created marginal slavery, revolution nevertheless did not occur. This is understandable. For a revolutionary situation to have arisen, the enslaved population would have had to be in the majority and sufficiently concentrated to render a revolution possible. We can only guess what the effect of size would have been on a revolutionary movement in Black Africa. Yet, there is reason to believe that such outbreaks would have failed like those that actually took place in a similar territorial setting: in Egypt, for example, after the sacking of Memphis under the Sixth Dynasty, or in China under the Tang Dynasty in 883 A.D.

Like those countries, Black Africa did not have slave, feudal, or capitalist economies in the Western sense. During the period of the slave trade, slavery operated in a way very different from the customary mode that had preceded it. As its States were taking shape, Africa passed through a phase of military democracy or, more accurately, tribal kingdoms. The originality of the Greek societies in the northern Mediterranean is thus easier to understand. Two factors contributed to making possible the revolutionary explosion and its success: First, a social regime or, more precisely, an exceptionally cruel slave system, which gave man no choice except a struggle to the death. Secondly, a small territory, limited to the dimensions of a single city, easily capturable because the revolutionary class was in the majority. Under such circumstances, the ideological structure quickly loses its influence on the minds of the enslaved class.

Even relatively less harsh social regimes have engendered uprisings all over the world. In that sense, all societies have developed sufficiently to generate seeds of disruption. Apparently, the failure of these authentic revolutions, everywhere except in the Greco-Roman world, may be attributable to a single residual factor: the more or less appropriate size of the national territory involved. It was easier for a Greek city to become saturated with slaves because of the smallness and proximity of the cities and because of the Greek constitutions which, without exception, made every alien a slave.

Perhaps the moment is not far distant when we will begin to have the elements of a satisfactory reply to the problem caused by the peculiar nature of Greco-Latin political and social evolution. Perhaps the final explanation will simply lead to a factor of individualistic nomadic selfishness, the blindness of which could not fail to create social catastrophe early, if not immediately. That social catastrophe (capitalist slavery) compelled man to forge the political instruments for his liberation, to find a way out for the entire human species.

*   *   *

Yoruba society, as described by Leo Frobenius in *Mythologie de l'Atlantide* (Chapter IV), is one that could furnish a mine of important information on the politico-social African past. Toward the end, the king exercised a purely nominal authority over all the cities that made up his kingdom. Each city was in reality an autonomous unit, governed by a president (or *balé*) and a senate formed by the assembly of notables. Next to the king, who lived in Oyo, the capital, the high priest, the Oni of Ife, was a venerable personage whose prestige and power practically equaled the king's.

It would be helpful to know whether this shrinkage of royal power preceded or resulted from the British occupation. In the former case, it could be a matter of a budding federation or the decline of a kingdom that had already reached its apogee. The city regimes were mere constitutional kingdoms; whatever Frobenius may think, they were not republics in the Greco-Latin sense of the word. The fact that not one of them attempted its "revolution" and the homogeneity of their politico-social structure attest to an ancient federal link, effective through relatively discreet. As a matter of fact, real autonomy at that time would have increased the possibility of social upheaval because of the urban structure. Could the extraordinary development and relative individualism of Yoruba society be linked in part to that peculiar political structure?[14] . . .

In the final analysis, the common denominator found in economies of the Asiatic type (Black Africa, China, India, pre-Columbian America, Iran, etc.) is the absence of slavery in the full sense of the term, as a means of production. Thus, the resulting social situations are hardly revolutionary. Secondly, the size of the territory condemns insurrectional movements in advance, even if the situation happens to be explosive. In the Western sense, the feudal system is but a poorly disguised variant of the slave system. This is the fundamental determining factor of historico-social evolution in that it invariably creates capitalist production which leads to revolution that in turn gravitates to socialism.

Consequently, to understand the revolutionary situation of antique societies, we must study the factors that have restricted the growth of this system in certain societies, or stimulated its development in others. . . . The Greek State was founded from birth on slavery and the intangibility of private land ownership. In contrast, the appearance of a State with an Asiatic economic system, as described by Marx and Engels, shows that it did not spring abruptly from the brutal contact of two races, one of which enslaved the other and thus created, from the outset, the conditions for the development of the class struggle and private property. It is the result of organizing, howsoever, a common sedentary life among "citizens" of the same territory. These initial conditions are unfavorable to the appearance of national slavery or the selfish, ill-regulated, overgrown development of private property.

For obvious reasons, this second type of State has existed more often than the first, and the reasons for it are more clearly visible. That is why the Greco-Latin State was a historical exception as against the more general type. The Indo-Europeans were unable to create a slave regime in Iran and India as extensively as in Greece and Rome, because they were unable to occupy those countries in sufficient numbers.

In sum, it suffices for societies with an Asiatic mode of production to be reduced into slavery . . . for them to insert themselves into the historic cycle of humanity. The worldwide emancipation of all the former European colonies which, without exception, were dependent on that means of production, illustrates this idea. It was slavery, in the Western sense, that made a Prometheus of Toussaint Louverture.* . . .

---

*Toussaint Louverture (1743–1803), precursor of Haitian independence. Wendell Phillips called him "the soldier, the statesman, the martyr."

44.   The Sphinx and the Great Pyramid.

45. Monumental Entrances to Pharaoh Zoser's Mortuary Temple. With the step pyramid of Saqqara, they inaugurate the era of great architecture in hewn stone.

46. Cretan Art, Seventh Century B.C. This clearly shows Egyptian influence.

CHAPTER XI

Contribution of Ethiopia-Nubia and Egypt

According to the unanimous testimony of the Ancients, first the Ethiopians and then the Egyptians created and raised to an extraordinary stage of development all the elements of civilization, while other peoples especially the Eurasians, were still deep in barbarism. The explanation for this must be sought in the material conditions in which the accident of geography had placed them at the beginning of time. For man to adapt, these conditions required the invention of sciences complemented by the creation of arts and religion.

It is impossible to stress all that the world, particularly the Hellenistic world, owed to the Egyptians. The Greeks merely continued and developed, sometimes partially, what the Egyptians had invented. By virtue of their materialistic tendencies, the Greeks stripped those inventions of the religious, idealistic shell in which the Egyptians had enveloped them. On the one hand, the rugged life on the Eurasian plains apparently intensified the materialistic instinct of the peoples living there; on the other hand, it forged moral values diametrically opposite to Egyptian moral values, which stemmed from a collective, sedentary, relatively easy, peaceful life, once it had been regulated by a few social laws.

To the extent that the Egyptians were horrified by theft, nomadism, and war, to the same extent these practices were deemed highly moral on the Eurasian plains. Only a warrior killed on the battlefield could enter Valhalla, the Germanic paradise. Among the Egyptians, no felicity was possible except for the deceased who could prove, at the Tribunal of Osiris, that he had been charitable to the poor and had never sinned. This was the antithesis of the spirit of rapine and conquest that generally characterized the peoples of the north, driven, in a sense, away from a country unfavored by Nature. In contrast, existence was so easy in the valley of the Nile, a veritable Garden of Eden, between two deserts, that the Egyptians tended to believe that Nature's benefits poured down from the sky. They finally adored it in the form of an Omnipotent Being, Creator of All that Exists and Dispenser of Blessings. Their early materialism—in other words, their vitalism—would henceforth become a materialism transposed to the sky, a metaphysical materialism, if one may call it that.

On the contrary, the horizons of the Greek were never to pass beyond material, visible man, the conqueror of hostile Nature. On the earth, everything gravitated around him; the supreme objective of art was to reproduce his exact likeness. In the "heavens," paradoxically, he alone was to be found, with his earthly faults and weaknesses, beneath the shell of gods distinguished from ordinary mortals only by physical strength. Thus, when the Greek borrowed the Egyptian god, a real god in the full sense of the word, provided with all the moral perfections that stem from sedentary life, he could understand that deity only by reducing him to the level of man. Consequently, the adoptive Pantheon of the Greek was merely another humanity. This anthropomorphism, in this particular case, was but an acute materialism; it was characteristic of the Greek mind. Strictly speaking, the Greek miracle does not exist, for if we try to analyze the process of adapting Egyptian values to Greece, there is obviously nothing miraculous about it, in the intellectual sense of the term. At most we can say that this trend toward materialism, that was to characterize the West, was favorable to scientific development.

Once they had borrowed Egyptian values, the wordly genius of the Greeks, emanating basically from the Eurasian plains and from their religious indifference, favored the existence of a secular, worldly science. Taught publicly by equally worldly philosophers, this science was no longer a monopoly of a priestly group to be jealously guarded and kept from the people, lest it be lost in social upheavals:

> The power and prestige of the mind which, everywhere else, exercised their invisible empire, alongside of military force, were not in the hands of the priests, nor of government officials among the Greeks, but in the hands of the researcher and the thinker. As was already visibly the case with Thales, Pythagoras, and Empedocles, the intellectual could become the center of a circle in a school, an academy, or the living community of an order, drawing nearer first to one, then to the other, setting scientific, moral, and political goals, and tying it all together to form a philosophical tradition.[1]

Scientific, philosophical teaching was dispensed by laymen distinguished from the common people only by their intellectual level or social status. No saintly halo encompassed them. In "Isis and Osiris," Plutarch reported that, according to the testimony of all Greek scholars and philosophers taught by the Egyptians, the latter were careful about secularizing their knowledge. Solon, Thales, Plato, Lycurgus, Pythagoras encountered difficulty before being accepted as students by the Egyptians. Still according to Plutarch, the Egyptians preferred Pythagoras because of his mystical temperament. Reciprocally, Pythagoras was one of the Greeks who most revered the Egyptians. The foregoing is the conclusion of a passage in which Plutarch explains the esoteric significance of the name *Amon:* that which is hidden, invisible.

As Amélineau observes, it is strange that we do not place more stress on the Egyptian contribution to civilization:

> I then realized, and realized clearly, that the most famous Greek systems, notably those of Plato and Aristotle, had originated in Egypt. I also realized that the lofty genius of the Greeks had been able to present Egyptian ideas incomparably, especially in Plato; but I thought that what we loved in the Greeks, we should not scorn or simply disdain in the Egyptians. Today, when two authors collaborate, the credit for their work in common is shared equally by each. I fail to see why ancient Greece should reap all the honor for ideas she borrowed from Egypt.[2]

Amélineau also points out that if certain of Plato's ideas have become obscure, it is because we fail to place them in the context of their Egyptian source. This is the case, for example, with Plato's ideas on the creation of the world by the Demiurge. We know, moreover, that Pythagoras, Thales, Solon, Archimedes, and Eratosthenes, among others, were trained in Egypt. Egypt was indeed the classic land where two-thirds of the Greek scholars went to study. In reality, it can be said that, during the Hellenistic epoch, Alexandria was the intellectual center of the world. Assembled there were all the Greek scholars we talk about today. The fact that they were trained outside of Greece, in Egypt, could never be overemphasized.

Even Greek architecture has its roots in Egypt. As early as the Twelfth Dynasty, proto-Doric columns are found (Egyptian cliff tombs of Beni Hasan). Greco-Roman monuments are mere miniatures as compared with Egyptian monuments. Notre-Dame Cathedral in Paris, with all its towers, could easily be placed in the hypostyle hall of the temple of Karnak; the Greek Parthenon could fit into those walls even more easily.[3]

The typically Negro—or Kushite, as Lenormant writes—kind of fable, with animals as characters, was introduced into Greece by the Egyptian Negro, Aesop, who was to inspire the fables of the Frenchman La Fontaine. Edgar Allan Poe, in "Some Words with a Mummy," presents a symbolic idea of the scope of scientific and technical knowledge in ancient Egypt.

From Egyptian priests, Herodotus had received information revealing the basic mathematical data on the Great Pyramid of Cheops. Several mathematicians and astronomers have produced works on that pyramid; their sensational revelations have not failed to unleash a flood of arguments which, as expected, are not expressed in the form of a coherent, scientific account. Without venturing into what might be considered excessive pyramidology, we can cite the following:

Astronomers have noted in the Great Pyramid indications of the sidereal year, the anomalistic year, the precessions of the equinoxes "for 6,000 years, whereas modern astronomy knows them for only about 400 years."[4] Mathematicians have detected in it the exact value of "pi," the exact average distance between the sun and the earth, the polar diameter of the earth, and so on.

We could prolong the list by citing even more impressive statistics. Could this result from mere chance? As Matila C. Ghyka writes, that would be inconceivable:

> Any single one of these items could be a coincidence; for them all to be fortuitous would be almost as unlikely as a temporary revision of the second principle of thermodynamics (water freezing over fire) imagined by physicists, or the miracle of typewriting monkeys . . . Nevertheless, thus completed and perfected, thanks to the research of Dieulafoy, E. Mâle, and Lun, the hypothesis of Viollet-le-Duc on the transmission of certain Egyptian diagrams to the Arabs, then to the Clunisians, through the intermediary of the Greco-Nestorian school of Alexandria, is quite plausible. Astronomically, the Great Pyramid can be the "gnomon of the Great Year," as well as the "metronome" whose harmony, often misunderstood, echoes throughout Greek art, Gothic architecture, the

first Renaissance, and in any art that rediscovers the "divine proportion" and the pulsation of life.[5]

The author also quotes Abbé Moreux's opinion that the Great Pyramid does not represent the "groping beginnings of Egyptian civilization and science, but rather the crowning of a culture that had attained its apogee and, before disappearing, probably wished to leave future generations a proud testimonial of its superiority."

This astronomical and mathematical knowledge, instead of completely vanishing from Black Africa, has left traces that Marcel Griaule was perceptive enough to detect among the Dogon, however astounding that may seem today.

On numerous occasions, reference has been made to the fact that the Greeks borrowed their gods from Egypt; here is the proof: "Almost all the names of the gods came into Greece from Egypt. My inquiries prove that they were all derived from a foreign source, and my opinion is that Egypt furnished the greater number."[6]

Since the Egyptian origin of civilization and the extensive borrowing of the Greeks from the Egyptians are historically evident, we may well wonder with Amélineau why, despite those facts, most people stress the role played by Greece while overlooking that of Egypt. The reason for this attitude can be detected merely by recalling the root of the question. As Egypt is a Negro country, with a civilization created by Blacks, any thesis tending to prove the contrary would have no future. The protagonists of such theories are not unaware of this. So it is wiser and safer to strip Egypt, simply and most discreetly, of all its creations in favor of a really White nation (Greece). This false attribution to Greece of the values of a so-called White Egypt reveals a profound contradiction that is not the least important proof of Egypt's Negro origin.

Notwithstanding the opinion of André Siegfried, the Black is clearly capable of creating technique. He is the very one who first created it at a time when all the white races, steeped in barbarism, were barely fit for civilization. When we say that the ancestors of the Blacks, who today live mainly in Black Africa, were the first to invent mathematics, astronomy, the calendar, sciences in general, arts, religion, agriculture, social organization, medicine, writing, technique, architecture; that they were the first to erect buildings out of 6 million tons of stone (the Great Pyramid) as architects and engineers—not simply as unskilled laborers; that they built the immense temple of

Karnak, that forest of columns with its famed hypostyle hall large enough to hold Notre-Dame and its towers; that they sculpted the first colossal statues (Colossi of Memnon, etc.)—when we say all that we are merely expressing the plain unvarnished truth that no one today can refute by arguments worthy of the name.

Consequently, the Black man must become able to restore the continuity of his national historic past, to draw from it the moral advantage needed to reconquer his place in the modern world, without falling into the excesses of a Nazism in reverse for, insofar as one can speak of a race, the civilization that is his might have been created by any other human race placed in so favorable and so unique a setting.

CHAPTER XII

Reply to a Critic

I propose here to answer the critical review by Mr. Raymond Mauny, which appeared in the *Bulletin de l'IFAN* (Bulletin of the Fundamental Institute of Black Africa) in the July–October 1960 issue, relative to *Nations nègres et culture*. . . . We apologize for returning to notions of race, cultural heritage, linguistic relationship, historical connections between peoples, and so on. I attach no more importance to these questions than they actually deserve in modern twentieth-century societies. Only my concern about scientific objectivity compels me to direct attention to these themes so long as certain of their aspects are challenged.

As will be seen, our account is devoid of any passion and we ask nothing better than to yield to factual evidence. What we shall try to combat in the name of scientific truth, and what forces us to utilize a notion as delicate as that of race, is a group of arguments that have become so habitual as to pass for scientific truths, which they definitely are not. It is the whole body of hypotheses, distorted into factual experiences, that are likely to lead to error and are still more dangerous than outright dogmatism. . . .

* * *

Mr. Mauny's criticisms begin near the end of his introduction:

What was permissible for the student or the young lycée teacher is no longer allowed the Doctor of Letters, whose title could authorize him tomorrow to teach at the University. And so, despite all my sympathy for the author, whose acquaintance I have made, I consider it my duty, no matter how much it may pain me and him, to say aloud what others are keeping silent out of politeness or for some other motive.

Obviously, Mr. Mauny intends to pull no punches in his attempt to demolish the adverse thesis. If, in spite of that, his arguments should happen to reveal an unexpected fragility, it would be entirely involuntary on his part. As for me, I shall try to reply as objectively as possible, with equal serenity, to all the criticisms formulated here. The reader will be the judge.

According to C. A. Diop, the examination of the bone remains and mummies shows that we are dealing with Negroes: "I affirm that the skulls from the most ancient epochs and the mummies from the dynastic epoch differ in no respect from the anthropological characteristics of the two Negro races existing on earth: the straight-haired Dravidian and the woolly-haired Negro." And later: "When we scientifically cleanse the skin of the mummies, the epidermis appears pigmented exactly like that of all other African Blacks . . . I add that at the present time there are infallible scientific procedures (ultraviolet rays, for example) to determine the amount of melanin in pigmentation. Now, the difference between a White and a Black in this respect is the fact that the white organism secretes enzymes which absorb the melanin. The Negro organism does not secrete any enzymes. The same is true of the ancient Egyptians. That is why invariably, from prehistory to the Ptolemaic epoch, the Egyptian mummy has remained Negro. In other words, throughout Egyptian history, the skin as well as the bone structure of all Egyptians of all social classes (from Pharaoh to Fellah) has remained that of authentic Negroes."

Let us separate the two ideas contained in the preceding passage quoted by Mauny: A. "According to C. A. Diop . . . African Blacks." This is exact; in August 1961 I brought back from Paris samples of mummies that I have indeed cleansed and kept in glass jars at the IFAN. They are at the disposal of all scholars who might be interested and Mr. Mauny, especially, may examine them at his leisure, whenever he so desires.[1]

B. "Now the difference between a White and a Black . . . The Negro organism does not secrete any enzymes." Mauny thinks he is quoting me. Nevertheless, scientific precision requires a clear distinction to be made . . . between ideas expressed by me in *Nations nègres et culture* and those collected [from me] by a journalist unfamiliar with the subject at a mere interview in the Latin Quarter [which M. Mauny interweaves with them]. On reading Mauny's critique, we get the distinct impression that the quoted passage occurs in *Nations nègres et culture;* this is not so. He could easily have avoided the confusion since both documents are available. It is to be regretted that throughout the critique he combines two texts that cannot be placed on the same plane. . . .

All animal and plant organisms contain enzymes; this is a classic question of biochemistry. It is the condition of activation of the enzymes that can differ; sometimes it depends on hereditary factors. Thus, a preponderant racial factor intervenes in the oxidation of tyrosine and its transformation into melanin (in the human epidermis), according to a chemical reaction catalyzed by tyrosinase.

It is also correct that one could trace back, so to speak, to that racial factor and determine its importance, starting from the "dosage of the amount of melanin" contained in the epidermis, especially in the epidermis of an Egyptian mummy. It is also certain that such a study would classify Egyptians among Negroes, according to the samples available to me and that I have selected entirely at random.

> I am not an anthropologist, nor is the author, but I refer the reader to one of the best books on the subject of ancient Egypt: Carleton S. Coon, *The Races of Europe* (New York: Macmillan, 1939, pp. 91–98 & 458–462). In it the racial components of Ancient Egypt are analyzed (Mediterraneans in the Preneolithic, Whites; Tasians on the Abyssinian plateau, Browns with Negroid tendency, Naqada, related but less Negroid; Mediterraneans of Lower Egypt, Whites; and from 3000 B.C. to the Ptolemaic epoch, the history of Egypt shows "the gradual replacement of the Upper Egyptian type by that of Lower Egypt" (p. 96). The later invaders (Hyksos, peoples of the sea, Semites, Assyrians, Persians, Greeks), all belong to white races, with the exception of the Twenty-fifth Dynasty, of Nubian ancestry, as is known.

Coon's work contributes nothing new. If all the specimens of races and sub-races described by him lived in New York today, they would reside in Harlem, including those whose heads and faces "are those of a smoothly contoured fine Mediterranean form"; no anthropologist will dispute me on this. Even Coon would agree with me. But, since the ancient Egyptian is dead, discussion seems possible.

So, let us discuss. Coon's volume is dated 1939. Surprisingly enough, the facts in it with which Mauny challenges me conform basically to my own conclusions. It is merely a question of variants of Negroes and Negroids. Insofar as we adhere strictly to the facts,

Egyptian archeology excludes the idea of an early occupancy of Lower Egypt by a White race. This idea seemed so natural to the first Egyptologists that they stated it almost spontaneously, without trying to base it on the slightest scientific or archeological certainty. A study of Narmer's Tablet would not allow us to affirm it since, in the final analysis, the indecisive nature of the persons depicted and the thinness of documentation would be disproportionate to the importance of the conclusion. All Moret's theories on the anteriority of Lower over Upper Egypt are taken from Egyptian legends of the Greek epoch and freely interpreted.[2]

In Lower Egypt, archeological diggings dating back to the predynastic have failed to uncover the existence of a White type. The Whites of Lower Egypt were transplanted there at a well-known, precise historical epoch; it was during the Nineteenth Dynasty, under Merneptah (1300 B.C.), that the coalition of Indo-Europeans (peoples of the sea) was conquered; the survivors were taken prisoner and scattered over the Pharaoh's various construction sites. Between 1300 and 500 B.C., these populations had time to spread from the Western Delta to the outskirts of Carthage. In Book II of his *History,* Herodotus explains how they were distributed along the coast. Consequently, when Coon speaks of Whites inhabiting Lower Egypt, his statement is not based on any document. It would even remain to be proved that Lower Egypt existed as inhabitable *terra firma* in remote times.

As for the white invaders: Hyksos, Assyrians, Persians, Greeks, etc., the Egyptians always represented them as races apart and were never influenced by them, for the simple reason that the invaders' civilization was less advanced than their own. No one has ever thought seriously of proposing scientifically the influence of any one of these peoples on Egyptian civilization.

Still according to Coon, the conventional representations reveal a slim body, narrow hips, small hands and feet. The head and face "are those of a smoothly contoured fine Mediterranean form"; numerous upper-class types represented by these portraits "looked strikingly like modern Europeans" (p. 96). On the contrary, the type of certain Pharaohs, like Ramses II, appears related to the Abyssinian type.

. . . If the reader, after carefully examining all the reproductions [of Pharaohs and other dignitaries] and noting the social significance of some and the insignificance of others in Egyptian society of that day, then rereads the above passage . . . he will have cause to meditate on the scientific validity of the conventional texts.

The pigmentation of the Egyptian "was usually a brunet white; in the conventional figures the men are represented as red, the women often as lighter, and even white" and the daughter of Cheops, builder of the Great Pyramid, was "a definite blond." Toward the south, near Aswan, the population was evidently darker (brownish-red, brown).

In their paintings and sculptures, the Egyptians depicted foreigners with their racial characteristics: "Besides the Libyans, who have Nordic features as well as coloring, Asiatics, with prominent noses and curly hair, sea peoples from the Mediterranean, with lighter skins and a more pronounced facial relief than the Egyptians are also shown, as well as Negroes," and later . . . "The Mediterranean pigmentation of the Egyptians has probably not changed during the last 5,000 years" (p. 98).

That is the opinion of an anthropologist; I leave it up to you to draw a conclusion. But I cannot help finding it difficult to maintain that a people whose principal components were Mediterranean could be Negro, especially after all the details provided by Coon who, incidentally, nevertheless recognizes Negro contributions.

Singling out Cheops' daughter as "a definite blond" would prove that this was rare, if accurate. The Egyptians were so little white, that when they encountered a white person with red hair, they killed him immediately as a sick person unable to adapt to life. This was certainly a regrettable but comprehensible prejudice between two different races during those remote epochs of history. However, we have an opportunity to scrutinize the profile of Chephren (Cheops' son or brother), which is identified with that of the Giza Sphinx. As we look, we are easily convinced that the hypothetical daughter of Cheops did not owe the color of her blond hair to her father.

As early as the Sixth Dynasty, under Pepi I and his chancellor Uni, Egypt began to import white women from Asia . . . Moreover, Cheops is supposed to have gone so far as to prostitute his daughters to finish building his pyramid: the Great Pyramid that would become his grave. Was it not perhaps rather a question of importing foreign girls for purposes of prostitution?

Concerning Mauny's conclusion, need I recall that, according to the most recent anthropological studies, a plurality, 36 percent, of the Egyptian population was "Negroid" in the protodynastic epoch? Mauny is mistaken about the term "Mediterranean"; it is a euphemism for "Negroid," when used by the anthropologists. In any case, it means "non-white," as is evident from what precedes. What is involved here is the "brown race" (in the melanodermic sense) of Sergi and Elliot Smith. This conclusion is not even a faithful reflection of the forecited facts from Coon's volume, for we cannot see how the principal components are "Mediterranean" in the Cro-Magnon sense of the word, since they are only brown Whites, brown reds, browns of the Abyssinian type, browns with Negroid tendency, the less Negroid Naqada type, and so on.[3]

According to C. A. Diop, ancient authors have also stated that the Egyptians were Negroes. Herodotus, the "Father of History," who wrote about 450 B.C., is quite rightly called upon, for he visited Egypt. But are C.A. Diop's examples as convincing as he thinks? For example, it is not to Egypt that Herodotus is referring (II, 22) when he says, "they are black from the heat," but to the inhabitants of the southern lands, the Ethiopians . . .
"By calling the dove black, they indicated that the woman was an Egyptian" (II, 57). Were not the Greeks (the Hebrews had the same reaction) inclined to call the Egyptians "Blacks" because the latter were darker than they, which is true? Do we not use the same expression in France (whence the family names: Morel, Moreau, Lenoir, Nègre, etc.) to designate persons darker than the average? A Nordic is clearly aware of having lighter skin than a Spaniard or Southern Italian; he will speak of dark skin, brown skin, even black skin, just as we do, moreover, with regard to bathers who acquire suntans on the beaches in summer. Neither of these is a Negro.
Is the example of the Colchians any better? The author quotes a passage from Hèrodotus: "The Egyptians said that they believed the Colchians to be descended from Sesostris' army. My own conjectures were founded, first, on the fact that they are black-skinned and have woolly hair." But why did Mr. Diop fail to include the rest of the passage: "This amounts to but little, since several other nations are so too"? And the adjective *melanochroes* used by Herodotus does not necessarily mean "black." In 1948 Legrand

translated it: "having brown skin." On this subject, cf. also F. M. Snowden, *The Negro in Ancient Greece,* 1948, p. 34.

In the next example, concerning the Indians of the south, I see nowhere mentioned the fact that the Egyptians were Blacks. It is solely a question of Ethiopians.

What precisely is remarkable is that in a digression on the sources of the Nile, Herodotus happens to apply the same ethnic adjective *melanochroes* to the Ethiopians reputed to be black and to the Egyptians that one would like to whiten and consider as leucoderms. To translate *melanochroes* as "having brown skin," is to take a liberty justified only by *a priori* ideas on the skin color of the Egyptians. This is the strongest term existing in Greek to denote blackness; strictly speaking, it should be translated as Negro (*niger-gra-grum*).

The attitude which consists of resorting to an insane misinterpretation of texts instead of accepting the evidence, is typical of modern scholarship. It reflects the special state of mind that prompts one to seek secondary meanings for words rather than give them their usual significance, for that is how deeply embedded *a priori* ideas have become. It is necessary to reread Herodotus' passages in context to know that no scholar whatsoever is entitled to give words a meaning differing from their real connotation. Herodotus was aware that he was describing a Negro race, in the proper sense of the term, a race whose morphological qualities are diametrically opposed to his own (in the sense of opposites: black-white, frizzy-straight, etc.). For him it was not a question of tonalities or nuances within a single race, as Mauny would understand it, for instance, as a distinction between Nordic and Spaniard.

The fact that Egyptians had black skin was for Herodotus an evident truth that he posits, like a mathematician, as an axiom to lead subsequently to the demonstration of more complex facts. Thus the doves in question are only symbols of two women whom the Phoenician traders allegedly took from Thebes to sell them, one in Libya (Oracle of Amon), the other in Dodona, in Greece. . . .

Herodotus wished to show the profound influence of Egypt on Greece, especially in religion. In this particular case, he wanted to prove that the Oracle of Amon and that of Dodona are of Egyptian origin and were founded by women kidnapped from the capital of Upper Egypt, Thebes. He draws this conclusion from the fact that the women were black. To attribute any other meaning to the text does not reflect scientific scholarship; it merely indicates an imperious determination to skirt around the facts, to hold on to what one wants to believe. All the passages from Herodotus are equally explicit from this point of view.

I shortened the second quotation because the rest added nothing to my demonstration. I needed to prove that the Egyptians were black; it mattered little to me to know (I already knew it) that they had this blackness in common with other peoples. Herodotus made that observation solely because he wanted to add a supplementary proof corresponding to this description of the Egyptians. If we continue to the end of the paragraph, we shall see that for Herodotus, the Egyptian had black skin, woolly hair, and was circumcized. Specifically because the Colchians possessed those three characteristics, he considered them Egyptians.

Coming back to the case of the Nordic who judges the populations of Southern Europe as rather dark "without being Negroes," I can only refer to a passage at the end of Chapter I of my *Antériorité des civilisations nègres,** where we discuss the difference in attitude of European and African researchers. In reality, it is evident that, when discussing one's own society, one analyzes without fragmenting it, one grasps traditions almost instinctively, one treats them objectively; nowhere does one dig deep ditches or set up impassable barriers; one does not clutter the investigated terrain with watertight partitions; one is inclined to seek the coherence of facts and usually finds it. When dealing with any other reality, the trend is to pulverize, for in all objectivity there is no more difference between Mauny's Nordic and a Spaniard than between the Ethiopian and the Egyptian on the one hand and the other West African Blacks on the other. To be sure, without ceasing to belong to the same ethnic universe, they are all well aware of the nuances that distinguish them.

Can Mauny state positively that in the Middle Ages, in the days of Barbary, when proper names were being formed in modern Europe, particularly in France, the Morels, Moreaus, Lenoirs, and Nègres did not indeed have some ancestor who justified that appellation? Names were not created gratuitously; one was called "de Vallon" when he came from the valley, "Dupont" if he lived near the bridge, and so on. Why should names implying ethnic origin be applied without any reason? Persons interested in kitchen gossip can easily show that au-

*Chapter XIII of the present volume.

thentic Negro elements were found in various European families during that epoch in France, Germany, and Italy, even if we discount the
Arab influence.

The third quotation criticized by Mauny involves the Padaean
Indians who were never subjugated by Darius. Herodotus describes
their skin color with the same ethnic adjective that he uses for Egyptians and Ethiopians; they are all Blacks (*melanochroes*) and this is
what Mauny fails to see. Such is the logical justification for that quotation.

The passage from Diodorus of Sicily concerning the Ethiopians'
claim that their civilization preceded that of the Egyptians, is interesting historically for the opinion that the Egyptians probably descended from the Ethiopians. It therefore poses the problem of the
Negro's contribution to the formation of ancient Egypt. So, I consider this text more important than those from Herodotus, Strabo,
or the authors of Genesis in this connection. But I insist on saying
at once that archeology proves superabundantly that Egypt was the
civilizing factor on Ethiopia, and not the reverse. I believe it impossible to prove that architectural constructions in Nubia, to cite
but one example, are earlier than those of Upper or Lower Egypt
in the epoch of the pyramids. This does not mean that the Ethiopians had no part in forming Egyptian civilization; I am even
convinced of the contrary. It is for the ethnologists, sociologists,
and others to spell out the importance of that contribution.

This passage from Diodorus was quoted to show that the first
Egyptians who filtered farther north in the Nile Valley, were only a
fragment, a "colony," detached from an early trunk: the Ethiopian
community located farther south. Diodorus reports this as a general
opinion in his day. Rightly or wrongly, the Ethiopians always thought
themselves to be the biological ancestors of the Egyptians. They also
claimed, as Diodorus reports, the paternity of the early cultural creations from which Egypt later benefited. Cailliaud, one of the first moderns to study the Nubian civilization in depth, shared that opinion. In
his view, the earliest attempts were made in Ethiopia and then perfected in Egypt. Having thus become masterpieces, the rough
sketches probably went back up the valley, like the reflux of the tide.
Consequently, it was never our intention to dispute the belated influence of Egypt on Nubia. As we reread the text of *Nations nègres et*

culture, we readily perceive that there is no need to confuse this issue.

From Mauny's critique, one gets the impression that I was the one who wrote somewhere: "the architectural constructions in Nubia, to cite but one example, are earlier than those of Upper or Lower Egypt." Since I never wrote any such thing, why does he make that insinuation? The best way to criticize objectively, in my opinion, is not to ascribe to authors ideas that they have not expounded, in order the better to attack them.

In the following quotation from Strabo: "Egyptians settled in Ethiopia and Colchis," I fail to see anything to prove that the Egyptians were black; they colonized parts of those two countries, and that is all there is to it.

Perhaps the logical connection (that escapes Mauny, he says) is too implicit? Yet, the passage just quoted from Herodotus could have helped him to grasp the meaning of that sentence.

During Antiquity, scholars considered Ethiopians, Egyptians, and Colchians as Negroes belonging to the same race. Nobody can cite a denial of this in the ancient texts. But the chapter from Strabo's *Geography,* which reports these facts, deals with migrations of peoples. The author simply wanted to describe the dispersion of populations; for him, the point of departure was Egypt, rather than Ethiopia. He thought that it started from an early Egyptian nucleus, from which Ethiopians probably separated in the form of colonies. These Ethiopians supposedly migrated up the Nile Valley and the Colchians settled on the shores of the Black Sea. For that reason he says: "Egyptians settled in Colchis and Ethiopia." As the blackness of Ethiopians and Colchians could be accepted *a priori* as indisputable (and remains so even today), one could deduce from Strabo's remark that the Egyptians were consequently also black.

The same observation on the passage from Genesis IX, 18–X, 20, where, as a matter of fact, the Egyptians (Mesraim) are classed among Ham's descendants. But the latter is a legendary personage like Noah, Shem, and Japhet, and the division worked out in the Bible only concerns the various races then known by the author or authors of Genesis: Indo-Europeans (Japhet), Semites (Hebrews, Arabs, some of the Mesopotamians, etc.), and Hamites (or the group of peoples who, to their knowledge, were darker than the Semites: Kush, Egyptians, Put, Canaan).

Moreover, Genesis, which is not an anthropological treatise but a collection of Hebraic, Mesopotamian, and Egyptian legends, referring *inter alia* to the origin of the human races as the Hebrews of the second millennium imagined them, nowhere mentions the black color of the descendants of Ham (Cham) or Canaan; the Israelites were conscious of being lighter than they, and that is all.

A great step forward has been taken: the Egyptians are no longer deliberately confused with Indo-Europeans or Semites, but ranked in the great family of Ham and Canaan, in conformity with the Biblical text. Naturally, no scholar would be so bold as to take the Biblical quotes literally. But, alas! That has been done only too often. If we assembled end to end all the Biblical quotations in Western works referring to the curse on Ham's progeny, they would without exaggeration be numerous enough to fill a library. In contrast, rare are the quotations pointing out the fact that the Egyptians belong among Ham's descendants. Thus, the Bible is complacently quoted when it is a matter of confirming opinions acquired from tender infancy on the inequality of human races. But it does not do to press the consequences to the limit. One is careful not to uncover the mine buried, so to speak, in the very text cited.

Nevertheless, the "Biblical legends" of which Mauny speaks are often surprisingly true: for example, the antediluvian civilization of El Obeid [in Central Sudan] discovered by modern archeology. It proves that the story of the flood is not unfounded, and that the overflowing of the Tigris and Euphrates, even if it failed to submerge the whole earth about 4000 B.C., must have given the riparian populations that impression. Napoleon, in turn, barely missed learning, at his expense, the truth of the passage about the crossing of the Red Sea. This does not diminish the fact that it is a compilation of texts from different sources: the role of Egyptian traditions in the formation of the Biblical text has begun to be stressed. Certain passages are almost copies of the Egyptian texts.

Returning to the question of whether the Bible designated Ham's descendants and the Egyptians by a term indicating their skin color, we can answer affirmatively. The very name "Ham" (Cham) is an ethnic term:

In Hebrew, Kham: son of Noah
        Khum: chestnut
        Khom: heat
        Khama: heat, the sun
In ancient Egyptian, Khem: black, burned
        Ham: hot, black
In Wolof, Khem: black, burned.

Thus, the ethnic designation of Ham and his progeny is implied in the etymology of the word used in Genesis.

Mauny's reservation is quite prudent, because it concerns Genesis alone. The inattentive reader could believe that nowhere in the Bible are Canaanites or Egyptians referred to as Blacks, which would obviously be incorrect. Genesis is not the whole Bible. In The Song of Songs, the poem ascribed to Solomon, there is no doubt that the alleged daughter of the Pharaoh is black. The Bible abounds in similar examples. Why should it be important then, to observe that in one of its books the ethnic term for the Canaanites is not explicitly stated?

From an examination of the ancient texts cited by the author, not much is left to persuade us that the ancient Egyptians were Negroes. Archeology leads us to believe the contrary, supported precisely by a text from Herodotus. It was only after the Egyptian deserters settled in Ethiopia that "the Ethiopians adopting Egyptian manners, became more civilized" (II, 30).

Furthermore, hypotheses on the origin of the Egyptians are not in short supply. C. A. Diop did not innovate in this field. Here is the passage in which Gabriel Hanotaux (*Histoire de la nation égyptienne,* 1931, I, 14) discusses it: "What were these early people (of the Nile Valley)? Celts, replied Poinsinet de Sivry—Negroes, said Volney—Chinese, thought Winckelmann—Indo-Polynesians, claimed Moreau de Jonnes—Africans from Ethiopia and Libya, declared Petrie, supported by the naturalists Hott, Morton, Perrier, Hamy—Asiatics from Babylonia, with an advanced civilization, affirm archeologists and orientalists Brugsch, Ebers, Hommel, de Rougé, de Morgan. For this variety of opinions there is doubtless a cause: it is that in Egypt there was a melange of various races."

Egypt, land of a mixture of races and of civilizations at the crossroads of three continents, such is indeed the logical vocation of that country. Any attempt to monopolize the whole for the benefit of a single component distorts the truth. It is for us, historians of Black Africa, to detect the part played in the formation of ancient Egypt by the Negro and the Brown (Africans from Ethiopia and Libya, as Petrie says), a truth widely admitted already, as we have seen.

The reader can appreciate how much "is left from an examination of the texts" involved. It is up to him to see whether or not our argument is strengthened by this critique, and whether the criticism has not made him more aware of the soundness of our position.

Mauny seems to confuse civilization and race. The passage from Herodotus, also cited in *Nations nègres et culture,* is absolutely silent on race. At most, it informs us that, at a given moment, dissatisfied Egyptian soldiers defected to the service of the king of Nubia, and that the result produced a civilizing (Egyptian) influence on Nubia. It is absolutely impossible to extract, despite what Mauny says, the slightest conclusion about races. Nothing justifies it. On the other hand, it can rightly be noted that these Egyptian soldiers, during that period of disarray and anarchy, turned toward Upper Egypt and Nubia; this was a constant of Egyptian Pharaonic policy. In troubled periods, princes of the blood and Egyptian tradition always took refuge in Upper Egypt, not the Delta. Ethiopia was the land of the gods, of the ancestors, the land of Punt, of legitimacy, the early habitat of the race, according to the most authentic Egyptian traditions. . . . In the ritual, Upper Egypt always took precedence over Lower Egypt; Egyptian society was legitimist until its decline. We recall that only a Nubian princess could be attached to the sanctuary of the god Amon at Thebes. The reaction of the Egyptian troops was a legitimist reaction. What it involved was a deliberate choice between Egypto-Nubian tradition and adventurous usurpers who had seized the throne of Egypt. There can be no doubt on this score; it suffices to refer to that part of Egyptian history to be convinced.[4]

Psammetichus I, Twenty-sixth Dynasty, was considered by the people as a usurper who delivered Egypt "to the dregs of the nations," to foreigners, by facilitating their installation. In particular, he surrounded himself by Greek mercenaries and conferred upon them the highest civil and military posts in the court. That was when the garrisons of the National Egyptian army, out of frustration and as legitimists (this was a part of the army composed of loyal citizens), went to place themselves at the disposal of the king of Nubia (Khartoum, Sudan). They numbered 200,000 and were assigned to the region between Bahr-el-Azrek and Bahr-el-Abyad. They multiplied and became the *automoles* mentioned by Herodotus.[5]

Egypt was no more a melting pot of races than Europe was, and the long quotation from Hanotaux can be applied word for word to that part of the world as well. There we find Celts, Ligurians, Pelasgians, Italiotes, Etruscans, Germans, Angles and Saxons, Slavs, Huns, Iberians, Arabs, Lapps, Cro-Magnon men and Grimaldi Negroids, Chancelade men, to cite only a few, of all races: white, black, yellow, "brownish-yellow," "brunettes"(?) gradually mixed in that relatively narrow area of Western Europe. Everyone knows this, but it did not prevent the different European nationalities known today—Italian, German, French, etc.—from aspiring to a certain racial homogeneity. Nevertheless, each of these nations claims and protects what it considers to be its cultural heritage.

No school of history has so far attempted seriously to deride those attitudes and to pulverize those crystallizations of historical errors. The permanence of somatic characteristics despite thousands of years of crossbreeding in a primitive people settled on a terrain is one of the most extraordinary facts noted by modern anthropology. The three great ethnic sectors of Europe (Nordic, Alpine, and Mediterranean of prehistory) still subsist, notwithstanding the incalculable number of peoples who have come to alter the original substratum.

All the anthropologists (Vallois, Haddon, Elliot Smith) who have studied Egypt reach the same conclusions. Similarly, in the passage quoted by Mauny, Coon reports that the pigmentation of the Egyptians has probably not changed appreciably during the last five millennia. To be sure, Egyptian crossbreeding spread out like a fan in the course of history, as no one denies, but it has never succeeded in overturning the racial constants of the early population, that of Upper Egypt in particular. The color of the Egyptians has become lighter down through the years, like that of West Indian Negroes, but the Egyptians have never stopped being Negroes. While all Egyptian civilization is directly linked to the cultural forms of Black Africa, a specialist would have great difficulty in demonstrating any cultural identity of Egypt with Europe or with Semitic or Chinese Asia.

For all these reasons, the Black Africans can and must exclusively lay claim to the cultural heritage of the old Egyptian civilization. They are the only ones today whose sensitivity is able to blend easily with the essence and spirit of that civilization which the Western Egyptologist finds so hard to understand. The intellectual and affective dispositions of present-day Blacks are the same as those of the people who edited the hieroglyphic texts of the pyramids and other monuments and sculptured the bas-reliefs of the temples. Starting from Black Africa, from its conception of the universe, from its cultural forms, its linguistic realities, and its types of politico-social organization, we can gradually bring back to life all those forms of Egyptian civilization that today are dead to European consciousness.

Mauny's repeated contention that the Black's role in Egyptian civilization is already recognized, could apply only to the time elapsed since we exhumed certain documents in *Nations nègres et culture*. The whole effort of modern science, until the past few years, has consisted in denying, despite the facts, this role of the Negro in the acquisition of civilization. The method was simply to silence the facts, as Breasted and so many others did. A second attitude, more cautious and shrewder, consisted of citing a few facts, so as not to be caught at fault, and then demonstrate their minor, negligible significance. Africans, especially those of my generation who have been the greatest victims of that cultural alienation, are in a good position to know whether the Negro's contribution to civilization has been recognized and integrated in the teaching programs, whether an attempt of that nature was even thinkable before the publication of *Nations nègres et culture*.

The cultural unity of Egypt and Black Africa, an essential fact for the history of humanity and the peoples of Black Africa today, has just been recognized officially by Egyptology. It must also be admitted that, as we said earlier, this was the only way for Egyptology to cure its sclerosis, to escape from the impasse and set forth toward a fruitful perspective.

As for the rest of Black Africa, the harvest of archeology is admittedly meager at present. How can C. A. Diop explain that the Egyptians whom he claims as Negroes and Nubians, spiritual sons of Egypt, were the only ones to be civilized before the first millennium B.C., the first to be civilized in all Africa? We cannot see why the inhabitants of the Nile Valley could have been in the vanguard of humanity while the Negroes remained in a "primitive" state, just like their European contemporaries. And if West African Blacks are descendants of the Egyptians, why have they become "decivilized" between 500 B.C., when Diop says they left Egypt, and 900 A.D., after which we have texts depicting them as being rather "retarded"? Where did they go? How is it that no ancient author has spoken of that migration, undertaken, according to the author, during the historical epoch? And how is it that they left no trace of their passage?

I am astounded that Mauny asks those three questions. Since these queries and their answers were discussed in my text, I am tempted to assume that perhaps Mauny has not read the whole of the book he is criticizing.

Why were the Nubians and Egyptians already civilized while the rest of the world, especially all Europe, was plunged in barbarism? That is a fact which has been observed, not the fruit of imagination. Nor is it a miraculous, inexplicable fact. Accordingly, the historian need not be astonished by it; his role ought to be that of seeking out and presenting plausible explanations for such phenomena.

The same question could be asked about the Greeks as compared with the rest of Europe. After their early contact with the world to the south and the cultural exchanges with Egypt and Crete, they escaped from barbarism in the twelfth century and became civilized between the twelfth and fifth centuries B.C. With the Etruscans, they remained the only civilized people in all Europe. The other European peoples, farther away from the southern cultural centers, remained steeped in barbarism until the Middle Ages, with the exception of the Latins, who also became civilized by contact with the Etruscans and Greeks.

Obviously, instead of regarding Greek civilization as an unusual and more or less miraculous phenomenon, we can easily explain it by placing it in historical and geographical context. A similar explanation can also be given for Egypto-Nubian civilization.

Concluding the first part of *Nations nègres et culture,* I emphasized that Egyptian civilization did not indicate any racial superiority, but was almost the result of a geographical accident. It was the special character of the Nile Valley that conditioned the politico-social evolution of the peoples who migrated there. The extensiveness of the floods of the Nile forced all the inhabitants of the valley to face the annual event collectively, to regulate their whole life in its smallest details on the inundation. To survive, each clan had to rid itself early of its selfishness. When the flooding began, no clan was able to meet the situation alone; each needed the others' assistance, the solidarity of all clans for the survival of the community. These were the working conditions that soon led the clans to unite and favored the rise of a central authority to coordinate all social, political, and national activity. Until the invention of geometry, none of the material and intellectual activity of the Egyptians was done for its own sake. In its beginnings geometry was an invention enabling them to locate scientifically the exact boundaries of each inhabitant's property after the floods. Nowhere was dependence on the geographical setting and the way of life so close. This imperious necessity seems to explain, at least in the essentials, the anteriority of the Egyptians and Nubians on the road to civilization.

All other peoples, Blacks or Whites, who were subjected to less stringent living conditions requiring a less formal collective action, attained civilization later than the Egyptians. Accordingly, why should it be surprising that certain Blacks and certain Whites became civilized while others were in barbarism? Peoples placed in more favorable conditions are civilized earlier than others, whatever their color, independently of their ethnic identity, and that is all.

We have never invoked any peculiar genius or special aptitudes of the Black race to explain why it was the first to attain civilization. That erroneous conception of the causes of man's evolution led European specialists to the theory of the Greek miracle. However erroneous, it is nevertheless so deeply rooted in the minds of its partisans that, even today, they consider any claim that Africans may legitimately be entitled to the moral advantage of Egyptian civilization as a claim of racial superiority, whether one admits it or not. But such is not the case; those who think so are interpreting it through their own intellectual and moral inclinations.

Why were the Africans "decivilized" en route? asks Mauny. Regression is also an historico-sociological phenomenon that the specialist has a duty to explain, whenever it is objectively detected. This is indeed pertinent here. Let us remain in the valley of the Nile, where the phenomenon is even more apparent. The current populations of that valley are rightly considered the authentic descendants of the ancient Egyptian. Yet, those populations, who never left their homeland, have been "decivilized" on their own soil, losing all the ancient Egyptian wisdom and no longer able to read hieroglyphics, an invention of their ancestors. Why, then, is it astonishing that a population of emigrants should be in a similar situation?

How many times have we heard it said: "If the Blacks are descendants of the Egyptians, why haven't they preserved writing?" On referring to my *Nations nègres et culture* and *L'Afrique Noire précoloniale,* one will see that the usage of writing never disappeared from Black Africa.

What layman or Martian descending on earth could have guessed that Greece is the distant mother of modern American technique and of Western civilization in its most refined and profound aspects? Western Europe has experienced the same regression. During the Middle Ages, all the knowledge of Antiquity took refuge in a few monasteries where it vegetated until the Carolingian Renaissance with Alcuin (735–804). Techniques were lost, architectural know-how in particular. Not only had they forgotten everything about ancient science; they could not even erect the least complicated building. We can get an idea of this regression by comparing the Ptolemaic map showing the geographical knowledge of Antiquity with that of the Middle Ages for the same Mediterranean area.

According to the satirical Latin poet, Juvenal, who wrote during the second century A.D., the Egyptians themselves had retrogressed immeasurably. Even if we take into account the fact that Juvenal hated Orientals, especially Egyptians, it must be noted that in his review of events dating from circa 127 A.D., Egyptian society was already bending under the weight of totemic deities and retribalization. As a consequence of uninterrupted colonization by Persians, Greeks, and Romans, the country which had civilized the world was reverting to "barbarism," if we are to believe Juvenal. Egypt, which under Queen Hatshepsut (Eighteenth Dynasty) had plowed the seas in high-decked ships, "no longer knew how to sail anything but clay boats with tiny sails and to crouch over short oars . . . " (Satire XV). Juvenal describes the bloody, fratricidal conflicts between two clans or tribes (the cities of Denderah and Hombos) with inimical totems; these conflicts allegedly ended in a cannibalistic scene that could only be described as a ritual orgy.

Where did the Black populations go? When we expounded, in *Nations nègres et culture,* the thesis of a Negro Sahara, we encountered considerable hostility from those who considered themselves experts on the subject. Today, with the recent discoveries of Henri Lhote, refutation is no longer possible. In the section of *Nations nègres et culture* on the peopling of Africa from the Nile Valley, the route from Egypt to the southwest now assumed special significance. In fact, it passes just south of Tassili N'Ajjer, where Lhote made the most important find of cave paintings of the century, after that of the Lascaux cave. This find enables us to affirm that, contrary to the ideas imposed on the world by scholars for 150 years, Egyptian cultural influences spread for thousands of kilometers in the direction of Black Africa. Tassili N'Ajjer was probably only one stop, located 3,000 kilometers (some 1,875 miles) from the Nile Valley. Those paintings establish an evident link between Egypt, the Sahara, and the rest of Black Africa. It is certain that Nubia also was a great center for the diffusion of cultural influence from the Nile Valley, a kind of hinge between Egypt and other parts of Black Africa. . . .

Let us point out that there are artificial mounds in the region of the Niger Delta, not pyramids, as the author thinks. [We report this] not because of any desire "to disparage African values," but because a pyramid is a mass of well-defined form, while the mounds are on a round or oval base and in a roughly hemispheric shape. The former are found especially in Egypt, Nubia, and Central America; the latter, in Black Africa and Europe.

I know, from experience, that the Serer tombs, called *m'banâr,* were originally perfect cones; with time the construction materials settle and the tomb takes the shape of a mound. . . . The tombs of the ancient emperors of Ghana, as described by Arab authors, have become mounds. No one disputes that. The tombs of the Askia are veritable pyramids. But this question is really of secondary importance, for one cannot see how the essence of a pyramid, to speak in the Platonic sense, could be more noble than the essence of a cone.

As for calling the signs engraved on the baobabs in Diourbel hieroglyphics, the author is now back home and is familiar enough with the question, I suppose, to judge for himself whether writing is really involved (and the oldest inhabitants can inform him) or whether, as seems likely, these are simply graffiti engraved on the soft bark.

I went back to the foot of the baobab last year. I was quite disappointed because I hardly recognized the signs that I easily identified during my childhood; the bark of the baobab had developed since then. A little boy and girl passed by and enlightened me. They helped me to locate the signs which, as a matter of fact, are riddles, ideograms: a kettle, a sword, a goatskin, a camel's foot, a string of prayer beads, and so on, memorializing the visit of a great religious leader of yesteryear, presumably the Prophet. If Mauny returns to the site one day, he will find no problem in being informed as I was about those signs; their meaning is not yet lost.

It is not writing in the phonetic sense of the word, but a series of drawings. The fact that this practice dates from the post-Islamic epoch tends to suggest that it reflects ancient habits about to disappear. On the baobab, along with the prayer beads, sword, and camel's foot, there was an inkstand and even a pen; so Arabic writing was known, but is absent from the bark of the baobab. This is similar to the attitude of Njoya, the sultan of Cameroon who, although a Moslem, utilized hieroglyphic writing, perhaps because of ancestral tradition, excluding Arabic characters, to take a census of the population of his kingdom, to transcribe all the literature, the oral tradition, and the history of his country.

What is rather remarkable is that Mauny also visited the same Diourbel area, after the publication of *Nations nègres et culture,* and found there both the mounds and the same baobab tree with its "mysterious signs." But he failed to remind the reader that the baobab of his article is the same one indicated in *Nations nègres et culture;* he could not have suspected its existence but for data provided in that volume. Strangely enough, Mauny was able to criticize that passage of our book without mentioning the assistance he drew from it for his personal research. Thus, the uninformed reader, picking up both texts separately, would be compelled to think that two absolutely distinct baobabs were involved. Moreover, Mauny entitled his article: "Discovery of . . . " What a strange "scientific" method for working on and elaborating documents intended to educate posterity! The layman must surely be taken in by it.[6]

Another problem understandably preoccupies Mr. Diop: the skin color of the Egyptians, as represented on the tomb paintings and other documents. In his view, "the so-called dark red color of the Egyptians is none other than the color of the Negro." To support this, he cites Champollion the Younger. But Champollion distinguishes clearly between Egyptians (dark red), Negroes (Nahasi),

Semites (Namou) who are flesh color verging on yellow, Medes and Assyrians with tanned complexion, and Indo-Europeans (Tamhou) with white skin.

Before me lie two volumes with numerous illustrations: A. Lhote's *Les Chefs-d'oeuvre de la peinture égyptienne* (Paris: Hachette, 1954), and Arpag Mekhitarian's *La Peinture égyptienne* (Geneva: Skira, 1954). In my view they support the statements of Champollion the Younger and of many others as well concerning the extreme variety of races represented. I shall note but one thing: when the artist wished to paint Negroes, he simply gave them a black or gray color. And the dark red personages, to mention them alone, are, with some exceptions, not Negroes, but tanned, brown, as is easily detected by the simple fact that the black color is found everywhere on the paintings to depict the hair, not the skin. The Egyptians were absolutely conscious of the difference in skin color between themselves, Blacks, and Asiatics.

We have seen earlier that an anthropologist, C. S. Coon (1939, p. 98), described the usual color of Pharaonic Egyptians as "brunet white." This is also true of the average modern Egyptian of the Delta; the Southerner is darker (reddish-brown to medium brown).

Nahasi, Namou, and Tamhou are not terms designating color in the Egyptian language, as Mauny's exposé could lead us to believe. The Egyptians never distinguished themselves from other African Negroes by such terms as white, black, tan, etc., since they all belonged to the same race. There is no need to open the Lhote volume at which Mauny was looking. The illustration on the cover, representing Osiris, god and ancestor of the Egyptian people (as Orpheus was for the Greeks) and painted coal black, could be an excellent subject for the critic to think about.

Is it necessary to remind Mauny of the conclusion reached by Champollion on the modest origins of the white race: ". . . a veritable savage tattooed on various parts of his body"?

Finally, what is the value of all these assumptions on the so-called conventional color of the Egyptians, as compared with the clinical examination of samples taken from the epidermis of mummies? That examination enables us to classify them unquestionably among the most authentic Blacks. At present Mauny is living in Senegal. Let him look around; if one painted all the shades observable on different Senegalese individuals, it would also be possible to distinguish in the same way a black Senegalese type, a dark brunet Senegalese type, etc. We can detect the artificial nature of such an approach because we are living in the midst of the people involved and reality imposes limitations on the excesses of our intellectual freedom. It is not the same when we are dealing with dead Egyptians.

Despite these risky hypotheses presented as accepted, irrefutable proofs, and his lack of information on recent studies concerning West Africa, Mr. Diop's work marks an important date. This is the first general work on African history by a French-speaking Black and, in addition to an impressive documentation, it includes some excellent pages. It has the great merit of not following beaten paths and of compelling Egyptologists and others to take a stand and to be precise about certain of their opinions. But, written in Paris before 1955, it is necessarily a militant book, impregnated with the spirit of those years of struggle, during which Africans, especially students exiled in Paris in the midst of the colonizing people, were frustrated about their national history, and were preparing the paths to independence by exalting Negritude;* sometimes—and this is normal—at the price of perhaps unconsciously twisting impartiality, and scientific truth. They recognized only that which provided arguments for their thesis, their cause. all this was considered "cricket" and, indeed, the results of that general struggle of the various strata of those African peoples can speak for themselves.

Today, in 1960, the situation is different. This is the year of Independence for numerous Black African countries, Mali† among others. The African historian, without disavowing in the least his political opinions during the years of opposition to colonialism, owes it to himself, to science, and to his country, to place himself, if not already there, on a plane of strict objectivity, which excludes neither political commitment nor the utilization of hypotheses to be

---

*Negritude has been defined by its theoretician, Léopold Sédar Senghor, as "the sum total of the values of the Negro–African world." The word was first used by Aimé Césaire, poet, essayist, and dramatist. As a literary and cultural movement, it is perhaps best illustrated by the works of its three founders: Senghor of Senegal, Césaire of Martinique, and Damas of Guiana. Essentially it stresses the Black man's past, present, and future potential contribution to the world.

†A reference to the short-lived Federation of Mali (1959–1960), which included Senegal and the "French" Sudan.

verified. Without that objectivity, one cannot speak of history, research or scientific knowledge of history. Otherwise, one risks bringing discredit on the whole new school of African history and publicizing a group of errors, exaggerations which would do harm to the Africans themselves. For now, with good reason, the curriculum of African history is going to be revised so that Black youngsters may learn their own history rather than that of the colonizer. It is no longer a matter of convincing audiences of Parisians or African students in Paris—the former, almost totally incompetent on the subject, and the latter, obviously predisposed by anti-colonialist reaction preceding the rapid acquisition of independence, to applaud this veritable Negro Gobinism. It is now a question of the author's submitting his ideas to examination by scholars who alone are qualified to say what should be retained. Or else let him return to the arduous task of historical research to verify many of his own hypotheses.

When we read under the signature of modern Egyptologists that C. A. Diop is right and that ancient Egypt was "Negro," only then must textbooks be revised in that sense. The cultural unity of Africa, from the Egyptian to the Bushman, Wolof, Moroccan, Tuareg, Teda, Pygmy, Zulu, Somali, and Abyssinian? Why not? On condition that ethnologists, sociologists, and others affirm it.

Linguistic connections between ancient Egyptian and Wolof? Specialists in African languages will be able to tell us someday whether this hypothesis is valid. However, only on condition that they specialize in them and be so certified.

The reader who has followed us this far will be able to verify whether or not the special conditions under which we labored in Paris or the requirements of the political and social struggle forced us at any time to twist scientific truth or prevented us from holding to a course of strict objectivity. It will also be for the reader to decide whether our attitude and its results cast discredit or honor on the "new school of African history"; whether it "publicizes a group of errors," or destroys once and for all a body of myths that scholars had imposed on the world throughout 150 years of erudition; whether it is a case of "Black Gobinism" or a rectification of human history.

If we had to wait for "specialists" to make all the rectifications contained in *Nations nègres et culture,* there would perhaps be time enough to see whole nations disappear under the weight of alienation. The reverse procedure is the real solution; each day these possessors of knowledge, supporting the new ideas, become more numerous. Has not Egyptology just recognized the cultural unity of Black Africa and ancient Egypt? This was not the case six years ago. As Professor Jean Leclant [a noted French Egyptologist] himself. has observed, this fact is perhaps more important than somatic relationship. Consequently, if battle there was, it has been won, the cause has been heard. One can find the facts distasteful, but no specialist will now risk a rebuttal of the cultural and linguistic relationship between ancient Egypt and Black Africa. By the same token, the assertion that the ancient inhabitants of the Sahara were Negroes and that they played a preponderant role in peopling Black Africa and Egypt no longer arouses an impassioned outcry, for the facts are there.

But all those truths had to be stated before those who call themselves specialists would even consider them. The history of these recent years fully demonstrates this. We have never spoken of any cultural unity other than that of Egypt and Black Africa; consequently, Mr. Mauny's list of disparate peoples reflects displeasure over the facts, a feeling of resignation in the presence of what one is unable to destroy, more so than it reflects the serene, convincing arguments that we would have expected. Henceforth, the textbooks can be revised in line with Mauny's criteria, at least in the direction of Egypto-African cultural unity. The condition has been met. Will it simply be ignored?

To criticize *Nations nègres et culture,* a very imperfect work, one should not attack its structure, for that approach will be unproductive. Its structure is solid, its perspectives valid. Instead, the target should be the small details, for then it will be possible to detect numerous shortcomings. . . .

CHAPTER XIII

Early History of Humanity: Evolution of the Black World

Insofar as the known facts permit, we shall try in this chapter to retrace the major stages in the evolution of the Black world since *Homo sapiens* appeared on the scene. In addition to providing a reference system for the young African researcher, the picture thus presented, with its inevitable gaps, its uncertainties, but also its areas of clarity, will give him an idea of the seriousness and magnitude of his task. I have directed my efforts to the period of the African past ranging from prehistory to the appearance of modern States at the end of the Middle Ages, for this is the span that poses the greatest number of problems for understanding the history of mankind.

Priority of the Negro Factor in the History of Humanity

The results of archeological finds,[1] especially those of Dr. Louis Leakey in East Africa, enable us every six months or so to penetrate more deeply into the obscurity of the first rough outlines of humanity. Thanks to dating methods based on the dosage of potassium 40/Argon, we can go back 1,700,000 years. Nevertheless, there is continued agreement that *Homo sapiens,* modern man, appeared about 40,000 years ago, during the Upper Paleolithic. This first humanity, belonging to the lower layers of the Aurignacian, was probably related morphologically to the current Black type of humanity.

The characteristics of that Grimaldi race have been summarized as follows by Marcellin Boule and Henri Vallois in *Fossil Men,* translated into English by Michael Bullock:

When we compare the dimensions of the bones of their limbs, we see that the leg was very long in proportion to the thigh, the forearm very long in proportion to the whole arm; and that the lower limb was exceedingly long relative to the upper limb. Now these proportions reproduce, but in greatly exaggerated degree, the characters presented by the modern Negro. Here we have one of the chief reasons for regarding those fossils as Negroid, if not actually Negro.

The Negroid affinities are likewise indicated by the characters of the skull. These are large; the crania are very elongated, hyperdolichocephalic (indices 68 and 69) and, seen from above, they present a regular elliptically shaped contour, with flattened parietal bosses. The skulls are also very high, so that their capacity is at least equal to that of the average Parisian of our day: 1,580 cubic centimeters in the case of the young man, 1,375 cubic centimeters in the case of the old woman. The mastoid apophyses are small.

The face is broad but not high, while the skull is excessively elongated from the front backwards; so that the head might be called unbalanced or dysharmonic.

The forehead is well developed and straight; the orbital ridges project only slightly. The orbits are large, deep and sub-rectangular; their lower border is everted toward the front.

The nose, depressed at the root, is very broad (platyrrhinian). The floor of the nasal fossae is joined to the anterior surface of the maxillary by a groove on each side of the nasal spine, as in Negroes, instead of being bordered by a sharp edge, as in the white races. The canine fossae are deep.

The upper maxillary projects forward in very marked fashion. This prognathism especially affects the subnasal or alveolar region. The palatal arch, though only slightly developed in breadth, is very deep.

The jaw is strong, its body very thick; the ascending branches are broad and low. The chin is not greatly developed; a strongly marked alveolar prognathism, correlated with the upper prognathism, gives it a pronouncedly receding appearance.

The majority of these characters of the skull and face are, if not Negritic, at least Negroid.[2]

. . . The other types found in Europe probably belonged to the Cro-Magnon race: the Predmost man (in Moravia) and the Brunn man (near Vienna) were perhaps Cro-Magnoids with "Ethiopian" characteristics. . . .

Such are the facts revealed by archeology. On the strength of this evidence, we must recognize in all objectivity that the first *Homo sapiens* was a "Negroid" and that the other races, white and yellow, appeared later, following differentiations whose physical causes still escape science. Refusing to accept these facts, scholars substitute hypotheses for them. Here is one that I heard expressed by a great modern scientist during the summer of 1963 in Paris:

> The morphological differences between Blacks, Whites, and Yellows are so deep that it would be absurd to make them date back less than 40,000 years, by supposing the two latter-named races to be the product of a differentiation in a primitive Negro substratum. At that period the three races must necessarily have already existed on earth with their own well-defined characteristics; archeology will one day find specimens of white men as old as the first Negro Aurignacians. When the latter lived in Europe, the white race must have been elsewhere, in some location not yet excavated. But its existence at that period cannot be doubted.

Though the hypotheses of scholars often prove true, the fact remains that at the present moment, while awaiting new discoveries to prove the contrary, the sole scientific conclusion conforming to the evidence is that the earliest humans, the very first *Homo sapiens,* were "Negroids." Obviously, the term "Negroid" is specious;[3] in scientific writing, it belongs to that group of words used to gloss over the facts. Any Negro type that stands unquestionably at the origin of a civilization is, for that very reason, described by the most distinguished scholars as a Negroid or Hamite, as we have seen. Thus, the first humans were probably quite simply Negritic.

The existence of an archaic *Homo sapiens* (Swanscombe man and Fontéchevade man*), as early as the Lower Paleolithic, would not change these facts one iota. In the Upper Paleolithic, the archaic *Homo sapiens* either disappeared or else evolved into the Grimaldi man, for only the latter has been found, without any parallel branch of *Homo sapiens* until the belated appearance of the Cro-Magnon and Chancelade races.[4]

Pierre Legoux's note in the proceedings of the French Academy of

---

*The Swanscombe skull was discovered in the Thames valley in 1935. The Fontéchevade skull fragments were found near Angoulême, France, in 1947.

Sciences for October 1962 (pp. 2276–2277) does not weaken those conclusions. In an effort to demonstrate that the Grimaldi race did not exist, he tried to continue Verneau's study on *Les Grottes de Grimaldi* that Boule and Vallois had utilized. Unfortunately, he was evasive in his attempt to refute the main points of the long text quoted earlier. Without denying the existence of prognathism, he tried to justify it. In the old woman, "it is a question of an old bilateral loss of mandible molars. This loss usually causes functional prognathism." Next he discusses the arrangement of the adolescent's teeth, claiming that these had been dislocated with time and that the skull is necessarily damaged, in order to say that it was probably prognathous on one side and orthognathous on the other. This is false when it is a matter of facial prognathism, of the jawbones, which is unquestionably the case in the adolescent as in the old woman. The author does not help his reader to avoid this confusion. Instead, he leads us to think he is discussing facial prognathism when he is merely discussing alveolar prognathism of the adolescent's teeth. He is no less vague on another characteristic: "the proportions of the limbs"; "characteristics one to three are concerned with the size of the individuals and the proportions of their long bones. These are not presented in their real state on the plates. Their respective proportions therefore rest on hazardous opinions."

The author, who has had access to the original pieces in the Monaco Museum, should certainly have provided the numerical measurements of the long bones of upper and lower limbs and should have demonstrated that they are not Negritic. Nothing should have been easier for him, yet he fails to do it. He is content with the vague, unusable observations quoted above. One always creates a malaise by omitting precise details when these are available. We would like him to present photographic reproductions not only of a "fragment of the dental apparatus" of one skull, but of both entire skulls, in profile, to prove the absence of prognathism in the originals. And we would like him to juxtapose these reproductions with those published by Professor Vallois to show how they differ from the originals. He does not comment on Vallois's important observation concerning "the floor of the nasal fossae"—an observation which suffices to ruin his whole theory. If Mr. Legoux wants to convince us, he must produce those proofs (including the numerical measurements of the proportions of the limbs) which are all available to him. We may hope soon to have an opportunity to examine these precious documents.

Extent of the Negro Substratum of Humanity

The Negroid human substratum is as extensive as it is durable. Haddon shows how Elliot Smith and Sergi identify that substratum. Concerning Sergi's Eurafrican race, he writes:

> Two variants may be noted: (1) with wavy hair, large measurements, and strong physique; (2) with rather close curly hair, prognathism, and smaller measurements; this type with almost Negro characters may be connected with the Grimaldi type.
> This type has been described by Sergi, Giuffrida-Ruggeri and by Fleure, who found it in the Plynlimmon and other districts of south Wales. It has been noted among the living in Algeria, Somaliland, north Abyssinia, Egypt, north Italy, Sardinia, north Portugal, Traz os Montes, and Spain (west of the Pyrenees) and other scattered places in Europe. It is evidently a very ancient type that has persisted in out-of-the-way spots.[5]

Similarly, Elliot Smith finds the type of his "brown" race "among the ancient Neolithic inhabitants of the British Isles, France, on both shores of the Mediterranean, the proto-Libyans, ancient and modern Egyptians, Nubians, Beja, Danakil, Hadendoa, Abyssinians, Galla, Somali, throughout the Arabian peninsula, on the coasts of the Persian Gulf (southern Persia, the land of Sumer?), Mesopotamia, Syria, the coastal regions of Asia Minor, Anau in Turkestan, and among the early Indonesians."

Haddon writes as follows about North Africa: "Taking North Africa as a whole, there seems little doubt that the substratum of the population is allied to the Hamite or Ethiopian, with a dark skin, fine face, and soft hair. This is overlaid by a stratum of leucoderm Mediterraneans." Quoting Balout and Vallois, Furon states that North Africa was inhabited by two races during the Upper Paleolithic, one of which, Ibero-Maurusian (man of Mechta el-Arbi in Tunisia), presented affinities with Cro-Magnon man. This race probably occupied only the coast and Tell without penetrating the interior. It gradually diminished in number and partially survived into the Neolithic. Present-day Guanches in the Canaries could be its last survivors. The other race was "Negroid" and lived in the Capsian: "They appear to be Mediterranean prototypes, often showing Negro characteristics."[6]

During the same Capsian period, another Negroid race, called Natufian by Miss Garrod, lived in Palestine. Perhaps the Natufian was the distant ancestor of the Canaanite, but prudence compels us not to affirm this categorically. The roundheaded men in the Saharan cave drawings, observed and described by Lhote, closely resemble the roundheaded man in the famous fresco on the Cogul rock (Catalonia), from the Magdalenian age. The sorcerer dancing in the grotto of the three brothers (south of France) and the one in Afvallingskop (Orange Free State, South Africa) present curious similarities which have already been noted. All of these are evidence that the Negroid substratum of humanity is very extensive and durable. In certain parts of western Asia—southern India, southern Persia and ancient Elam, southern Arabia, Phoenicia, Canaanland, etc.—it has lasted until the historical epoch.

Despite this abundance of archeological facts authentically attesting the anteriority of "Negroids," some scientists and researchers continue to pose the problem in unexpected fashion. Apropos the Palestinian Mesolithic, Furon reports:

[The caves of Erq-el-Ahmar] . . . produced 132 individuals for Miss Garrod. All these Natufians share the same physical type, completely different from that of earlier Palestinians. They are short, about 160 cm.* and dolichocephalic. They were probably Cro-Magnoid Mediterraneans, presenting certain Negroid characteristics attributable to crossbreeding . . . These notions about crossbreeding are all the more interesting because one finds Negroids in western Europe and Africa, but still no true Negroes.[7]

The Natufian straddled the Mesolithic and Neolithic, about the sixth millennium.

After Furon, Cornevin supports the same point of view on the genesis of the Negro world: *"Homo sapiens* did not definitely appear until the Upper Gamblian; he was of the Cro-Magnoid type: the Mechta man, the Kenya man of the Capsian.† At that point he was only slightly differentiated and showed no Negroid characteristics. He

---

*Approximately 5 feet 2 inches.

†The Gamblian was the second of the great pluvial periods recognized from the geological strata of Kenya. Kenya Capsians lived about 8000 B.C. (Cf. Winick's *Dictionary of Anthropology* and Cottrell's *Concise Encyclopedia of Archeology*.)

practiced the blade industries of the Maghreb [North Africa] and East Africa: Capsian of the Maghreb, Capsian of Kenya."[8] These two authors and all who belong to their school would thus like to demonstrate, despite the facts, that the Negro did not appear on earth until about the sixth millennium. Consequently, their thesis is supported only by a difficult, wearisome, unscientific argumentation.

According to Furon's conclusions, the Natufian, a cross between White and Black, probably antedated his Negro ancestor, who would still not have been born by the sixth millennium B.C.! And the author finds these "notions" interesting! For his part, Cornevin apparently forgets that the most distinguished prehistorians and anthropologists nowadays—Abbé Breuil, Professor Arambourg, Dr. Leakey, etc.—consider Africa the cradle of humanity. Africa has known the Paleolithic, which was prolonged into the Capsian, corresponding to the Solutrean and European Magdalenian, in archeological succession. Certain authors suppose that, in general, a time gap must elapse between corresponding European and African archeological periods.[9] It is difficult to square this with the almost certain fact that the Aurignacians came from Africa and were "Negroids." "Aurignacian culture was brought into Western Europe from North Africa by new types of men, and these and all subsequent races and their cultures have been termed Neanthropic; usually all these races are grouped under the designation *Homo sapiens* of Linnaeus. We know that the Aurignacians were superior in every way to the old Neanderthal group of men whom they conquered and probably exterminated."[10]

Cornevin seems to ignore the depth of morphological differences that exist between the Black and the White when he dates these differences back to an Antiquity as recent as the eleventh millennium B.C. By so doing, he opposes the one hypothesis at the disposal of scholars to confer upon the Whites an antiquity equal to that of the Blacks. He errs most regrettably in claiming that the Asselar man* looks more like the Cro-Magnoid European of Grimaldi and the Bushman than like modern Blacks. By definition, the Grimaldi Negroid is not Cro-Magnoid, and he is the only one the Asselar man could possibly resemble; he shares no feature with the so-called Cro-Magnon man who lived later in the same cave and is the prototype of the White race as the "Negroid" is the prototype of the Black race.

---

*The remains of the Asselar man were discovered in the Sahara by Théodore Monod in 1927.

There is also good reason to point out that the similarities too often cited between the Grimaldi Negroid and the Bushman are tendentious and stem more from an interpretation of Aurignacian art than from actual archeological measurements. That art reveals a steatopygic female type. This morphological feature has been made a monopoly of the Bushman and Hottentot since Cuvier's studies on the Hottentot Venus at the Musée de l'Homme in Paris.[11] The almost exclusive relationship between these races and the Grimaldi "Negroes" has been claimed. But the morphological characteristics, steatopygia included, which seem common to Hottentots and Bushmen, are found to be generally true of all Negroes. We have only to read the following text:

> As for me, I have been much impressed by the resemblance between the Grimaldi Negroids and the Bushman-Hottentot population of South Africa. The comparisons I have been able to make from the elements at my disposal, especially from the skeleton of the Hottentot Venus, have led me to observe, for example the same dolichocephaly, the same prognathism, the same platyrrhinia, the same wide facial development, the same form of the mandible, the same macrodontism; the only differences lie in the stature and perhaps the height of the skull.[12]

None of the features cited in that passage distinguishes Bushmen from other Negroes. The slope of the pelvis and steatopygia, which seems to be its corollary, exist in almost all black races. But one can maintain with assurance that this morphological characteristic derives from a deformation of the spinal column at the level of the hips from transporting the baby, for it is very ancient and dates back to the Upper Paleolithic. (See Fig. 48.)

Steatopygia is often latent during the girl's adolescence and does not develop noticeably until after her first children are born. There are hundreds, even thousands of girls of all Black African races, once thin as skeletons, who become steatopygic as they mature after marriage. Often this morphological characteristic in Aurignacian races from Western Europe to Lake Baikal (Soviet Union) has been challenged in order to avoid reaching the logical conclusion that would follow: namely, the area over which Negroids were scattered on the face of the globe:

Since all these statuettes seem to have a "family resemblance," it is necessary to accept the idea of a fertility cult, for it would be incredible that France, Italy, and Siberia could have been inhabited by people of the same Negroid race, all of whose women were steatopygic. . . .
There were rites to obtain the fertility of the herds, necessary to the very life of these hunting tribes.[13]

In reality, by reasoning in this way we avoid one difficulty only to fall into a greater one. The fertility cult during the Aurignacian period could not concern cattle since it was not yet domesticated, nor could farming be involved, since it was not yet invented. As for animals, the most one has detected has been scenes of bewitchment connected with the hunt. It could simply be a question of woman's fertility and, therefore, the development of the "human family," but we must stress the rather earthy nature (according to our present standards) of the statuettes.

The human skeletons discovered by Leakey near Elmenteita (Kenya) in the grotto called Gamble's Cave II, and which probably belonged to the same human type as the Olduvai man (northern Tanzania) of the Capsian, have caused much ink to flow. "It is certain that these are not true Negroes, in the usual sense of the word. These are men comparable to the Nilotics in the Great Lakes region, or else comparable to the lighter-skinned populations of those territories. A skeleton recently found at Naivasha (Kenya) obviously belongs to the same type."[14]

From these discoveries, prehistorians, historians, and ethnologists draw conclusions of varying importance concerning the early peopling of Black Africa. In the Olduvai man, Cornevin sees the ancestor of the Nilotic, of the Shilluk, Dinka, Nuer, and Masai. He makes him a Caucasoid. His existence, Cornevin contends, "proves that it is useless to make the East African, improperly called Nilo-Hamitic, come from India or Arabia."[15] Finally, referring to the Naivasha man just mentioned, on the next page he writes that archeological research reveals affinities with the Cro-Magnon race: "tall stature, low, wide face, broad forehead, rectangular sockets, thin nose, little prognathism."

There was no Cro-Magnon man in sub-Saharan Africa. At an interview that Professor Vallois was kind enough to grant me at the Paris Institute of Human Paleontology, this scientist was categorical

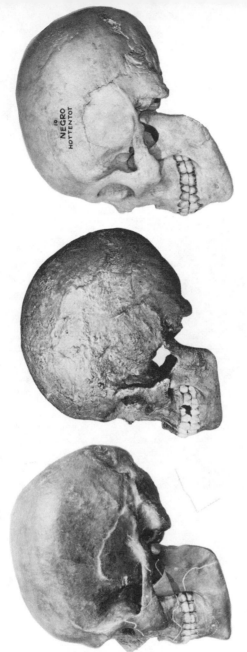

47. Three Skulls: *Lower* Cro-Magnon; *Middle* Grimaldi; *Top* Modern Sudanese (Mali). Compare *Middle* with *Lower* and *Top*, especially for any resemblance to *Lower* or difference from *Top*.

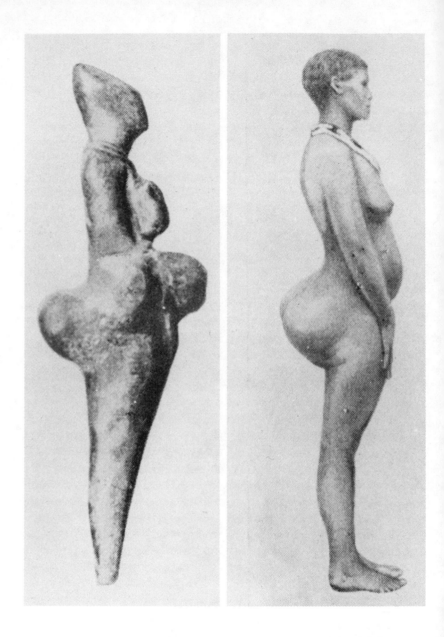

48. The Hottentot Venus. Left, a steatopygic Aurignacian statuette; right, the Hottentot Venus mold (cf. Boule and Vallois, *Fossil Men*).

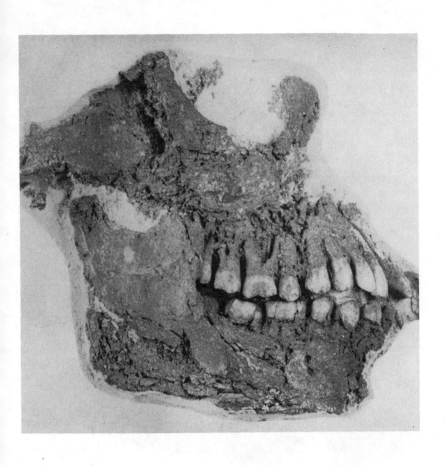

49.   Leakey's Crushed Aurignacian Skull from
Gamble's Cave II.

50.   Sahara Cave Painting of a Negro Woman. (From
J. D. Lajoux, *Les Merveilles du Tassili n'Ajjer.* Paris: Editions du Chêne.)

about this. Only the Boskop man (Transvaal Province, South Africa) was, for a time, considered as a Cro-Magnoid having affinities with the Bushman. But this opinion was later abandoned by its partisans. Cornevin, unfortunately, continues to confuse Grimaldi man—a "Negroid" with marked prognathism and broad nose—with Cro-Magnon man, who is not at all prognathous but presents in hypertrophic fashion typical European traits: thin lips, prominent chin, narrow nose. There is reason to reexamine the documents. (Cf. fig. 47.)

The theory that makes Causcasoids of the Dinka, Nuer, Masai, etc., is the most unwarranted. Suppose an African ethnologist insisted on recognizing only blond Scandinavians as Whites and systematically refused all other Europeans—especially Mediterraneans, French, Italians, Greeks, Spaniards, and Portuguese—membership in the White race. Just as Scandinavians and Mediterraneans must be considered as the two poles, the two extremes of the same anthropological reality, it would be only fair to do the same for the two extremes of the reality of the Black world: Negroes of East Africa and those of West Africa. To call a Shilluk, a Dinka, or a Masai a Caucasoid is as devoid of sense and scientific validity for an African as it would be for a European to claim that a Greek or a Latin are not White. The desperate search for a non-Negro solution sometimes leads to talk about "a primitive stock that might not yet have assumed a differentiated Black or White character," or to whitening Negroes such as the Masai. All the human types found in Kenya from the Paleolithic to the end of the Neolithic, are perfectly distinguishable as Negroes.

Dr. Leakey,* who has studied nearly all of them, knows this. He knows that all the skeletons that have fallen into his hands have Negritic proportions in the full sense of the word. He also is aware that the obervation by Boule and Vallois on the "floor of the nasal fossae" is applicable to all the skulls that he has studied. One can understand why anthropologists are silent on these determining points. On the contrary, they readily expand on cranial measurements, for in this domain, except in extreme cases, it is harder to distinguish a Negro from a White. They admit, for example, that from the Paleolithic to our day Kenya, East Africa, and the Upper Nile have been inhabited by the same population which has remained anthropologically unchanged, with the Masai as one of the most authentic representative types.[16]

---

*This was written some time before the death of Louis S. B. Leakey in 1972.

To the anthropologists, he is the very type of the undifferentiated Negro. Whenever they discuss the late appearance of the "true Negro," we must remember that this is because they do not consider him as such, for he has been there since the beginning of time, since the Paleolithic. All the skull specimens considered non-Negroid, following the measurements of Leakey and other anthropologists, are really those of his archeological forebears from whom he does not differ morphologically. Dr. Leakey and all the anthropologists will confirm this.

If he were not a living reality, his skull would have come out whitened or, in any case, "denegrified" by their measurements, with an orthognathous face held high, a thin nose, high forehead, etc. Even alive, he is not a Negro in the view of the so-called specialists, but the authentic type of the Nilo-Hamite. I invite the reader to verify this. He will simply find these facts confirmed.[17]

Anthropologists have invented the ingenious, convenient, fictional notion of the "true Negro," which allows them to consider, if need be, all the real Negroes on earth as fake Negroes, more or less approaching a kind of Platonic archetype, without ever attaining it. Thus, African history is full of "Negroids," Hamites, semi-Hamites, Nilo-Hamitics, Ethiopoids, Sabaeans, even Caucasoids! Yet, if one stuck strictly to scientific data and archeological facts, the prototype of the White race would be sought in vain throughout the earliest years of present-day humanity. The Negro has been there from the beginning; for millennia he was the only one in existence. Nevertheless, on the threshold of the historical epoch, the "scholar" turns his back on him, raises questions about his genesis, and even speculates "objectively" about his tardy appearance: "It is quite possible that the Negro type, 'the true Negro' of the anthropologists, who now inhabits West and Equatorial West Africa, has existed since 10,000 B.C. Unfortunately, the conditions of the tropical soil do not readily permit the fossilization of bones and it is hardly probable that interesting finds will be made. For a long time to come this will leave the field open for any and all hypotheses concerning the populations of those regions." (Cornevin, *op. cit.,* p. 81.)

On carefully rereading Baumann and Westermann's *Les Peuples et les civilisations de l'Afrique,* the only ethnological synthesis on Black Africa, Mr. Cornevin will realize that he is mistaken and that Central and West Africa are inhabited almost exclusively by Eastern Hamites, if we are to accept the conclusions presented in that volume.

The difference in the intellectual approach of the African and European researcher often causes these misunderstandings in the interpretation of facts and their relative importance. The scientific interest of the European scholar with regard to African data is essentially analytical. Seeing things from the outside, often reluctant to synthesize, the European clings basically to explosive, more or less biased microanalysis of the facts and constantly postpones *ad infinitum* the stage of synthesis. The African scholar distrusts this "scientific" activity, the aim of which seems to be the fragmentation of the collective historical African consciousness into minute facts and details.[18]

If the African anthropologist made a point of examining European races "under the magnifying glass," he would be able to multiply them *ad infinitum* by grouping physiognomies into races and subraces as artificially as his European counterpart does with regard to Africa. He would, in turn, succeed in dissolving collective European reality into a fog of insignificant facts.

Conclusion

The condensation of our work that you have just read has by no means exhausted the subject; it is merely a progress report, prepared on the basis of documents available to us at the time. It is also an indication of the direction in which future generations of Black African scholars must continue calmly to work, for salvation lies at the end of that effort. Our various publications are rough outlines, successive stops in a scientific attempt to get closer and closer to the facts analyzed. It is therefore understandable why we never rewrite a work once it has been published. We prefer to pass along to the following stage with a new publication. Meanwhile we never fail to reply to the body of criticism addressed to us, without concealing all the difficulties raised by our adversaries; in this connection one can refer to the second part of *Antériorité*.

Research has made a prodigious leap forward in recent years with the emergence in French-speaking Africa of a young generation of scientists harnessed to the task of delving into the most diverse questions relative to human sciences: *L'Afrique dans l'Antiquité* by Théophile Obenga; *Pouvoir politique en Afrique* by Pathé Diagne; the writings of Boubacar Ly, Sossou N'Sougan, and others, inaugurate a new scientific era in Black Africa. The Africans are determined to show that this immense effort of cultural renewal will never depart from the scientific level to descend to the emotional. This is one reason why, at the plenary session of the International Scientific Committee on editing a general history of Africa—a meeting held in Paris in April–May 1971 under the auspices of UNESCO—I proposed three preconditions to the preparation of volume II (on African Antiquity). All three proposals were accepted:

1. An international colloquium, assembling Egyptologists and Africanists in Egypt for the first time to compare points of view of the anthropological identity of the ancient Egyptians;

2. An international colloquium on the decipherment of Meroitic, the ancient writing of Nubia (two meetings scheduled for Cairo, November 1973);

3. An aerial survey of Africa to retrace the ancient network of roads.

If, by scientific knowledge, we can eliminate all forms of the frustrations (cultural and others) which victimize peoples, the sincere rapprochement of mankind to create a true humanity will be fostered. May this volume contribute to that lofty objective!

Cheikh Anta Diop

Notes

CHAPTER I

1. *The History of Herodotus,* translated by George Rawlinson. New York: Tudor, 1928, p. 88.
2. *Ibid.,* p. 101.
3. *Ibid.,* p. 115.
4. *Ibid.,* p. 184.
5. *Histoire universelle,* translated by Abbé Terrasson. Paris, 1758, Bk. 3, p. 341.
6. Bk. 1, Chap. 3, par. 10.
7. The Colchians formed a cluster of Negroes among white populations near the Black Sea; that is why the problem of their origin intrigued scholars during Antiquity. One may suppose that "black" has a weakened meaning here to denote the "Semitic" tint of the Egyptian. But then the following question arises: Why did the Greeks reserve the term "Negro" for Egyptians alone, of all Semites? Why did they never apply it to Arabs, who are Semites par excellence?

   Did the Egyptians have "Semitic" features so close to those of other African Negroes that the Greeks found it natural to confuse them by using exclusively the same ethnic term (*melanos*), the strongest existing in Greek to denote a Black? This is the root used even today whenever one wishes to indicate a Negro type without ambiguity. Example: melanin, pigmentation that colors the skin of a Black; Melanesia, a group of islands inhabited by Negroes.

   As a matter of fact, the Greeks were very sensitive to color nuances and distinguished them clearly wherever they existed. In the same epoch, they designated the ancient Canaanites, then strongly mixed, by the Phoenician term which probably meant red and was thus perhaps an ethnic word. Strabo goes even further in his *Geography* and attempts to explain why Egyptians are blacker than Hindus (the famous dark red race of the moderns). Evidently, then, the Ancients distinguished Egyptians and Ethiopians from Semites and so-called dark red races. No scholarly interpretation of terms allows us to escape the truth by consciously obscuring that which is obvious. By indulging in such acrobatics to avoid accepting simple facts, one raises unsurmountable difficulties without realizing it.
8. Gaston Maspero, *Histoire ancienne des peuples de l'Orient.* Paris: Hachette, 1917, p. 15, 12th ed. (Translated as: *The Dawn of Civilization.* London, 1894; reprinted, New York: Frederick Ungar, 1968.)
9. Genesis, X, 6–16. New Catholic Edition of the Holy Bible. New York, 1953.
10. *Herodotus,* p. 236.
11. *Ibid.,* pp. 133–134.
12. *Ibid.,* pp. 88–89.
13. *Sciences et Avenir,* No. 56, October 1951.
14. Cornelius de Pauw, *Recherches philosophiques sur les Egyptiens et les Chinois.* Berlin, 1773, II, 337.
15. J. J. Bachofen, *Pages choisies par Adrien Turel,* "Du Règne de la mère au patriarcat." Paris: F. Alcan, 1938, p. 89.
16. Cf. Exodus, I, 7–14, 16–17.

17. D. P. de Pédrals, *Archéologie de l'Afrique Noire*. Paris: Payot, 1950, p. 37.
18. Genesis, XV, 13. If the Biblical version is even slightly accurate, how could the Jewish people be free of Negro blood? In 400 years it grew from 70 to 600,000 individuals in the midst of a Negro nation that dominated it throughout that period. If the Negroid traits of Jews are less pronounced today, this is very likely due to their crossbreeding with European elements since their dispersion. At present it seems almost certain that Moses was an Egyptian, therefore a Negro.
19. Pédrals, *op. cit.,* p. 27. Here he is quoting Louis J. Morié.

CHAPTER II

1. What we find in the Sahara shows that it was inhabited by Negroes: "Steatopygic female bodies, as the ethnologists say. As Jean Temporal describes them, 'with backsides quite full and round.'" Théodore Monod, *Méharées, exploration au vrai Sahara* (Paris: Ed. "Je sers," 1937, p. 108).

"Peasants, perhaps Negro peasants, innumerable oxen, fields of millet, pots made of terra cotta, fresh fish, an abundance of game, a green countryside, and solidly built canoes, all well and good. But that was not to last. The humid period had been preceded by a hot, barren interlude that would gradually be replaced by a new desiccation. The desert reconquered its kingdom, draining lakes, drying up grass, obliterating the countryside.

"And what about the people? Hard times for them and serious debates in Parliament: Should they remain there and let themselves die, or migrate, or adapt? No one opted for suicide, adaptation did not get a single vote; the unanimous choice was exodus." (*Ibid.,* p. 128.)

Prehistoric skeletons found in the Sahara are of the Negro type: the Assclar man, south Sahara.

2. "Negro, Negress (Latin *niger:* black), man, woman with black skin. This is the name given especially to the inhabitants of certain countries in Africa . . . who form a race of black men inferior in intelligence to the white or Caucasian race." *Nouveau Dictionnaire Larousse*, 1905, p. 516.

3. "If, with the Greeks and the most competent authorities on the subject, we agree that exaltation and enthusiasm are inseparable from artistic genius and that genius, when complete, borders on madness, we shall not seek the cause of creativity in any well-organized, reasonable sentiment of our nature, but rather in the depths of sensual upsurges in those aspiring thrusts which lead them to blend spirit with appearances, in order to produce something more pleasant than reality . . . Accordingly, we reach this inescapable conclusion: that the source of the arts is foreign to the civilizing instincts. It is hidden in the blood of the Blacks . . . This, you will agree, is quite a lovely crown that I place on the deformed head of the Negro, a very great honor for him to have the harmonious chorus of the Muses grouped around him. [Yet] the honor is not so great. I have not said that all the Pierides are assembled there. The noblest ones are absent, those which depend on serious thought, those which prefer beauty to passion . . . Let us translate for [the Black] verses of the *Odyssey*, especially the encounter of Ulysses and Nausicaa, the most sublime example of thoughtful inspiration, and he will fall asleep. For sympathy to be aroused in any human being, his intelligence must first have understood, and that is where the difficulty lies with the Negro . . . His artistic sensibility, though powerful beyond expression, will necessarily remain limited to the most wretched uses . . . And so, of all the arts that the black creature prefers, music ranks

first, insofar as it caresses the ear with a succession of sounds and requires no response from the thinking part of his brain. . . .

"Picture a Bambara listening to one of the melodies that please him. His face lights up, his eyes shine. He laughs and his wide mouth, sparkling in his dusky face, shows his white pointed teeth. A sexual climax occurs . . . Inarticulate sounds try to escape from his throat, choked by passion, big tears run down his fat cheeks; a little more and he would scream. The music stops; he is exhausted.

"With our refined habits, we have made art something so intimately connected with sublime mental meditations and scientific ideas, that it is only by abstraction and a certain effort that we are able to include the dance [among the arts.] For the Negro, the dance, along with music, is the object of the most irresistible passion. This is because sensuality means almost everything, if not everything in the dance.

"Consequently, the Negro possesses in the highest degree the sensual faculty without which no art is possible. On the other hand, the absence of intellectual aptitudes makes him completely powerless to cultivate art, even to appreciate the loftiest work that this noble application of the human intelligence can produce. To develop his faculties, he must unite with a race differently endowed.

"Artistic genius, similarly alien to the three great types [races], has appeared only as a result of union between Whites and Blacks." Comte de Gobineau, *Essai sur l'inégalité des races humaines*. (Paris: 1853, Bk. II, Chap. VII, first edition.)

4. This sentence first appeared in Léopold Sédar Senghor's essay: "Ce que l'Homme noir apporte," in *L'Homme de couleur* (Paris: Plon, 1939, p. 295). The exact wording is: "L'emotion est nègre, comme la raison hellene." "Does this mean, as certain young people would llke to interpret my remarks," Senghor asks many years later, "that the Negro African lacks discursive reason, that he has never used any? I have never said so. In truth, every ethnic group possesses different aspects of reason and all the virtues of man, but each has stressed only one aspect of reason, only certain virtues." (Senghor, *On African Socialism*. New York: Praeger, 1964, p. 75.) *(Tr.)*

5. Aimé Césaire, *Soleil cou coupé*. Paris: Editions K, 1948, p. 66.

6. Aimé Césaire, *Return to My Native Land*, translated by Emile Snyders. Paris: Présence Africaine, 1968, pp. 99 & 101. This quotation does not in the slightest weaken my deep admiration for the author.

7. C. F. Volney, *Voyages en Syrie et en Egypte*. Paris, 1787, I, 74–77.

CHAPTER III

1. *L'Océanie*. Paris: Collection l'Univers, 1836, vol. I.

2. The yellow race as well was probably the result of crossbreeding between Blacks and Whites at a very ancient time in the history of mankind. In fact, the yellow peoples have the pigmentation of mixed breeds, so much so that comparative biochemical analysis would be unable to reveal any great difference in the quantity of melanin. No systematic study of blood groups in mixed breeds has been made to date. It would have permitted an interesting comparison with those of the yellow race.

The ethnic features of yellow peoples, lips, nose, prognathism, are those of the mixed breed. Their facies (high cheekbones, puffed eyelids, Mongolian pucker, slant eyes, depression at the bridge of the nose) could merely result from the effect of thousands of years in a climate that blows cold winds on the face. The crispation of the face as a result of the wind would suffice to explain the prominent cheekbones and puffed eyelids, which form two correlative ethnic traits.

Beating against the face in cold weather, the wind can escape through the corner of the ey·e only by following an oblique upward movement, after the molecules of air have been warmed. In the long run, this mechanical force could produce a deformation of the eye in the same direction. Such an action by the climate could be even stronger on a young organism like that of a child. This explanation obviously assumes the heredity of acquired characteristics.

It is known, moreover, that these features, called Mongolian, change from northern to southern Asia, following to some extent a climatic curve. And it has been observed that, wherever there are yellow-skinned peoples, one still finds small pockets of Blacks and Whites who seem to be the residual elements of the race. This is the case throughout southeast Asia: the Mois in the mountains of Viet-Nam where, in addition, it is curious to encounter such names as Kha, Thai, and Cham; the Negritos and Ainus in Japan, etc. According to a Japanese proverb: "For a Samurai to be brave, he must have a bit of Black blood." Chinese chroniclers report that a Negro empire existed in the south of China at the dawn of that country's history.

Proto-Aryan + Proto-Dravidian + cold climate = Yellow?

3. Champollion-Figeac, *Egypte ancienne*. Paris: Collection l'Univers, 1839, pp. 30–31.

The oldest Egyptian monuments which depict all the races of the earth—the bas-reliefs of Biban-el-Moluk, for example—show that during those early epochs only the so-called Nordic race was tattooed. Neither Negro Egyptians nor other African Blacks practiced tattooing, according to all known Egyptian documents. Originally, tattooing made no sense except on a white skin where it produced a difference of tint. With the white Libyans, it was introduced into Africa, but would not be imitated by Negroes until much later. Since the blue-white or any other contrast cannot possibly be realized on a black skin, they resorted to scarification.

Unfortunately, we have been unable to publish a reproduction of Champollion's bas-reliefs.

4. Champollion-Figeac, *ibid.*, p. 27.

5. *Ibid.*, pp. 26–27.

6. *Ibid.*, p. 27.

7. Figeac was unaware that all frizzy hair is woolly. Keratin, a chemical substance basic to wool, makes hair curly. Thus, his argument is worthless.

8. Marius Fontanes, *Les Egyptes (de 5000 à 715)*. Paris: Ed. Lemerre, n.d., p. 169.

9. Champollion-Figeac, *ibid.*, p. 27.

10. *Ibid.*

11. Chérubini, *La Nubie*. Paris: Collection l'Univers, 1847, pp. 2–3.

12. Chérubini alludes to this passage from Diodorus of Sicily:

"The Ethiopians call themselves the first of all men and cite proofs they consider evident. It is generally agreed that, born in a country and not having come from elsewhere, they must be judged indigenous. It is likely that located directly under the course of the sun, they sprang from the earth before other men. For, if the heat of the sun, combining with the humidity of the soil, produces life, those sites nearest the Equator must have produced living beings earlier than any others. The Ethiopians also say that they instituted the cult of the gods, festivals, solemn assemblies, sacrifices; in short, all the practices by which we honor the gods. For that reason they are deemed the most religious of all men and they believe their sacrifices to be the most pleasing to the gods. One of the most ancient and the most respected poet in Greece renders them this homage when he introduces Jupiter and other gods en route to Ethiopia (in the *Iliad*) to attend the feast and annual sacrifices prepared for them all by the Ethiopians:

Jupiter today, followed by all the gods,
Receives the sacrifices of the Ethiopians. (*Iliad*, I, 422)

"They claim that the gods have rewarded their piety by important blessings, such as never having been dominated by any foreign prince. In fact, thanks to the great unity that has always existed among them, they have always kept their freedom. Several very powerful princes, who tried to subjugate them, have failed in that endeavor. Cambyses came to attack them with numerous troops; his army perished and he ran the risk of losing his own life. Semiramis, the queen, known for her cleverness and exploits, had scarcely entered Ethiopia when she realized that her plan could not succeed. Bacchus and Hercules, after crossing the whole earth, abstained from fighting the Ethiopians, either through fear of their power or respect for their piety. . . . (*Histoire universelle*, Bk. I, 337–341.)

13. Chérubini, *ibid.*, pp. 28–29.
14. *Ibid.*, p. 73.
15. *Ibid.*, p. 30.
16. *Ibid.*
17. *Ibid.*, p. 32.
18. Nahas: "good-for-nothing," in Wolof.
19. According to Marius Fontanes, *ibid.*, p. 219.
20. Fontanes, *ibid.*, pp. 44–45.
21. *Ibid.*, pp. 47–48.
22. Maspero, *ibid.*, p. 19. Maspero observes that this is also the thesis of naturalists and anthropologists such as Hartmann, Morton, Hamy, and Sergi.
23. Raymond Furon, *Manuel d'archéologie préhistorique*. Paris, 1943, p. 178.
24. *Ibid.*, p. 371.
25. *Ibid.*, pp. 14–15.
26. *Ibid.*, p. 15.
27. Dumoulin de Laplante, *Histoire générale synchronique*. Paris, 1947, p. 13.
28. Cf. the passage from Furon which we quote in note 26.
29. Abbé Henri Breuil, "L'Afrique du Sud", *Les Nouvelles littéraires*, April 5, 1951.
30. Abbé Breuil, *ibid.*
31. *History of Herodotus*, p. 256.
32. Fontanes, *ibid.*, pp. 60–61.
33. Cf. Hardy, *Histoire d'Afrique*, pp. 28–29.
34. These two plural forms in *n* and *a* also existed in old High German.
35. Abderrahman es-Sa'di, *Tarikh es-Sudan*.
36. Maspero, *ibid.*, p. 15.
37. According to Amélineau, the Egyptians designated the heart of Africa by the word *Amami*: land of the ancestors; *Mamyi*: ancestors, in Wolof.
38. Maspero, *ibid.*, p. 16.
39. *Ibid.*
40. *Ibid.*, pp. 16–17.
41. *Ibid.*, pp. 17–18.

42. Abbé Emile Amélineau, *Nouvelles Fouilles d'Abydos*. Paris: Ed. Leroux, 1899, p. 248.
43. *Ibid.*, p. 271.
44. Amélineau, *Prolégomènes à l'étude de la religion égyptienne*. Paris: Ed. Leroux, 1916, part 2, 124.
45. Hieroglyph: an arrow with two feathers or reeds.
46. Amélineau, *Prolégomènes*, pp. 124–125.
47. *Ibid.*, pp. 257–258.
48. *Ibid.*, p. 330.
49. Jean Capart, *Les Débuts de l'art en Egypte*. Brussels: Ed. Vromant, 1904, fig. 14, p. 37.
50. Cf. Amélineau, *Prolégomènes*, p. 413.

CHAPTER IV

1. Cf. V. Gordon Childe, *New Light on the Most Ancient East*. London: Kegan Paul, Trench, Trubner & Co., Ltd., 1934.
2. Capart, *ibid.*
3. Childe, *ibid.*, pp. 85–86.
4. *Ibid.*, pp. 100–101. (On pp. 12–13 of this volume, Childe explains "S.D." as Sequence Dates, a numerical scale worked out by Sir Flinders Petrie, going from 30 to 80. The period between S.D. 30 and S.D. 77 is ordinarily called Predynastic. S.D. 30 is assumed to equal 5000 B.C.—ED.)
5. Alexandre Moret & Georges Davy, *From Tribe to Empire*. New York: Cooper Square Publishers, Inc., 1970, pp. 132–133. This is V. Gordon Childe's translation of *Des clans aux empires*. Paris: Ed. La Renaissance du Livre, 1923.
6. In "Isis and Osiris," Plutarch related that Osiris was born on the first of the intercalary days, as Moret writes. That is, on the 361st day of the year, which corresponds to the 26th of December, when we take into account the reform of the calendar. Pope Julius I (fourth century) fixed December 25th as the birthday of Christ, but we know that Christ had no vital statistics; no one knows the date of his birth. What could have inspired Pope Julius I to choose that date—only one day removed from the birthday of Osiris—unlesss it be the Egyptian tradition perpetuated by the Roman calendar? This becomes evident when the idea of a tree is associated with the birth of Christ. That would seem arbitrary if we did not know that Osiris was also the god of vegetation. Sometimes he was even painted green in the image of that vegetation, whose rebirth he symbolized. His symbol was a tree with cut branches set up to announce the resurrection of plant life. This was an impressive agrarian rite characterizing a sedentary society. The plant symbol of Osiris was called *Djed* in Egyptian. In Wolof, we have: *Djed:* standing, erect, planted upright; *Djan:* vertical; *Djed-Djed-âral:* very erect (intensification of *Djed); Djen:* a post.
Such, then, could be the remote origin of the Christmas tree. Once again we see, on retracing the course of time, that more than one feature of Western civilization, whose origin has been forgotten, loses its enigmatic character when linked with its Negro-African source.
Taking our inspiration from Plutarch, we could also establish a relationship between the birth of Nephthys (sister of Isis and Osiris), who enters the world through her mother's ribs, and that of Eve, created from the rib of Adam.
7. Alexandre Moret, *Le Nil et la civilisation égyptienne*, p. 122.

8. Amélineau, *Prolégomènes,* p. 203.
9. *Ibid.,* p. 104.
10. *Ibid.*
11. *Ibid.,* p. 105.
12. *Ibid.,* p. 106.
13. *Ibid.,* p. 102.
14. *Ibid.*
15. *Mam y alla:* Ancestor God, in Wolof. Although the Arabic word *alla* replaces the primitive African term, this expression still reveals the concept of an ancestral god.
16. Moret would like to prove that the Egyptian calendar was invented at Heliopolis. Existing documents testify to the contrary: "The priests at Thebes are reputed to be the most learned in astronomy and philosophy. They began the custom of telling time, not according to the revolution of the moon, but by that of the sun. To twelve months of thirty days each, they add five days a year. A certain fraction of a day is still left over, so to complete the duration of the year, they form a period comprising an even number of days . . . ; when the excess fractions are added, they make a whole day." (Strabo, Bk. XVII, Chap. 1, par. 22, 816.)
    This fraction (one-fourth of a day), when added up, amounts to one day every four years, one year every 1,460 years—whence the period of 1,461, at the end of which the ordinary year began again with the solar year (Sothic cycle).
17. Edouard Naville, "L'Origine africaine de la civilisation égyptienne," *Revue archéologique,* Paris, 1913.
18. *History of Herodotus,* p. 113.
19. Moret & Davy, *ibid.,* pp. 338–339.
20. *Ibid.*
21. *Ibid.,* p. 170.
22. The Tehenu or black Lebou was probably the ancestor of the modern Lebou of the Cap-Vert Peninsula. The Blacks preceded the Temehou or white Libyans (people of the sea) in that region of the western Delta. The existence of that first black inhabitant, the Tehenu, made it possible to create confusion over the term "brown Libyan." Although really designating the Negro indistinguishable, except in civilization, from other Egyptians, he was to serve in official textbooks as a hypothetical ancestor of the Berber. . . .

CHAPTER V

1. Moret & Davy, *op. cit.,* p. 122.
2. James H. Breasted, *The Conquest of Civilization.* New York: Harper & Brothers, 1926, fig. 57.
3. *Ibid.,* p. 128, note 1.
4. Cf. Diodorus, *Histoire universelle,* Bk. 1, Sect. 1, 56–57.
5. Ferdinand Hoefer, *Chaldée, Assyrie, Médie, Babylonie, Mésopotamie, Phénicie.* Paris: Ed. Didot frères, 1852, p. 390.
6. Genesis, X, 9–11.
7. Georges Contenau, *Manuel d'archéologie orientale.* Paris: J. Picard, 1947, IV, 1850–1858.
8. François Lenormant, *Histoire ancienne des Phéniciens.* Paris: Lévy, 1890, pp. 96–98.
9. Contenau, *ibid.,* p. 97.

10. *Ibid.*, p. 98.
11. Quoted by Christian Zervos, *L'Art en Mésopotamie*. Ed. Cahiers d'Art, 1935. [In *Gods, Graves, and Scholars:* (New York: Knopf, 1967), C. W. Ceram calls the Gilgamesh Epic "the first great epic of world history" and quotes from this work "the primal version of the Biblical legend of the Deluge." ED.]
12. Contenau, *ibid.*, III, 1563.
13. Georges Contenau, *La Civilisation des Hittites et des Mitanniens*. Paris: Payot, 1934, I, 49.
14. Marcel Brion, *La Résurrection des villes mortes*. Paris: Payot, 1948, p. 65. Translated as *The World of Archeology*. New York: Macmillan, 1962.
15. Diodorus, Bk. 1, Sect. 2, 102.
16. Strabo, Bk. 15, Chap. 3, 728.
17. Genesis, XII, 1–6.
18. *Ibid.*, XXXIV, 20–21.
19. Hoefer, *op.cit.*, p. 158.
20. Lenormant, *op.cit.*, pp. 484–486.
21. Contenau, *Manuel d'archéologie orientale*, p. 1791.
22. The root of the word Thebes is not Indo-European. According to Greek orthography, it should be pronounced Taïba. In Black Africa today, in Senegal for example, there are several cities named Taïba. It is reasonable to assume that those cities got their name from that of the sacred ancient capital of Upper Egypt.
23. Lenormant, *ibid.*, pp. 497–498.
24. A few Germanic tribes knew the matriarchal system, but that was an exception among the barbarians, as Tacitus pointed out:
    "Yet the laws of matrimony are severely observed there; nor in the whole of their manners is aught more praiseworthy than this: for they are almost the only barbarians contented with one wife, excepting a very few amongst them; men of dignity who marry diverse wives, from no wantonness or lubricity, but courted for the lustre of their family into many alliances.
    "To the husband, the wife tenders no dowry; but the husband, to the wife . . .
    "Children are holden in the same estimation with their mother's brother, as with their father. Some hold this tie of blood to be most inviolable and binding, and in receiving of hostages, such pledges are most considered and claimed, as they who at once possess affections the most unalienable, and the most diffuse interest in their family. To every man, however, his own children are heirs and successors." (Tacitus, *Germany*, translated by Thomas Gordon, *Harvard Classics*. New York: P. F. Collier & Son, 1938, XXXIII, 103–104.)
    It is rather probable that this trait of Negro culture was introduced among the Germans, then half-sedentary, at the same time the worship of Isis was imported. Tacitus stresses the foreign origin of this cult: "Some of the Suevians make likewise immolations to *Isis*. Concerning the use and origin of this foreign sacrifice I have found small light; unless the figure of her image formed like a galley, show that such devotion arrived from abroad." (*Ibid.*, pp. 97–98.)
    Caesar was born 155 years before Tacitus. He also wrote about the customs of Gauls and Romans, but nowhere mentioned matriarchy, or the presence of priests and other religious aspects noted by Tacitus.
25. Caesar and Tacitus describe the warlike, savage customs of the nomadic or semi-nomadic Germans before they acquired a sense of land ownership:

"They do not apply themselves to farming and live mainly on milk, cheese, and meat. No one has a piece of land of his own with fixed limits; but each year the magistrates and chiefs assign to different small tribes and families a certain amount of terrain in whatever district they deem appropriate. The following year they are forced to move elsewhere. This they justify by several arguments: they fear that the force and attraction of habit may make them lose their taste for war and prefer agriculture. . . . The greatest honor for cities is to be surrounded by devastated frontiers and vast wilderness. They believe that the mark of courage is to compel neighboring tribes to desert their territory and to see no one dare to settle nearby. At the same time they feel safer with no sudden invasions to fear. . . . There is nothing shameful about theft committed beyond the frontiers of the city; this serves, they say, to provide exercise for the young men and to lessen laziness." (Caesar, *Commentaries,* French ed., Bk. 6, Chap. 22, 23.)

"The most glaring disgrace that can befall them, is to have quitted their shield. . . . Their wounds and maims they carry to their mothers, or to their wives, neither are their mothers or wives shocked in telling, or in sucking their bleeding sores. Nay, to their husbands and sons whilst engaged in battle, they administer meat and encouragement. . . . Many of the young nobility, when their own community comes to languish in its vigor by long peace and inactivity, betake themselves through impatience to other States which then prove to be in war. For, besides that this people cannot brook repose, besides that by perilous adventures they more quickly blazon their fame, they cannot otherwise than by violence and war support their huge train of retainers. . . . " (Tacitus, *Germany, Harvard Classics,* XXXIII, 97–107 passim.)

26. "Our ancestors did not allow women to handle any business, even domestic, without special authorization. They never failed to keep women dependent on their fathers, brothers, or husbands. As for us, if it pleases the gods, we shall soon permit them to participate in the direction of public affairs, to frequent the Forum, to hear the speeches and to become involved in the proceedings. List all the legislation by which our ancestors tried to curb women's independence and keep them submissive to their husbands; then see, despite all these legal obstacles, how much trouble we have in restricting them to their duties. If you let them break those restrictions one after another, free themselves from all dependence, and place themselves on a par with their husbands, do you think it will be possible for their husbands to stand them? Women will no sooner become our equals than they will dominate us." (Livy, *Histoire romaine,* Bk. 34: "Cato's speech on maintaining the Oppia Law against the luxury of women." 195 B.C.)

27. Joseph Vendryes, *Les Religions des Celtes, des Germains et des anciens Slaves.* Coll. "Mana," III, 244.

28. The intolerance of the Church during the Middle Ages rules out placing its origin in that period. To relate it to the return of the Crusaders would be to assume that those who went off to fight one "heresy" brought back another.

29. Pierre Hubac, *Carthage.* Paris: Ed. Bellenand, 1952, p. 170.

30. Walter von Wartburg, *Problèmes et méthodes de la linguistique.* Paris: Presses Universitaires de France, 1946, p. 41.

31. Lenormant, *op.cit.,* p. 543.

32. *Ibid.*

33. *Les Races et l'histoire,* p. 409.

34. *Ibid.*, p. 411.
35. *Ibid.*, p. 407.
36. *Les Phéniciens,* pp. 368ff. Lenormant gained this information from al-Masudi, *Les Prairies d'or.* Paris: Imprimerie impériale, 1861–1917. 9 vols.
37. Lenormant, *ibid.*, p. 373.
38. *Ibid.*, p. 374.
39. Far from having introduced the caste system in India, the Aryas seem to have adopted it, as Lenormant observes. If this system rested on an ethnic base, there would be, at most, as many castes as races; but such was not the case. According to ancient writers, Strabo in particular, the system stemmed directly from the division of labor in society, as is true among all other Kushites. Strabo lists as follows the seven castes then existing: 1. philosophers; 2. farmers; 3. shepherds and hunters; 4. artisans and workmen; 5. soldiers; 6. those who scour the country to inform the king on whatever is happening; 7. the king's advisors and courtiers. (Bk. 15, Chap. 1, par. 29–38.)
Strabo states that the castes did not mix, but there was as yet no mention of "pariahs." Thus this caste seems to result from a recent transformation of Indian sociey with the decline of Dravidian supremacy. The texts on which the existence of an untouchable caste in earliest Antiquity is based are probably apochryphal.
A Dravidian can be a Brahmin, in other words, a Negro can belong to the highest class or caste in society. This remains true no matter how far back in time one may go. It is therefore absurd to try to assign an ethnic base to the caste system.
It would seem that Buddha was an Egyptian priest, chased from Memphis by the persecutions of Cambyses. This tradition would justify the portrayal of Buddha with woolly hair. Historical documents do not invalidate this tradition. "Koempfer, in his *Histoire du Japon,* claims that the Saçya Buddha of India was a priest from Memphis, who fled from Egypt when Cambyses invaded it. . . . Koempfer wanted to reduce everything to a dominant idea: the diffusion of Egyptian doctrines in Asia by priests from Thebes or Memphis exiled by Cambyses or fleeing his persecution. A modern author gets the same results by another road. William Ward, who published some years ago a vast compilation of various documents on Hindu religion, history, and literature, based on extracts from books in Sanskrit, included a biographical account of Buddha, establishing that he could not have appeared until the sixth century B.C. . . . Buddha is given the surname Goulama, which is that of the usurper's race." (M. de Marlès, *Histoire générale de l'Inde.* Paris, 1928, I, 470–472.)
There is general agreement today on placing in the sixth century not only Buddha but the whole religious and philosophical movement in Asia, with Confucius in China, Zoroaster in Iran. This would confirm the hypothesis of a dispersion of Egyptian priests at that time spreading their doctrine in Asia. It is difficult to explain this religious movement by a simultaneous evolution of the different countries involved.
40. Lenormant, *op.cit.,* p. 384.
41. Ernest Renan, *Histoire des langues sémitiques,* quoted by Lenormant, p. 385.
42. Lenormant, *ibid.*, p. 361.
43. *Ibid.*, pp. 429–430.
44. Lenormant betrays himself when he speaks about relations between Egypt and Ethiopia: at that time he uses Kushite as a synonym for Negro. Let us remember that Kush is a word of Hebrew origin, meaning Negro.

CHAPTER VI

1. Massoulard, *op. cit.*, pp. 420–421.
2. Breasted, *op. cit.*, p. 113.
3. Pédrals, *op. cit.*, p. 6.
4. *Géographie, classe de 5ᵉ.* Collection Cholley, Ed. Ballière et fils, 1950.

CHAPTER VII

1. *History of Herodotus*, p. 115.
2. The probability of encountering men with black skin and woolly hair, without any other ethnic feature common to Negroes, is scientifically nil. To call such individuals "Whites with black skin" because they allegedly have fine features, is as absurd as the appellation "Negroes with white skin" would be if applied to three-fourths of the Europeans who lack Nordic features. That is why such an attitude is only pseudo-scientific, even if the person who adopts it claims to be strictly scientific; it consists of generalizing from infinitesimal exceptions.
3. Marcel Griaule, *Dieu d'eau*. Paris: Editions du Chêne, 1948, pp. 187, 189.
4. Baumann & Westermann, *Les Peuples et civilisations de l'Afrique*, followed by *Les Langues et l'éducation*. Paris: Payot, 1948, p. 328.
5. Paul Masson-Oursel, *La Philosophie en Orient*, supplement to Emile Bréhier's *Histoire de la philosophie*, p. 42.
6. *Ibid.*, p. 43.
7. The name Meroë does not seem to derive from an African root. It is probably what foreigners used after Cambyses to designate the capital of Ethiopia (in the Sudan). Quoting Diodorus, Strabo reports that the wife—or sister—of Cambyses was killed in Ethiopia and was buried there when this conqueror tried unsuccessfully to take the country by force. Her name was Meroë.
8. Mahmoud Kâti, *Tarikh el Fettach*, p. 80, French translation by O. Houdas and M. Delafosse. Paris, 1913.
9. *Voyage au Soudan*, translated by Slane, p. 12.
10. The term "Ethiopian" was applied essentially to Black populations, to the civilized Negroes of the Meroitic Sudan as well as to those rather savage Negroes who were their neighbors: the Strutophagi (ostrich eaters), Ichthyophagi (fish eaters), "elephant riders," etc. Their skin color was not simply "browned," "reddened," "bronzed," or "suntanned"; it was pitch black, like that of the god Osiris; they were free of any White admixture.
11. They would never have foreseen that a reversal of the situation could one day bring a Sudanese king to "take pride in" the title Lion of Judah. Less than 111 centuries separate them from the epoch of the Queen of Sheba; yet their perfectly Negro features show that the racial mixture of the emperors of Ethiopia, far from going back to an alleged union between Solomon and the Queen of Sheba (reigning over Ethiopia and a colonized Arabia), came much later. A laconic passage in the Bible informs us that the Queen of Sheba visited Solomon, was well received, asked him riddles that he solved, and then returned home. No known historical document authorizes us to speak today of a marriage between Solomon and the Queen of Sheba.
12. Chérubini, *op. cit.*, p. 108.
13. Pédrals, *op. cit.*, pp. 18–19.
14. Maurice Delafosse, *Les Noirs de l'Afrique*. Paris: Payot, 1922. This was

translated by F. Fligeman as *The Negroes of Africa*. Washington, D.C.: Associated Publishers, 1931.

15. "Before leaving Nubia, I shall take the liberty of jotting down a few observations capable of establishing the anteriority of its civilization to that of Egypt. This question, still unanswered by historical documents, acquires in my view much clarity when we carefully examine the monuments and natural productions of Ethiopia or Upper Nubia. I am not so presumptuous as to think that my ideas will remove all doubt on a subject that has long been controversial; my sole aim is to inspire better ideas. I have reported a great number of ancient usages which have continued in Nubia but have left no traces in Egypt. We cannot, I agree, draw from this any proof that these usages were not born in Egypt. But if we are able to establish that the principal objects used in the cult of the ancient Egyptians were products belonging exclusively to Ethiopia, one will be led to recognize that this cult was not created in Egypt. It is rightly said that migrations of peoples seeking a settlement go down river. Adopting this natural trend, we could not refuse to conclude that Ethiopia was inhabited before Egypt. Thus, Ethiopia was the first to have laws, arts, writing, but these civilizing elements, still crude and imperfect, were greatly developed in Egypt, which was favored by the climate, the nature of the soil, and the geographical position. In Egypt, the sculptor's chisel was able to present in more regular form the emblems of the primitive beliefs of his fellow citizens, in order to decorate those temples, those monuments that astonish us by their imposing massiveness, of which the territory of Thebes offers such magnificent examples. As several scholars have written, Mr. Jomard among others, arts perfected in Egypt returned up river. . . . Such, in fact, was my opinion in 1816, on seeing the monuments of Lower Nubia, most of which are recognized today as being later than the monuments of Thebes." (Frédéric Cailliaud, *Voyage à Méroë*, 1836, III, 271ff.)

16. *Ibid.*, III, 165.

17. Delafosse, *The Negroes of Africa*, pp. 125–126.

18. "Africa long remained a mystery and, yet . . . was it not one of the cradles of history? An African country, Egypt, thousands of years old, still presents, practically intact today, the most venerable monuments of Antiquity. At a time when all Europe was only savagery, when Paris and London were swamps, and Rome and Athens uninhabited sites, Africa already possessed an antique civilization in the valley of the Nile; it had populous cities, the labor of generations on the same soil, great public works, sciences, and arts; it had already produced gods." (Jacques Weulersse, *L'Afrique Noire*. Paris: Ed. Arthème Fayard, 1934, p. 11.)

CHAPTER VIII

1. Leo Frobenius, *Mythologie de l'Atlantide*. Paris: Payot, 1949.

2. Here is the famous passage from *The Book of the Dead*, in which the deceased renders an accounting of his earthly acts before the Tribunal presided over by the god Osiris. It is readily seen that Judaism, Christianity, and Islam, later religions, have taken the dogma of the Last Judgment from this text: "I have not sinned against men . . . I have done nothing to displease the gods, I have indisposed no one against his superior. I have not let anyone go hungry. I have not made anyone weep. I have not killed, nor ordered anyone to kill. I have made no one suffer. I have not cut down on food for the temple. I have not touched the bread of the gods. I have not

stolen offerings to the blessed dead. I have not reduced the measure of grain. I have not shortened by one cubit nor cheated on weights. I have not taken milk away from the mouth of the child. I have not removed cattle from the pasture. I have not dammed flood water during its period. . . . I have done no damage to herd, property, or temple funds. Be praised, O God! See, I come to you without sin, without evil. . . . I have done what is pleasing to the gods. I have given bread to the hungry, water to the thirsty, clothes to the naked, a boat to him who had none. I have made offerings to the gods and funeral gifts to the blessed dead. Save me, protect me. You will not accuse me before the Great God. I am a man with pure mouth and pure heart. Those who see me say, Welcome!"

3. Frobenius, *Histoire de la civilisation africaine.* Paris: Gallimard, 1938.
4. Ibn Battuta, *op. cit.,* pp. 25–26. This is quoted from Gibb's *Ibn Battuta, Travels in Asia and Africa.* London, 1929, pp. 326–327.
5. This testimony of Ibn Battuta confirms what the ancients (Herodotus, Diodorus, *et al.*) have taught us about the virtues of the Ethiopians.
6. *Op. cit.,* p. 36. Translated by Basil Davidson, from the French of C. Défremery & B. R. Sanguinetti, in *The African Past,* p. 82.
7. *Op. cit.,* p. 10.
8. Delafosse, *Les Noirs de l'Afrique,* p. 62.
9. Quoted by Pédrals, *op. cit.,* p. 7.

CHAPTER IX

1. The word *Kondrong,* a dwarf inhabiting the forest, with a good-luck utensil on his head, suggests the memory of cohabitation with the Pygmy in a forest area before the installation of the Wolof on the plains of Cayor-Baol, where there were neither forests nor Pygmies.
2. Armand d'Avezac-Macaya, *L'Afrique ancienne.* Paris: Didot, 1842, p. 26.
3. Edouard Schuré no less surprisingly reports a portion of these legends about early domination by Blacks: "After the red race, the black race ruled the globe. . . . The Blacks invaded southern Europe during prehistoric times. Their memory has been completely erased from our popular traditions. Nevertheless, they have left indelible traces. . . . At the time of their domination, the Blacks had religious centers in Upper Egypt and India. Their gigantic cities crenelated the mountains of Africa, Caucasia, and central Asia. Their social organization was an absolute theocracy. Their priests possessed profound knowledge, the principle of the divine unity of the universe and the cult of the stars which became Sabaeanism among the Whites . . . an active industry, especially the art of handling colossal masses of stone by ballistics and of smelting metals in immense furnaces worked by prisoners of war. . . .

"The white race had just been awakened by the attacks of the black race which was beginning to invade southern Europe. At first it was slaughter. The Whites, half-savage, leaving their forests and lakeside huts, had no weapons other than their bows, spears, and stone-tipped arrows. The Blacks had iron weapons, bronze armor, all the resources of an industrial civilization and their Cyclopean cities. Crushed by the first onslaught, the Whites were taken into captivity and became en masse the slaves of the Blacks, who forced them to work on stone and to carry ore to their furnaces. Escaped prisoners took back to the fatherland the arts and fragments of the science of their conquerors. From the Blacks they had learned two essentials: the smelting of metals, and sacred writing, hieroglyphics. What saved the Whites was their forests where, like wild animals, they could hide and then spring out at the propitious moment." (*Les Grands Initiés*, Paris, 1908, pp. 6–13.)

4. Because of its laconic nature, Hannon's travel account teaches us very little about the Negro populations who had reached the coast by the fifth century B.C. when the Carthaginians, threatened by the rapid development of the Indo-European States on the northern Mediterranean, fell back on Africa and tried to found colonies all along the coast. According to Auguste Mer, a mariner who claimed to know those coasts intimately, the deserted area noted by Hannon would be the stretch of shore extending from Saint-Louis-du-Sénégal to Dakar. He also shares the opinion of those who think that the Theon Ochema (Chariot of the gods) which marks the farthest point reached by Hannon, was probably Mount Cameroon. . . .

5. Bory de Saint Vincent, *Histoire et description des Iles de l'Océan*. Paris: Didot, 1839.

6. *Rom*: man, in Egyptian. *Ya-ram*: body, in Wolof. Based on the etymology given *Ya* by the author, *Ya-ram* probably meant living body, living man.

7. Mandu: a saint who practices religion to the letter, in Wolof.

8. Joseph Maes, "Pierres levées de Tundi-Daro," *Bull. Com. Et. A. O. F.*, 1924.

9. In Egypt, because of geographical conditions—the absence of rain and the fecundation of the soil by the "earthly" water of the Nile—the sexual role of the divine couple was reversed: the Sky was the goddess, the Earth the male god.

10. The Egyptian hieroglyph designating the tomb is a Nubian pyramid (great height on a narrow base), which is read: *Mr*. In Serer, the same type of tomb is called *m'banar*. Among Wolof and Serer, however, kings are buried in deep, hidden wells, not to avoid desecration of their bodies by subjects mistreated, but to prevent a rival dynasty from performing magic there which might extinguish the line of the dead kings once and for all. The Egyptians proceeded in the same manner and buried their kings in similar wells, the site of which was also unknown to the public. It may thus be assumed that they were motivated by similar reasons. Consequently, we see that, even in details, African tradition can throw new light on Egyptian tradition.

11. Tundi-Daro is inhabited by the Rimaïbe. The village is located on the northeastern shore of Tundi-Daro lake, about sixteen kilometers (ten miles) northwest of Niafunké, county seat of the Issaber Circle, "French" Sudan.

12. Aniaba, an alleged son of this king, was ennobled by Louis XIV. Later it was claimed that this was a slave whom the African monarch had entrusted to a European ship captain.

CHAPTER X

1. Informed specialists take pains to photograph Egyptian figures only at "artful" angles that mask or attenuate the Negro features.

2. Cf. Sir Flinders Petrie, *The Making of Ancient Egypt*. London: Sheldon Press; New York: Macmillan, 1939.

3. Cf. Jacques Pirenne, *Histoire de la civilisation de l'Egypte ancienne*. Paris: Albin Michel, 1963, I, 16.
"All Egyptians, men and women, have equal rights; marital power and paternal authority no longer exist; all families, except the king's, are strictly

monogamous, and the wife can dispose of her property without the husband's authorization. In public law, bureaucracy has completely replaced the ancient hereditary feudal system. Administrative services are manned by a corps of officials appointed and paid by the king, rigorously classified and obliged to work their way up from the lowest to the highest government posts. Justice, dispensed exclusively in the name of the king, is entrusted to royal tribunals. Cities still enjoy a certain autonomy, although integrated in the general administrative system of the country; the former feudal principalities have become provinces.

"The pomp of the court, royal buildings, religious structures, and the enormous development of the administration, require increasingly large resources. Taxes rise, falling ever more heavily on the income of the citizens. They try to escape it; then fiscal constraint intervenes. The Administration is superimposed on the nation and the high officials enter the 'order' of the nobility. High office is in fact hereditary. Lands allocated to remunerate the great officers of the crown remain their private patrimony, because the posts are inherited. Honorary titles are accompanied by royal donations which increase from one reign to the next. A class of great landowners is created; these are simply the agents of royal power. Temples now used to celebrate the royal cult receive huge subsidies. The king becomes a prisoner of the system he has built up to ensure his omnipotence. The new nobility, created to support that omnipotence, stifles and destroys it. The individualism on which centralized monarchy was constructed is en route to ruin. At the close of the Fifth Dynasty Egyptian society is divided into social classes. A titled aristocracy, endowed with great domains, hereditarily holds the high posts. Absolute power exists in name only. It is no longer anything but a formula poorly disguising the oligarchy created to its disadvantage. Under the Sixth Dynasty this evolution accelerates. Inheritance of high office is decreed into law. Provincial governors, having become hereditary, are transformed into princes. The high duties of the clergy become the appanage of a tiny oligarchy. The temples, whose priests have also made themselves hereditary, are exempted from taxes and endowed with immunity. . . . Imitating the king, the provincial 'princes' are surrounded by a court and a harem. Like the land, the family stagnates, either on noble possessions or on 'perpetual' tenure granted by a lord. The wife falls back under the guardianship of her husband and even adult children are under parental authority. Meanwhile, male privilege reappears, favoring sons in the inheritance of land, to the disadvantage of daughters."

4. "Admonitions d'un sage," quoted by Pirenne, p. 328.
5. As a matter of fact, the Greeks, Herodotus included, often confused the conquests of Tuthmosis III, Sesostris I, and Ramses II.
6. Cf. C. A. Diop, *L'Afrique Noire précoloniale.* Paris: Présence Africaine, 1960.
7. The vassalage stemming from the conquests of the Eighteenth and Nineteenth Dynasties produced one result that is often misrepresented by historians. It has been claimed that those two dynasties inaugurated the era of political marriages between foreigners and Egyptians. Note, however, that it was the Asiatic vassals who, to curry royal favor, gave their daughters to the Egyptian Pharaoh without any *quid pro quo.* Not until the tenth century B.C. was the sole legend on this subject born in Solomon's "Song of Songs." In contrast, the Syrian kinglets, formerly so turbulent, were resigned to their fate and offered their daughters to be placed in the Pharaoh's harem (cf. Maspero, *op. cit.,* p. 242). There is general agreement

that Tai or Ty, mother of Amenophis IV (Akhnaton), was of foreign birth, Semitic or Libyan. In either case, she was merely a vassal's daughter, given unilaterally to the Pharaoh to serve his pleasure.

The marriage of Ramses II with the daughter of Khatousil III, during the Nineteenth Dynasty, had no other significance. Khatousil III, leader of the Hittites, had, in fact, just rebelled against Egyptian authority. But, routed everywhere, he sued for peace and, as soon as Ramses II accepted it, the Hittite gave him his daughter in "marriage." Because of her beauty, this daughter was able to win the Pharaoh's affection. She was white. But for her attractiveness, she would have remained a courtesan all her life. In the eyes of Egyptian legitimists, she was by no means a princess. Referring to Ramses II, Khatousil even seems proud to speak as a vassal. Thus he tells a chief: "Get ready, let us go to Egypt. The King has spoken, let us obey Sesostris (Ramses). He gives the breath of life to those who love him, and so the whole earth loves him, and Khati [the Hittite country] and he are one." (Quoted by Maspero, p. 269.)

8. The Hittites were the only Indo-European people in Antiquity to start "spontaneously" to write in hieroglyphics, some 1500 years after the official beginnings of writing in Egypt and immediately after their first contacts with Egypt. Efforts to discover originality and autonomy in Hittite hieroglyphs have led only to generalities linked to the structure and morphology of Indo-European languages.

The principle of hieroglyphic writing certainly originated with the Egyptians, but applied to a quite different linguistic reality, it evolved on its own. The Egyptians taught writing to all the peoples they colonized, especially the Phoenicians, who later carried it to Greece and throughout the Mediterranean in alphabetical form.

Furthermore, it is claimed that the Hittite country was the center for the diffusion of iron during Antiquity. This poses an enigma that will have to be resolved before the notion can be accepted. The fragility of the Hittite State is proved by the fact that it disappeared immediately without even leaving any structural traces, on contact in Asia Minor with the successive waves of the Dorian invasion in the twelfth century B.C. The Dorians, who came from Illyria, on the other side of the strait, had iron weapons. Where did they get their supply? Did they go down surreptitiously to get it from the Hittites and then return home to pillage all ancient Greece and cause the destruction of the Hittite nation? . . .

Egypt was familiar with the use of iron as early as the predynastic period; pearls of meteoric iron (5 percent to 20 percent nickel) have been found in Gerzean tombs of the fourth millennium. From the Fourth Dynasty (2900 B.C.), Egypt knew how to extract iron from iron ore. As a matter of fact, in the Great Cheops Pyramid at Giza, a sample of sponge iron has been found. Another, from the Sixth Dynasty, has been found at Abydos (circa 2500 B.C.). It too resulted from treating the ore.

According to M. I. Attia, inscriptions on a sandstone stela in Nubia, two miles north of Aswan, indicate that iron ore in that region was already utilized, "worked" by the ancient Egyptians during the Eighteenth Dynasty. . . . Iron does not exist in the natural state; it must be extracted from the ore. What blast furnaces produced the metal that served to fashion Egyptian objects? In the third millennium there was no iron age in Europe or Asia. In Egypt, iron ore is nonexistent. Only Nubia and the rest of Black Africa could furnish an explanation.

In certain regions of Black Africa, the use of iron preceded that of any other metal. The usual stratification of the age of metals is not applicable here. A native center to diffuse iron ore probably existed; its age remains to be determined. Even those who contend that Egypt did not begin to smelt iron until the sixth century, admit that Nubia preceded it by a century. Yet, if the influences had to come from outside, from Asia Minor in particular, they would of necessity pass through Egypt.

Thus, the question of the diffusion of iron in Antiquity is far from settled. . . . New, unbiased research, taking into account all the new facts, which are numerous, is the only road to an acceptable conclusion. It will be necessary to date the exploitation of the iron mines in the Chad village of Télé-Nugar. There one finds a gallery more than one kilometer long, an underground room 22 meters by 10, other underground rooms with low ceilings supported by pillars and somewhat resembling a subterranean temple. . . . Numerous other mine sites have been discovered comparable to that of Télé-Nugar.

Except for gold and silver, which must have been the first metals discovered, the names of other metals in Wolof are preceded by the generic term for iron. Example: *ven-ug-handjar*=the iron of copper=copper metal, and so on.

9. In Egyptian, *Djahi* designated Phoenicia, meaning, of course, the land of navigation par excellence. In Wolof, it means navigation.
10. In Wolof, *Khekh* means war, to wage war.
11. *Histoire générale de la population mondiale.* Paris: Ed. Montchrestien, 1961, p. 23. The four authors cited were Hecataeus of Abdera, Diodorus of Sicily, Herodotus, and Flavius Josephus.
12. In Wolof, *djit* means the guide or leader.
13. This was the Napatan period of the Nubian (Nilotic) Sudan. The Ethiopia of the Ancients was really the Sudanese kingdom with its two successive capitals: Napata and Meroë. Modern Ethiopia is more directly the heir of the civilization of Axum, which corresponds to a later phase of which the Ancients were totally unaware. In fact, Axum was merely a peripheral province belatedly detached from the Sudanese kingdom. Since it corresponds to modern Ethiopia, the retention of that name to denote the Ethiopia of the Ancients inevitably creates confusion in the mind of the reader. Today the name Sudan is the only proper designation for the country the Ancients called Ethiopia.
14. Cf. Diop, *L'Afrique Noire précoloniale,* for a more detailed analysis of politico-social African structures and the search for the driving force of history.

CHAPTER XI

1. Ernst von Aster, *Histoire de la philosophie.* Paris: Payot, 1952, p. 48.
2. Amélineau, *Prolégomènes,* Introduction, pp. 8–9.
3. Despite the anatomy of the limbs, the facial rigidity of a Greek statue differs from subsequent Latin realism and is more related to the serenity of Egyptian art.
4. George R. Riffert, *Great Pyramid, Proof of God.* Haverhill, Mass.: Destiny Publishers, 1944, p. 90.
5. Matila C. Ghyka, *Esthétique des proportions dans la nature et dans les arts.* Paris: Gallimard, 1927, pp. 345, 367–368.
6. *Herodotus, op. cit.,* p. 99.

CHAPTER XII

1. Since those lines were written, this has been done. Raymond Mauny has had the time to examine all these samples in my laboratory. I leave it up to him to reveal his impressions if he deems it necessary.
2. One day soon, there will be second thoughts about the authenticity of the Tasian civilization, because of the restricted number, the fragility, and the almost artificial nature of the documents available to support its existence.
3. Among members of the African aristocracy, with an equal amount of melanin, the woman seems to have a lighter complexion than the man because she is less exposed to the weather, the sun in particular. This phenomenon, quite well known in Black Africa, might well be the origin of the Egyptian pictorial convention relative to the complexion of the women.
4. On the contrary, it is impossible to make Nubian civilization date back only to this event in the seventh century B.C. The documents oppose this with so much evidence that we are astonished to see a historian give the impression of believing it possible.
5. Cf. Gaston Maspero, *Histoire ancienne des peuples de l'Orient,* 12th ed. Paris: Hachette, 1917, pp. 578–579.
6. Cf. *Notes africaines,* no. 89, January 1961, p. 10: Raymond Mauny, "Découverte de tumulus dans la région de Diourbel."

CHAPTER XIII

1. *Zinjanthropus* and *Homo habilis* are the latest discoveries. Little is known about the hominians recently discovered in Palestine and about *Homo faber* allegedly found in South America. These finds have yet to be confirmed.
2. Marcellin Boule & Henri Vallois, *Les Hommes fossiles.* Paris: Masson, 1952, 4th ed., pp. 299–301. This text impresses by its objectivity, precision, and clarity. It leaves practically no doubt about the Negro character of the race described. [The translation is that of Michael Bullock: *Fossil Men.* New York: Dryden Press, 1957, pp. 285–289.]
3. Its opposite, "blancoid" or "leucodermoid," has not been coined. Thus, one detects the often unconscious sentimental basis of "scientific hypotheses."
4. In any case, the hypothetical existence of an archaic *Homo sapiens* has lost much support since the discovery that Piltdown man, one of the corner-stones of the structure, was a fake.
5. Alfred C. Haddon, *The Races of Man and their Distribution.* New York: Macmillan, 1925, pp. 24–25.
6. Furon, *Manuel de préhistoire générale.* Paris: Payot, 1958, p. 271. He quotes L. Balout, *Préhistoire de l'Afrique du Nord,* 1955, pp. 430, 437.
7. Furon, *ibid.,* p. 274.
8. Robert Cornevin, *Histoire des peuples de l'Afrique.* Paris: Berger-Levrault, 1960, p. 81.
9. African industries are generally considered the more recent.
10. Haddon, *ibid.,* p. 103.
11. Boule & Vallois, *ibid.,* p. 333.
12. *Ibid.,* p. 303.
13. Furon, *ibid.,* pp. 216, 214.
14. Boule & Vallois, p. 465.
15. Cornevin, *ibid.,* p. 88.

16. "In short, we can see that, aside from Africanthropus, the human remains found up to now in East Africa do not differ from the present inhabitants of that country or neighboring countries." Boule & Vallois, p. 466.
17. Cf. Louis S. B. Leakey, *The Stone Age Race of Kenya*. London: Oxford University Press, 1935.
18. One must take care, however, to avoid excessive generalization about these two attitudes.

Notes on Archeological Terms
Used in the Text

Though many of these terms are explained in the text, we list them here for purposes of ready reference. These brief notations are culled from various sources, especially:

1. Palmer & Lloyd, *Archaeology A to Z* (London & New York: Frederick Warne & Co., Ltd., 1968)
2. Bray & Trump, *A Dictionary of Archaeology* (London: Penguin, 1970)
3. Charles Winick, *Dictionary of Anthropology* (New York: Philosophical Library, 1956)
4. Leakey & Goodall, *Unveiling Man's Origins* (Cambridge, Mass.: Schenkman Publishing Co., 1969)
5. Michael H. Day, *Guide to Fossil Man* (Cleveland & New York: World Publishing Co., 1968)

AMRATIAN: "An early predynastic culture of Egypt characterized by finely worked implements of bone and stone." (Cf. Winick)

ASSELAR MAN: Discovered in the Sahara by Théodore Monod.

AURIGNACIAN: "A highly developed Upper Paleolithic Age culture, named after a cave at Aurignac (France) where artifacts were found. . . . Cro-Magnon man, Combe-Capelle man, and Grimaldi man all contributed to Aurignacian culture." (Cf. Palmer & Lloyd)

BADARIAN: An early Egyptian culture noted for its pottery, which is found beneath that of Amratian and later ages.

CHANCELADE MAN: Prototype of the yellow race; skeletons resemble those of modern Eskimos.

COMBE-CAPELLE MAN: Aurignacian skeleton found in Dordogne (France) in 1910; housed in Berlin Museum. (Cf. Day)

CRO-MAGNON MAN: An Upper Paleolithic man living in Europe during the Aurignacian-Magdalenian periods. "Tall and strong, with broad, high forehead and firm chin." Original home probably Asia. Named for rock shelter at French village of Eyzies. (Cf. Palmer & Lloyd)

ENEOLITHIC: Pertaining to Chalcolithic or Copper Age.

FONTECHEVADE MAN: Found in 1947 about 17 miles east of Angoulême (France). Fontéchevade man and Swanscombe man have been grouped as "Presapiens" hominids. (Cf. Day)

GAMBLIAN: The second of the great pluvial periods, recognized from the geological strata of Kenya. (Cf. Winick)

GERZEAN: "The late predynastic culture of Egypt which developed out of the Amratian circa 3600 B.C. Named after the site of El Gerza or Gereh in the Fayum (Egypt) and is well represented at the cemetery of Naqada in Upper Egypt." (Cf. Bray & Trump)

GLACIAL PERIODS: The four Glacial Periods of the Pleistocene Epoch: the Günz (790,000 years ago, lasted 250,000 years); the Mindel (480,000 years ago, lasted 50,000 years); the Riss (240,000 years ago, lasted to 175,000); the Würm (115,000 years ago, lasted 90,000 years). (Cf. Palmer & Lloyd)

GRIMALDI NEGROIDS: A prehistoric race of men whose remains were first found in cave (Grimaldi, Italy, near Menton, France). They are found in lower layers than Cro-Magnon men, whom they therefore preceded. "The Negroids of Grimaldi," writes Verneau, "are tall and their skull is extremely high." Grimaldi skeletons have been found in Western and Central Europe, but they probably originated in Africa. Noted for their realistic, steatopygic statuettes. (Cf. R. Verneau, *Les Grottes de Grimaldi,* Vol. 1, pt. 1, "Anthropologie," Monaco, 1906–1912, 2 vols.)

LASCAUX CAVE: A prehistoric cave in southwestern France, famous for its paintings of the Upper Paleolithic.

MAGDALENIAN: An Upper Paleolithic Age culture, which began in Western Europe before 15,000 B.C., so called because remains were first found in the rock shelter of La Madeleine (France). (Cf. Palmer & Lloyd)

MERIMDE: A site on the borders of the Libyan desert. V. Gordon Childe calls it a typical example of "Neolithic culture."

MESOLITHIC AGE: The Middle Stone Age.

NATUFIAN CULTURE: "The principal Mesolithic culture of Palestine." (Cf. Coon, *The Living Races of Man.* New York: Knopf, 1965.)

NEOLITHIC AGE: The New Stone Age. "Food production replaced food gathering, and hunting and fishing became less important. . . . Neolithic men were the first to plant and harvest crops, breed animals, spin and weave, and make pots . . ." (Cf. Palmer & Lloyd)

OLDUVAI GORGE: Site in Tanzania where Dr. Leakey and co-workers found remains of Zinjanthropus, *Homo habilis,* etc.

PALEOLITHIC: "In the earlier days of Prehistory, the Stone Age was divided into Paleolithic or Old Stone Age, and Neolithic or New Stone Age.

"After a time, it became clear that the Paleolithic spanned a very long period of time and it was divided into Lower Paleolithic, Middle Paleolithic, and Upper Paleolithic. Each of these cultural divisions corresponded roughly to the then accepted time divisions of the Lower Pleistocene, Middle Pleistocene, and Upper Pleistocene.

"Subsequently, the term Eolithic was introduced for some supposedly primitive stone age cultures that were thought to date back to the Pliocene. This term has been gradually abandoned and the earliest known cultures such as the Oldowan, from the lowest levels of the Olduvai Gorge, are now grouped with the Lower Paleolithic . . ." (Leakey & Goodall)

PITHECANTHROPUS: An extinct genus of apelike men, especially *Pithecanthropus erectus* of the Pleistocene epoch of Java.

PLEISTOCENE: Time division. "The start of the Pleistocene was once put at circa 500,000 but is now placed at 3 million." (Leakey & Goodall)

QUATERNARY: The Period following the Tertiary, which has lasted from about 1 million years ago to the present. . . . It is divided into Pleistocene and Holocene Epochs, the latter covering the last 10,000 years. (Cf. Palmer & Lloyd)

SINANTHROPUS: "Generic name formerly given to a group of Middle Pleistocene hominids found near Peking." (Cf. Day)

SWANSCOMBE MAN: "Part of a human skull and some flint hand-axes were found in a gravel pit near Swanscombe in Kent in 1934 . . . It dated from the Second Interglacial Period of the Middle Pleistocene Epoch. another piece of the skull was discovered in 1955 . . . oldest human remains so far found in England, and are older than Neanderthal man." (Cf. Palmer & Lloyd)

TASIAN: "A culture named after the site of Deir Tasa in Upper Egypt, a settlement of primitive farmers. It is now regarded as at best a variant of the Badarian culture." (Cf. Bray & Trump)

ZINJANTHROPUS: Also called "Nutcracker man" because of size of teeth in skull found by Mrs. M. D. Leakey (July 1959) in Olduvai Gorge, Tanzania. According to Leakey, Zinjanthropus is more than 1½ million years old.

ABSOLUTE DATING: "Only one direct method of absolute dating is in common use. Nitrogen in the upper atmosphere is bombarded by neutrons produced by cosmic radiation; this results in the formation of a known proportion of radioactive carbon which becomes incorporated in carbon dioxide. This is absorbed by vegetation and thence passes into animal tissues. When bones are buried the radioactive carbon (C14) begins to decay at a known rate. Measurements of the carbon14 content of buried organic matter can be translated mathematically to give an estimate of the age of the specimen. In practice the method is limited to material less than 60–70,000 years old since above this age the amount of carbon14 remaining is too small to estimate.

"Another radiometric method (the potassium-argon technique) depends on the fact that naturally occurring potassium contains a radioactive isotope; this isotope decays at a constant rate producing argon which is held within the crystals of some potassic minerals. Estimates of the argon content of a sample of these minerals, derived from a deposit containing fossil bones, will indirectly measure the age of the bones . . ." (Cf. Day, p. 12)

Brief Biographical Notes

Because many of the authors cited in this volume are unfamiliar to the average reader, we append these brief notes on some of Dr. Diop's sources. This material has been culled from various biographies and reference works. We are especially indebted here to Warren Dawson's *Who Was Who in Egyptology* (London, 1951), and to John A. Wilson's *Signs and Wonders upon Pharaoh* (Chicago: University of Chicago Press, 1964).

AMÉLINEAU, ABBÉ EMILE (1850–1915), French archeologist and Professor of the History of Religions at the Ecole des Hautes Etudes in Paris; excavated at Abydos and reportedly located the tomb of Osiris.

ARAMBOURG, CAMILLE (1885–   ), French paleontologist and anthropologist; Professor at the Paris Museum of Natural History.

BACHOFEN, JOHANN JAKOB (1815–1887), Swiss jurist and "philosopher of history."

BATTUTA, IBN (1304–1377), Muslim writer and traveler born in Tangier; visited the old kingdom of Mali in 1352. His "narrative remains one of the best travel books ever made," writes Basil Davidson in *The African Past*, p. 80.

BAUMANN, HERMANN (1902–   ), German anthropologist.

BORY DE SAINT-VINCENT, BARON JEAN-BAPTISTE (1778–1846), French naturalist, one of the editors of the 17-volume *Dictionnaire classique d'histoire naturelle* (Paris, 1822–31).

BOULE, MARCELLIN (1861–1942), French scientist; Director, French Institute of Human Paleontology; Professor, French National Museum of Natural History.

BREASTED, JAMES HENRY (1865–1935), American Egyptologist; Professor of Egyptology at University of Chicago from 1895; Director, Oriental Institute from 1919; prolific author.

BREUIL, ABBÉ HENRI (1877–1961), French archeologist, authority on the Paleolithic Age. He "studied every important cave of Europe, searched the Sahara for still more, and explored the decorated rocks of the Horn of Africa . . . " (Karl E. Meyer, *The Pleasures of Archeology*. New York: Atheneum, 1971, p. 37.)

BRION, MARCEL (1895–   ), French art critic and novelist. In addition to *The World of Archeology,* he has written on German painting, Romantic art, etc. Member, French Academy, 1964.

BRUGSCH, KARL HEINRICH (1827–94), German Egyptologist; from 1870–79 was head of Khedive's school of Egyptology in Cairo; Professor at Göttingen, 1868; published, among other works, a *Dictionnaire géographique de l'ancienne Egypte* (Leipzig, 1879–80).

BUDGE, SIR ERNEST ALFRED WALLIS (1857–1934), British scholar, collector of antiquities for British Museum; museum official.

CAILLIAUD, FRÉDÉRIC (1787–1869), French mineralogist and traveler; first went to Egypt in 1815 and was employed to find the emerald mines described by Arab historians; revisited Egypt in 1819; in 1821 ascended Nile and discovered ruins of Meroë.

CAPART, JEAN (1877–1947), Belgian Egyptologist, specialist in Egyptian art; Director, Royal Museum in Brussels; an adviser to Brooklyn Museum.

CHAMPOLLION, JEAN-FRANÇOIS, Champollion the Younger (1790–1832), has been called "Founder of Egyptology" because of his decipherment of hieroglyphics; a precocious and gifted linguist, had mastered half a dozen oriental languages as well as Latin and Greek by the age of 16; taught first at Grenoble; in 1831 appointed to Collège de France.

CHAMPOLLION-FIGEAC, JACQUES-JOSEPH (1778–1867), French philologist, interested in Egyptian archeology; educated his famous younger brother; professor of Greek and librarian at Grenoble; later in charge of manuscripts at Bibliothèque Nationale in Paris.

CHÉRUBINI, SALVATORE (1797–1869), Italian artist, son of the composer; accompanied Champollion to Egypt in 1828; naturalized French; Inspector of Fine Arts.

CHILDE, V. GORDON (1892–1957), British prehistorian; Professor of prehistoric archeology, University of Edinburgh; Director, Institute of Archeology, University of London, 1946–56. Works include: *Man Makes Himself* (1951) and *What Happened in History* (1954).

CONTENAU, GEORGES (1877–   ), French Orientalist, specialist on Persia (Iran) and Babylonia; official at Louvre Museum.

CORNEVIN, ROBERT (1919–   ), French historian and ethnologist; has produced volumes on Dahomey, the Bassari of northern Togo, the history of Africa, etc.

DELAFOSSE, MAURICE (1870–1926), French Africanist, author of *The Negroes of Africa* and other works primarily on "French" West Africa.

DESPLAGNES, LOUIS (1878?–1914), French archeologist.

DIEULAFOY, MARCEL-AUGUSTE (1844–1920), French archeologist, excavated at Susa.

DIODORUS SICULUS, Greek historian, first century B.C.; came from Sicily and lived in Alexandria and Rome.

FRAZER, SIR JAMES GEORGE (1854–1941), Scottish anthropologist who wrote on mythology and primitive religions, author of *The Golden Bough*.

FROBENIUS, LEO (1873–1938), German ethnologist; made 12 expeditions to Africa, 1904–35.

FURON, RAYMOND (1898–   ), French geologist, past president Geological Society of France; Professor, University of Paris; author of many books on such subjects as the geology of Africa, paleontology, Iran, the water problem, etc.

GOBINEAU, COUNT JOSEPH-ARTHUR DE (1816–1882), French writer and diplomat, whose racist theories influenced the Nazis.

GRIAULE, MARCEL (1898–1956), French ethnologist, authority on the Dogon ethnic group.

HADDON, ALFRED CORT (1855–1940), British anthropologist; professor of Zoology, Dublin, 1880; 15 years later named Lecturer in Physical Anthropology at his alma mater, Cambridge. "The life history of Alfred Cort Haddon is, to a great extent, the life history of modern anthropology" (A. H. Quiggin, *Haddon, the Head-Hunter*. Cambridge University Press, 1942).

HAMY, ERNEST-THÉODORE (1842–1908), French anthropologist; Professor, Paris Museum of Natural History; wrote on Stone Age in Egypt and on races of man seen on the monuments; member of the Institut.

HARTMANN, CHARLES DE (1842–1906), German philosopher, savant.

HERODOTUS (484?–425? B.C.), Greek historian, "Father of History."

HOEFER, FERDINAND (1811–78), French scholar; in addition to Chaldea, Assyria, Media, Babylonia, Mesopotamia, and Phoenicia, he also wrote on southern Africa, chemistry, botany, and mathematics.

HOUSSAYE, FRÉDÉRIC-ARSÈNE (1860–1920), French naturalist.

JEFFREYS, MERVYN DAVID WALDEGRAVE, former Senior District Officer, Bamenda, "British" Cameroons. By 1944 he had "worked among the Negroes of West Africa" for more than 25 years.

KATI, MAHMUD (1468–1593?), Soninké or Sarakolé scholar with Askia Muhammad; wrote the *Tarikh el Fettach*.

KHALDUN, IBN, fourteenth-century Arab historian.

LARREY, BARON DOMINIQUE-JEAN (1766–1842), Surgeon-in-chief, French army; member Napoleon's Commission in Egypt.

LEAKEY, LOUIS SEYMOUR BAZETT (1903–1972), British archeologist born in Kenya, son of English missionaries; Curator, Coryndon Memorial Museum, Nairobi, 1945–61; especially famous for his finds in Olduvai Gorge; Fellow of British Academy; awarded Royal Medal of Royal Geographical Society.

LENORMANT, FRANÇOIS (1837–1933), French archeologist; member, Academy of Inscriptions and Belles-Lettres; Professor, Paris Bibliothèque Nationale; founded *Gazette archéologique,* 1875.

LEPSIUS, KARL RICHARD (1810–1884), German Egyptologist; Curator, Egyptian collections in Berlin after 1865.

LÉVY-BRUHL, LUCIEN (1857–1939), French philosopher who wrote extensively on the primitive mentality and primitive soul.

LINNAEUS, CARL, eighteenth-century Swedish naturalist.

LLOYD, SETON (1902–   ), British archeologist; excavated in Egypt 1929–30, in Iraq 1930–37, in Turkey 1930–37; directed British Institute in Ankara 1949–61; professor of Western Asiatic Archeology, London University 1962–69, now Emeritus.

MAES, JOSEPH, Belgian ethnologist; published several studies on ethnic groups of ex-Belgian Congo, in addition to the 1924 article on the Serer quoted.

MANETHO OF SEBENNYTOS, an Egyptian priest (third century B.C.), who wrote a chronicle on Egypt in Greek.

MASPERO, SIR GASTON-CAMILLE-CHARLES (1846–1916), French Egyptologist; directed Service of Antiquities in Egypt, 1881–86, 1899–1914; Professor of Egyptology in Paris from 1869; prolific author; knighted by King of England, 1901; member, French Academy, 1883.

MAUNY, RAYMOND, French archeologist; Director of Archeology at IFAN in Dakar; most recent volume: *Les Siècles obscurs de l'Afrique Noire* (Paris: Fayard, 1971).

MONOD, THÉODORE (1902–   ), French geologist; for many years was Director of IFAN; one of pioneer explorers of Sahara; one of original sponsors of *Présence Africaine* and edited its special issue on *Le Monde Noir.*

MORET, ALEXANDRE (1868–1938), French Egyptologist; studied under Maspero; Director, Ecole des Hautes Etudes, 1899–1938; Professor, Collège de France, 1923; member, French Academy, 1927.

NAVILLE, HENRI EDOUARD (1844–1926), Swiss archeologist; studied under Lepsius; excavated in Egypt 1883–1913.

PÉDRALS, DENIS-PIERRE DE (1911–   ), French archeologist.

PETRIE, SIR WILLIAM MATTHEW FLINDERS (1853–1942), British Egyptologist, prolific author; began work in Egypt in 1880; directed British School of Archeology in Egypt, then in Palestine; Professor of Egyptology, University of London.

PIRENNE, JACQUES (1891–   ), Belgian historian; tutor of ex-King Leopold 1920–24; has taught at University of Brussels, Oriental Institute of Prague, Collège de France, University of Cairo, Grenoble, and Geneva; member, Royal Academy of Belgium, 1945.

QUATREFAGES DE BRÉAU, ARMAND (1810–92), French naturalist; Professor at Paris Museum of Natural History; member of the Institut.

QUIBBELL, JAMES EDWARD (1867–1935), British archeologist; best known for his excavations at Saqqara; worked in Services of Antiquities and at Cairo Museum; Petrie's assistant in 1894; discovered Narmer's Tablet.

REISNER, GEORGE ANDREW (1867–1942), American Egyptologist; has been called "the finest of excavators"; from 1910 was Curator of Egyptian Antiquities at Boston Museum of Fine Arts; Professor of Egyptology at Harvard from 1914; directed the Harvard Camp at the pyramids.

SCHURÉ, EDOUARD (1841–1929), French writer; studied law but left jurisprudence for career as music critic and historian. *Les Grands Initiés,* from which Dr. Diop quotes, is an essay on occult theories of founders of various religions.

SELIGMAN, CHARLES GABRIEL (1873–1940), British anthropologist; member Haddon's 1898 expedition to Torres Straits and New Guinea; appointed 1909 by government of Sudan to conduct ethnographic survey.

SERGI, GIUSEPPE (1841–1936), Ialian anthropologist.

SIEGFRIED, ANDRÉ (1875–1959), French economist and professor, author of various works on foreign lands, including the United States. In a lecture on the African, in 1952, he contended that the Black could be a good subordinate but made a poor director.

SMITH, SIR GRAFTON ELLIOT (1871–1937), British anatomist; Professor of Anatomy, School of Medicine, Cairo, 1900–09; authority on mummification.

TEMPELS, FATHER PLACIDE (1906–   ), Belgian missionary in the Congo; his famous book on Bantu philosophy was first published in Antwerp in 1946.

VALLOIS, HENRI-VICTOR (1889–   ), French anthropologist; Director, French Institute of Human Paleontology, Paris Museum of Man.

VENDRYES, JOSEPH (1875–   ), French Professor of Linguistics, stressing its importance as an "introduction to history"; edited *Etudes celtiques.*

VOLNEY, COUNT CONSTANTIN DE (1757–1820), French intellectual, member of the Estates-General, Constituent Assembly, French Academy, and Society of Friends of the Blacks. His *Voyage en Egypte et Syrie* was considered "the masterpiece of that genre"; a second work, *The Ruins, or a survey of the revolution of empires* (1791), was even more successful. Imprisoned during the Reign of Terror, he was appointed Professor of History at Paris Ecole Normale the following year. In 1795 went to the United States, was warmly welcomed by George Washington; returned home in 1798 denounced by John Adams as a secret agent to help France recover Louisiana. In 1803 he published a *Tableau du climat et du sol des Etats-Unis*. Napoleon named him a count in 1808; six years later was made a peer of France by Louis XVIII.

WOOLLEY, SIR LEONARD (1880–1960), British archeologist; excavated in Egypt, Iraq, Syria; during World War I, prisoner-of-war in Turkey; wrote volume on the ancient Orient for UNESCO World History.

Selected Bibliography

AESCHYLUS. *Complete Plays,* translated into English rhyming verse by Gilbert Murray. London: Allen & Unwin, 1952.

AITKEN, MARTIN J. *Physics and Archeology.* New York & London: Interscience Publishers, 1961.

AMÉLINEAU, ABBÉ ÉMILE. *Prolégomènes à l'étude de la religion égyptienne.* Paris: Ed. Leroux, 1916.

————. *Nouvelles Fouilles d'Abydos.* Paris: Ed. Leroux, 1899.

ARISTOTLE. *Politique.* Books I & II. Paris: Les Belles Lettres, 1960.

ARON, RAYMOND. *Les Étapes de la pensée sociologique.* Paris: Gallimard, 1967.

ASTER, ERNST VON. *Histoire de la philosophie.* Paris: Payot, 1952.

ATTIA, MAHMOUD IBRAHIM. Communication in *Actes du Congrès international de géologie, 1948.* 18th session. London: Butles, 1952.

BACHOFEN, JOHANN JAKOB. *Pages choisies par Adrien Turel.* Paris: F. Alcan, 1938.

BALOUT, LIONEL. *Préhistoire de l'Afrique du Nord.* Paris: Arts et Métiers graphiques, 1955.

BASSET, ANDRÉ. *La Langue berbère.* Paris: E. Leroux, 1929.

BATTUTA, IBN. See H. A. R. Gibb, *Ibn Battuta, Travels in Asia and Africa.* London: 1929. Also: *Les Voyages d'Ibn Battuta,* translated into French by C. Défremery & B. R. Sanguinetti. Paris: 1854.

BAUMANN, HERMANN & D. WESTERMANN. *Les Peuples et civilisations de l'Afrique,* followed by *Les Langues et l'éducation.* Paris: Payot, 1948.

BLOOMFIELD, LEONARD. *Language.* New York: Henry Holt & Co., 1933; first ed., 1914.

BOILAT, ABBÉ. *Grammaire de la langue wolofe. Paris,* 1858.

BORY DE SAINT-VINCENT, BARON JEAN-BAPTISTE. *Histoire et description des Iles de l'Océan.* Paris: Didot, 1839.

BOULE, MARCELLIN & HENRI V. VALLOIS. *Les Hommes fossiles.*

Paris: Masson, 1952. Translated by Michael Bullock as *Fossil Men.* New York: Dryden Press, 1957.

BREASTED, JAMES H. *The Conquest of Civilization.* New York: Harper & Brothers, 1926.

BREUIL, ABBÉ HENRI. "L'Afrique du Sud," *Les Nouvelles littéraires,* April 5, 1951.

BRION, MARCEL. *La Résurrection des villes mortes.* Paris: Payot, 1937–38. Translated by Miriam & Lionel Kochan as *The World of Archeology,* New York: Macmillan, 1962.

BUDGE, WALLIS. *The Egyptian Sudan.* Vols. I & II. London: Kegan, Trench & Co., 1907.

CAILLIAUD, FRÉDÉRIC. *Voyage à Méroë.* Paris, 1836.

CAPART, JEAN. *Les Débuts de l'art en Egypte.* Brussels: Ed. Vromant, 1904.

CAPPART, DENISE. "Origine africaine de la coiffure égyptienne," *Reflets du Monde,* Brussels, 1956.

CHAMPOLLION, JEAN FRANCOIS (ÇHAMPOLLION THE YOUNGER). *Grammaire égyptienne.* Paris: F. Didot frères, 1836–41.

CHAMPOLLION-FIGEAC, JACQUES JOSEPH. *Egypte ancienne.* Paris: Collection l'Univers, 1839.

CHÉRUBINI, SALVATORE. *La Nubie.* Paris: Collection l'Univers, 1847.

CHILDE, V. GORDON. *New Light on the Most Ancient East.* London: Kegan Paul, Trench, Trubner & Co., Ltd., 1934.

COHEN, MARCEL S. *Essai comparatif sur le vocabulaire et la phonétique du chamito-sémitique.* Paris: Librairie Honoré Champion, 1947.

CONTENAU, GEORGES. *Manuel d'archéologie orientale.* Paris: J. Picard, 1947.

————. *La Civilisation des Hittites et des Mitanniens.* Paris: Payot, 1934.

COON, CARLETON S. *The Races of Europe.* New York: Macmillan, 1939.

CORNEVIN, ROBERT. *Histoire des peuples de l'Afrique.* Paris: Berger-Levrault, 1960.

DAVIDSON, BASIL. *The Lost Cities of Africa.* Boston & Toronto: Little, Brown & Co., 1959.

———. *The African Past: Chronicles from Antiquity to Modern Times.* New York: The Universal Library, Grosset & Dunlap, 1967.

DELAFOSSE, MAURICE. *Haut-Sénégal, Niger.* Paris: Larose, 1912.

———. *Les Noirs de l'Afrique.* Paris: Payot, 1922. Translated by Frieda Fligeman as *The Negroes of Africa.* Washington, D. C.: Associated Publishers, 1931.

DIODORUS SICULUS (DIODORUS OF SICILY). *Histoire universelle,* translated by Abbé Terrasson. Paris, 1758.

DIOP, CHEIKH ANTA. *Nations nègres et culture.* Paris: Présence Africaine, 1954.

———. *L'Unité culturelle de l'Afrique Noire.* Paris: Présence Africaine, 1959.

———. *L'Afrique Noire précoloniale.* Paris: Présence Africaine, 1960.

———. *Les Fondements culturels, techniques et industriels d'un futur état fédéral d'Afrique noire.* Paris: Présence Africaine, 1960.

———. *Antériorité des civilisations nègres: mythe ou vérité historique?* Paris: Présence Africaine, 1967.

———. "L'Apparition de l'Homo-sapiens," *Bulletin de l'IFAN,* vol. XXXII, series B #3, 1970.

———. "La Métallurgie du fer sous l'ancien empire égyptien," *Bull. B. IFAN,* 1973 (on press).

———. "La Pigmentation des anciens Egyptiens: test par la mélanine," *Bull. B. IFAN,* 1973 (on press).

———. "Introduction à l'étude des migrations en Afrique occidentale et centrale. Identification du berceau nilotique du peuple sénégalais," *Bull. IFAN,* 1973 (on press).

DUMEZIL, GEORGES. *Mythe et épopée.* Paris: Gallimard, 1968.

———. *Idées romaines.* Paris: Gallimard, 1969.

DUMOULIN DE LAPLANTE. *Histoire générale synchronique.* Paris: 1947.

ERMAN, ADOLF & HERMANN GRAPOW. *Wörterbuch der Aegyptischen Sprache.* Berlin: Akademie-Verlag, 1971, 7 vols.

EVANS, ARTHUR J. *The Palace of Minos.* London: Macmillan, 1921–35, 4 vols.

FAGG, WILLIAM B. *Nigerian Images, the splendor of African Sculpture.* New York: Praeger, 1963.

FAIDHERBE, LOUIS. *Langues sénégalaises.* Paris: Leroux, 1887.

FAULKNER, RAYMOND O. *A Concise Dictionary of Middle Egyptian.* Oxford, 1964.

FONTANES, MARIUS. *Les Egyptes.* Paris: Ed. Lemerre, 1880 (?).

FRAZER, JAMES G. *The Golden Bough,* New York: Macmillan, 1951; first ed., 1922.

FROBENIUS, LEO. *Histoire de la civilisation africaine,* translated into French by H. Back & D. Ermont. Paris: Gallimard, 1952.

————. *Mythologie de l'Atlantide.* Paris: Payot, 1949.

FURON, RAYMOND. *Manuel de préhistoire générale.* Paris: Payot, 1958.

GARDINER, ALAN H. *Egyptian Grammar.* London: Clarendon Press, 1927.

GHYKA, MATILA C. *Esthétique des proportions dans la nature et dans les arts.* Paris: Gallimard, 1927.

GOBINEAU, COUNT JOSEPH ARTHUR DE. *Essai sur l'inégalité des races humaines.* Paris, 1853. Translated by Adrian Collins as *The Inequality of Human Races.* New York: G. P. Putnam's Sons, 1915.

GREENBERG, JOSEPH H. *Languages of Africa.* Bloomington: Indiana University, 1966.

GRIAULE, MARCEL. *Dieu d'eau.* Paris: Editions du Chêne, 1948.

GURVITCH, GEORGES. *Déterminismes sociaux et liberté humaine,* 2nd ed. Paris: Presses Universitaires de France, 1963.

HADDON, ALFRED C. *The Races of Man and Their Distribution.* New York: Macmillan, 1925.

HALÉVY, DANIEL. *Essai sur l'accélération de l'histoire.* Paris: A. Fayard, 1961.

HARDY, GEORGES. *Vue générale de l'histoire d'Afrique.* Paris, 1930.

HERODOTUS. *History,* Book II. Translated by George Rawlinson. New York: Tudor, 1928.

HOEFER, FERDINAND. *Chaldée, Assyrie, Médie, Babylonie, Mésopotamie, Phénicie.* Paris: Ed. Didot frères, 1852.

HOMBURGER, LILIAS. "Le Wolof et les parlers bantous," *Mémoires de la Société Linguistique de Paris,* vol. VII, #5.

―――. *Les Langues négro-africaines et les peuples qui les parlent.* Paris: Payot, 1941.

HUBAC, PIERRE. *Carthage.* Paris: Ed. Bellenand, 1952.

JAHN, JANHEINZ. *Muntu.* Paris: Ed. du Seuil, 1961. Translated by Marjorie Grene as *Muntu, an outline of neo-African culture.* New York: Grove Press; London: Faber & Faber, 1961.

JUVENAL. *Satires.* Paris: Les Belles Lettres, 1957.

KATI, MAHMOUD. *Tarikh el-Fettach,* translated into French by O. Houdas & M. Delafosse. Paris: Leroux, 1913.

LEAKEY, LOUIS S. B. *The Stone Age Races of Kenya.* Oxford: University Press, 1935.

―――. *The Progress and Evolution of Man in Africa.* Oxford: University Press, 1961.

―――. *Report to the VIIth Pan African Congress on Prehistory and the Study of the Quaternary.* Addis Ababa, 1971 (on press).

LECOQ, RAYMOND. *Le Bamiléké.* Paris: Editions Africaines, 1953.

LECLANT, JEAN. "Un Tableau du Proche-Orient à la fin du XVIIIᵉ siècle." *Bulletin de la Faculté des Lettres de Strasbourg,* Feb. 1961, #5.

―――. "Les Etudes méroitiques, état de la question," *Bulletin de la Société française d'égyptologie,* Dec. 1967, #50.

―――. Cf. also the series of bulletins on Meroë: Meroitic newsletter, Documentary Center of the Ecole pratique des Hautes Etudes (5th section), Paris.

LENORMANT, FRANÇOIS. *Histoire ancienne des Phéniciens.* Paris: Lévy, 1890.

LHOTE, HENRI. *A la découverte des fresques du Tassili.* Grenoble:

Arthaud, 1958. Translated by Alan Brodrick as *The Search for the Tassili Frescoes*. New York: E. P. Dutton, 1959.

LIVY. *The History of Rome,* Book 34.

MAES, JOSEPH. "Pierres levées de Tundi-Daro," *Bull. Com. Et. A.O.F.,* 1924.

MARX, KARL. *Le Capital,* Vol. III, Book I. Paris: Bureau d'Editions, 1939.

————. *Contribution à la critique de l'Economie politique.* Paris: Editions Sociales, 1957.

MASPERO, GASTON. *Histoire ancienne des peuples de l'Orient.* Paris: Hachette, 1917, 12th ed. Translated as *The Dawn of Civilization.* London, 1894.

MASSON-OURSEL, PAUL. *La Philosophie en Orient,* supplement to Emile Bréhier's *Histoire de la philosophie.* Paris: F. Alcan, 1938.

MASSOULARD, ÉMILE. *Préhistoire et protohistoire d'Egypte.* Paris: Institut d'Ethnologie, 1949.

MAUNY, RAYMOND. "Campagne de fouilles de 1950 à Koumby Saleh." *Bull. IFAN,* vol. XVIII, series B #1 & 2, 1956.

————. "Tableau géographique de l'Ouest africain au Moyen Age." Memoir IFAN, #61, 1961.

————. "Essai sur l'histoire des métaux en Afrique occidentale." *Bull. IFAN,* vol. XIV, #1, 1952.

————. *Les Navigations médiévales sur les côtes sahariennes antérieures à la découverte portugaise* (1434). Lisbonne: Centre des Etudes historiques ultra-marines, 1960.

MONOD, THÉODORE. *Majâbat al-Koubrâ.* Memoir IFAN, #52, 1960.

————. *Méharées, exploration du vrai Sahara.* Paris: Ed. "Je sers," 1937.

MONTAGU, ASHLEY. *An Introduction to Physical Anthropology.* Springfield (Illinois): Thomas, 1960, 3rd ed.

MORET, ALEXANDRE. *Le Nil et la civilisation égyptienne.* Paris, 1926.

———— & GEORGES DAVY. *Des clans aux empires.* Paris: Ed. La Renaissance du Livre, 1923. Translated by V. Gordon Childe as *From*

Tribe to Empire. New York: Cooper Square Publishers, Inc., 1970.

NAVILLE, HENRI EDOUARD. "L'Origine africaine de la civilisation égyptienne," *Revue archéologique,* 1913.

PAUW, CORNELIUS DE. *Recherches philosophiques sur les Egyptiens et les Chinois.* Berlin, 1773.

PÉDRALS, DENIS PIERRE DE. *Archéologie de l'Afrique Noire.* Paris: Payot, 1950.

PETRIE, WILLIAM MATTHEW FLINDERS. *The Making of Ancient Egypt.* London: Sheldon Press, New York: Macmillan, 1939.

PIRENNE, JACQUES. *Histoire de la civilisation de l'Egypte ancienne.* 3 vols. Paris: Albin Michel, 1963.

―――. *Les Grands Courants de l'histoire universelle.* Vol. I. *Des origines à l'Islam.* Paris: Albin Michel, 1959.

PITTARD, EUGÈNE. *Les Races et l'histoire.* Paris: Renaissance du Livre, 1924. Translated as *Race and History.* New York: Knopf, 1926.

PLUTARCH'S *Lives* (especially "Isis and Osiris").

RIENZI, DOMENY DE. *Océanie.* Paris: Collection l'Univers, 1836.

RIFFERT, GEORGE R. *Great Pyramid, Proof of God.* Haverhill, Mass.: Destiny Publishers, 1944.

SA'DI, ABDERRAHMAN. *Tarikh es Soudan,* translated into French by O. Houdas & Edmond Benoist. Paris, 1900.

SCHURE, EDOUARD. *Les Grands Initiés.* Paris, 1908.

SELIGMAN, CHARLES G. *Egypt and Negro Africa; a study in divine kingship.* London: Routledge, 1934.

SMITH, GRAFTON ELLIOT & WARREN R. DAWSON. *Egyptian Mummies.* London: G. Allen & Unwin, Ltd., 1924.

SNOWDEN, FRANK M., JR. *Blacks in Antiquity.* Cambridge, Mass.: Harvard University Press, 1970.

SUMMERS, ROGER. *Zimbabwe, a Rhodesian Mystery.* South Africa: Nelson, 1963.

SURET-CANALE, J. *Afrique Noire.* Paris: Editions Sociales, 1958.

―――. "Les Sociétés traditionnelles en Afrique tropicale et le concept de mode de production asiatique." *La Pensée,* #117, Oct. 1964.

TACITUS. *Germany,* translated by Thomas Gordon. *Harvard Classics,* vol. XXXIII. New York: P. F. Collier & Son, 1938.

TEILHARD DE CHARDIN. "L'Afrique et les origines humaines," *Revue des questions scientifiques* (Belgium), Jan. 1955.

TEMPELS, FATHER PLACIDE. *Bantu Philosophy.* Paris: Présence Africaine, 1959.

VAN GENNEP, ARNOLD. *L'Etat actuel de la question totémique.* Paris: Leroux, 1920.

VENDRYES, JOSEPH. *Les Religions des Celtes, des Germains et des anciens Slaves.* Paris: Collection "Mana."

VOLNEY, COUNT CONSTANTIN DE. *Voyages en Syrie et en Egypte.* Paris, 1787.

WARTBURG, WALTER VON. *Problèmes et méthodes de la linguistique,* Paris: Presses Universitaires de France, 1946.

WAUTHIER, CLAUDE. *L'Afrique des Africains.* Paris: Ed. du Seuil, 1964.

ZERVOS, CHRISTIAN. *L'Art en Mésopotamie.* Paris: Ed. Cahiers d'Art, 1935.

INDEX